The Perfectionist Predicament

THE PERFECTIONIST PREDICAMENT

How to Stop Driving Yourself and Others Crazy

MIRIAM ELLIOTT, Ph.D., AND SUSAN MELTSNER, M.S.W.

Produced by Cathy D. Hemming and The Philip Lief Group, Inc.

William Morrow and Company, Inc. / New York

Library of Congress Cataloging-in-Publication Data

Elliott, Miriam
    The perfectionist predicament / Miriam Elliott and Susan Meltsner.
        p.   cm.
    Includes bibliographical references.
    ISBN 0-688-09045-1
    1. Perfectionism (Personality trait)   I. Meltsner, Susan.
    II. Title.
    BF698.35.P47E45   1991
    155.2′32—dc20   91-7723
                                                     CIP

Printed in the United States of America

First Edition

1 2 3 4 5 6 7 8 9 10

BOOK DESIGN BY LINEY LI

We dedicate this book to the late Jamie Rothstein, who gave us more than she ever realized.

ACKNOWLEDGMENTS

I would like to acknowledge my husband, Bryan Elliott, for helping me find balance in my life, my mother and brother for helping me with my own perfectionism during this project, and my many professors who have influenced my thinking on perfectionism, especially Dr. Mary Frazier.

—Miriam Elliott

My heartfelt thanks to the many people in my life who know just how imperfect I am but have loved and encouraged me anyway, especially my mother, Judy Feinstein, who taught me that I could be anything if I set my mind to it and believed in myself.

—Susan Meltsner

CONTENTS

CONTENTS

· *Part One* ·

THE

PERFECTIONIST'S

PREDICAMENT

In Search of . . . Perfection

After just one year of setting up employee health and fitness programs, Marty, a twenty-seven-year-old exercise physiologist, had made quite a name for himself in the small midwestern city where he lived. His business was booming, and to top it all off, he had been asked to bid on a contract with a locally based national corporation. Marty was thrilled for exactly thirty seconds. Then he panicked. "Suddenly everything I'd done before seemed so minor-league," Marty explained. "But the corporate contract could launch me. I would finally be on my way." From where he stood, Marty saw his entire future on the line. He was determined not to waste what might be the best opportunity he'd ever get. "My proposal *had* to be perfect," he said.

To meet Marty's standards, the proposal not only had to outline the perfect program at the perfect price, but it also had to look perfect. "Two days before I had to turn the thing in, I realized that my computer printer just didn't cut it," Marty recalled. "I called just about everyone I knew, but their computers were either incompatible or their printers churned out copy that looked just as shoddy as mine. Finally I paid a secretary at one of the small companies I work with to type it on the best typewriter in the place." He found three typographical errors in the ten-page proposal.

"I can't turn it in this way," he told himself. "If they see those typos, they'll think I'm careless in general and give the contract to someone else." So Marty canceled an important meeting with another potential customer (whom he had been courting for months), decided not to attend his mother's fiftieth birthday party, rushed out to rent a typewriter, and proceeded to retype the entire proposal himself.

Even though he eventually got the contract, Marty's efforts to submit a perfectly typed proposal were entirely wasted. Not only did he have to spend several more months courting the other customer and several weeks convincing his mother to speak to him again, but in the end the neatness of the proposal made absolutely no difference to the corporate decision makers. They were going to award the contract to the lowest bidder no matter how many typos they found or what kind of printer was used.

Most of us know someone like Marty. Some of us are involved in close personal relationships with people like him, people who expect to be *consummate* professionals, conduct *exhaustive* research, have *impeccable* credentials, live in an *immaculate* house, raise *ideal* children, hear that every elaborate dinner party they give is an *unqualified success*, or have a *sublime* sexual experience each and every time they make love. Although we see, even love or admire, our perfectionist friend, lover, spouse, or relative's other attributes, his or her manic quest for success, penchant for neatness and order, or neurotic nit-picking drives us nuts nonetheless.

Or you may have been thrown into a professional situation with a perfectionist—a secretary who comes up with a new filing system every week, a boss who demands more than any human could deliver, a business partner who is still "organizing" his ideas ten minutes before you both have to pitch them to a prospective client.

Or you may be a perfectionist yourself. You set lofty goals and sky-high standards. You strain to reach them and expect other people to live up to them as well. Driven by "shoulds, musts, and have-tos," you overschedule, overwork, overdo in general, and come unglued when things don't proceed smoothly or according to your plans.

Is Perfectionism Really a Problem?

Your pursuit of perfection, craving for consistency, inability to tolerate other people's mistakes, and determination never to make them yourself leave you chronically dissatisfied, frustrated, anxious, or depressed. Yet you may be far from convinced that perfectionism is a problem. As Marty put it, "To a certain extent I'm proud of my perfectionism. If I hadn't been so driven, if I hadn't tried so hard to be the best and expected 110 percent of myself 100 percent of the time, I'd still be polishing the equipment and supervising singles' volleyball nights at the YMCA."

Jay, a thirty-one-year-old vice president for marketing at a Fortune 500 company, wholeheartedly agreed. "My standards set me apart," he said. "My grades were the highest. My friends were the friends everyone else only wished they could have. I went farther in my career faster than anyone dreamed possible and have plenty to show for it. How many people do you know who owned two condos, a Porsche, and their own twin-engine airplane by the time they turned thirty?" Not many.

There's no denying that when you count up material comforts, remarkable achievements, and other outward signs of success, perfectionism will seem to have served you well—especially in this day and age. We have been going through an era in which setting high standards and devoting an inordinate amount of

11

time and energy to attaining them is considered a prerequisite for success. More is better, we are told. Only the best is good enough. It's a jungle out there, and if you're going to survive, you need an edge, an advantage, an ace-in-the-hole. Perfectionism certainly *looks* like it will give you the winning hand and keep you one step ahead of your cutthroat competitors. But appearances can be deceiving.

Jay had been on the fast track to success since childhood, garnering scholastic honors, winning athletic competitions, completing his college and graduate school education in record time, and rising through the corporate ranks at a breakneck pace. He attributed his success to "sweating the small stuff." No detail escaped his attention. No job was complete until he had checked it, tinkered with it, brought it up to par—in short, perfected it—and the more responsibility he was given, the more meticulous he became. As a divisional vice president—the youngest one in his company's history—Jay was virtually obsessed with "the small stuff," prodding, advising, and overseeing his staff every step of the way and sometimes doing or redoing their work so that he could be absolutely sure it measured up to his standards.

But rather than paving the way for his next promotion, Jay's perfectionism earned his division the dubious distinction of having the lowest morale in the company and also being the least productive—a state of affairs that did not go unnoticed by his superiors. While Jay saw himself "going the extra mile" for the good of the company, the company's senior executives saw an ineffective manager whose inability to delegate responsibility or allow his staff to complete the tasks he did delegate had held up several key projects. At their last meeting they had seriously discussed asking for his resignation.

Under certain circumstances—when performing brain surgery, for instance, or building a freeway overpass—perfection is in fact a reasonable standard. No one wants to hand a scalpel to a surgeon who isn't committed to performing as flawlessly as humanly possible. Nor is it desirable to let a construction crew "wing it" and hope that the overpass does not collapse the first time a truck drives over it.

It is also true that in moderation many perfectionistic traits—responsibility, punctuality, neatness, attention to details, and so on—are assets. Society as a whole has long admired and rewarded people who are disciplined, reliable, and conscientious—up to a point. Unfortunately if you are a perfectionist, you go beyond that point, and moderation definitely isn't your style. You are driven to be above and beyond the best at everything you do and tend to be excessively devoted to work or other goals, overly conscientious, inflexible, and sometimes downright irrational about certain aspects of your life.

Barbara, a forty-five-year-old office manager, wife, and mother of three grown children, loved clothes. With a lean, lithe figure maintained by strict dieting and two-hour-daily workouts, she wore them well. "I subscribe to a dozen fashion magazines," Barbara told us. "I can look through catalogs for hours. Just ask me where to find the best buy on designer clothes. I know all the outlets. I keep track of all the department-store sales." Despite her penchant for bargain hunting, Barbara still spent a small fortune on clothing and accesories. She frequently exceeded the limits on her credit cards and admitted that she and her husband argued about money "constantly."

"But it all seems worth it when I put together the perfect outfit," she said. "I find one thing, a great pair of shoes, a stunning scarf, a suit that's been marked down to half its original price, and I can't pass it up. Then I get everything I need to go with it. Nothing feels as good as knowing I've come up with the perfect combination and that I'm going to look absolutely magnificent when I wear it."

The trouble was that Barbara saved her perfect outfits for perfect occasions—which never seemed to arrive. "I don't want to waste them on people who won't appreciate them," she explained. "What's the point of wearing a breathtaking outfit to sit behind a desk at work or to have dinner at a local restaurant with my husband or visit my kids at college?" The basic black dress she'd worn to countless social gatherings "will do," she decided each time she had a new event to attend. She'd wait until her old excercise wear had worn out before switching to any one of the six new spandex jumpsuits, matching leg warmers, and headbands she'd purchased in recent months. In fact, at least 50 percent of the perfect outfits she'd bought over the past five years had never been worn. They hung in Barbara's meticulously organized closets in the same plastic garment bags she placed them in the day she brought them home.

The Many Faces of Perfectionism

Our combined professional experiences—for Miriam ten years of research and work as an educational psychologist and for Susan nine years as a therapist and consultant to helping professionals prone to burnout—have taught us that perfectionism cuts across all religious, socioeconomic, professional, and racial lines, affecting both men and women of all ages. We have learned that perfectionists come in all shapes and sizes. Some are neatness freaks who have a place for everything and keep everything in its place—right down to separating paper clips by sizes or lining up eggs in the refrigerator. Others go overboard scheduling their time. They live by their "things to do today" list and even plan vacation itineraries right down to the minute. Some are perfectionistic about what they do. Others about how they look. Still others focus their attention on other people's imperfections or try to adhere to inhumanly rigid moral or ethical codes. There are "all-around" perfectionists as well. However, most of the people we have counseled or interviewed seem to be more perfectionistic in certain areas than others.

Regardless of the area in which they "specialize," perfectionists strive to achieve goals that are beyond the reach of any mere mortal *and measure their overall self-worth by their ability to attain them.* As one woman we interviewed put it, "I had to be the best, the cleverest, the most beautiful, the star. And if I was not, I felt that I must be the extreme opposite, the worst, the dumbest, the ugliest, and completely inconsequential."

Because they expect the impossible—to be perfect, complete, and flawless in all respects—perfectionists spend a great deal of their time feeling as worthless and disappointed with themselves as this woman did. In fact the harder they try to be perfect, the more aware of their own imperfections they become. Unfortunately it does not occur to them to acknowledge their own or a situation's limitations and adapt their standards accordingly.

"You should see some of the losers I've gone out with," Linda said with a sigh. "One guy actually showed up wearing white socks with dark pants and the most ludicrous tie. No taste, probably no class. Did I want to be involved with a guy like that? No way." Linda, a thirty-three-year-old literary agent, "suffered through" that date as she did so many others—mentally listing all the reasons why this man was not "the one."

"And you should see the men people fix me up with," she continued. "Short guys, bald ones, men who haven't read anything but the sports page since they graduated from high school. My mother even introduced me to an accountant, of all things. How boring can you get? He didn't even have his own apartment and was still driving the first car he'd ever bought. Doesn't anyone realize I have standards?"

Linda had standards, all right, standards so high that the chances of finding a man who met them fell somewhere between slim and none. She could spot a man's flaws from fifty paces, and as soon as she saw one—no matter how small—she eliminated that man, that imperfect specimen, from her list of potentially suitable mates. A decade of dismal dates, dashed hopes, and loneliness had not convinced her to look beyond the blemishes that immediately caught her eye or to consider the possibility that there might be more to a man than the faults she so easily found. "I won't settle for second best," Linda asserted.

15

"The perfect man for me is out there somewhere, and I intend to keep looking until I find him."

The Price of Perfectionism

Rarely will perfectionists recognize or admit what everyone around them can clearly see—that their expectations are too high and their relentless pursuit of perfection is actually reducing their chances for success. As a result many get trapped in an endless, self-defeating cycle of trying, failure, frustration, trying harder, failing again, feeling more frustrated, and trying harder still. Many are plagued by a diminished joy in living and an inability to cope with setbacks or mistakes. Some have even more serious problems: alcoholism, exercise addiction, eating disorders, high blood pressure, ulcers, and other gastrointestinal illnesses. Others are hooked on tranquilizers, which they originally used to calm their nerves, or cocaine, which they believed made them sharper and better able to perform various tasks. Many can point to at least one and often several failed relationships and many more that never got off the ground. A few have arranged their lives so that they have as little contact with other people as possible. Panic attacks are not uncommon, and almost all of the perfectionists we've spoken to report periodic bouts of depression.

Your perfectionism may not have taken you to such depths of despair. But if your efforts to be the best at all you do are keeping you in a constant state of anxiety, decreasing your productivity, or causing conflict in your personal or professional relationships, then perfectionism has begun to defeat you. This book can help you reverse the cycle and become a healthy, happy, well-rounded pursuer of excellence. It can teach you a new way to do your best, one that does not include the expectation to be the best at all you do.

The first section of this book will help you figure out if you are a perfectionist or have perfectionistic tendencies that may be defeating you—standing between you and the healthy, productive, well-balanced life you could be leading. We will describe how trying too hard ensures that you get less out of life and explain how you got into the habit of relentlessly striving for perfection in the first place.

The Perfectionist's Advantage

Despite the toll it has taken on you and the people around you, as problems go, perfectionism is one of the better ones to have. No matter how much hot water you're in right now, your troubles are the outgrowth of potentially positive attributes that you have taken to extremes or used in ways that ultimately make it more difficult to accomplish whatever you set out to do. By using this book's insights, information, and practical suggestions to learn how to look at yourself and your life a bit differently than you have in the past and to practice moderation, you will still end up ahead of the pack. In fact when you demand less of yourself than the unattainable perfection you have been seeking, you will find that you can actually do more and, more important, feel good about what you do.

Chapter One

Are You a Perfectionist?

Four Perfectionists on a Job Hunt

·

COLIN

When Colin, the managing editor of a magazine, learned that his company was declaring bankruptcy and he would be out of a job by the end of the year, naturally he was worried. "I hadn't actually applied for a job in years," Colin explained. "I just kept moving from one position to another in this one company, copy writing, editing, selling advertising, art designing for the different magazines the company owned. I didn't have a clue about selling myself on the open market." So Colin, thirty-seven, married and the father of an eight-year-old son, purchased a dozen books on job hunting.

After reading them all cover to cover, he updated his résumé, accumulated letters of recommendation, and put together a portfolio of meticulously annotated samples of his work. The months he devoted to this task seemed well spent when he spotted a newspaper advertisement for an in-house publications coordinator position with a major life and health insurance company.

He knew the job would be perfect for him. "And thanks to all my preparation, all I had to do was write a cover letter," he recalled.

But that proved easier said than done since everything Colin had read about the importance of cover letters came rushing to mind and convinced him that his had to "knock the personnel director's socks off, leaving absolutely no doubt in his mind that I was the perfect candidate for the job." Looking for a sample on which to model his own letter, Colin went through all of his books again. But nothing he found really "dazzled" him. He went through personnel files at work and again failed to find a "spectacular" cover letter. Two days passed before Colin decided to "wing it" and sat down to do just that. But when he began to actually compose his cover letter, he "drew a complete blank."

Colin stared at his legal pad for hours, doodling in the margins, chewing on his pencil, eventually writing a sentence, then crossing it out, rewriting it, and crossing it out again. "Sometimes I'd get through a whole paragraph only to tear off the page and rip it into little pieces," he admitted. When he was finally satisfied with the opening paragraph, he repeated the same agonizing process for each subsequent paragraph. Four days later he had a completed draft. "But I still wasn't happy with it," he said.

Knowing him well enough to realize that he could continue to tinker with the letter indefinitely, Colin's wife took matters into her own hands, typing the letter, signing Colin's name to it and, along with his résumé and portfolio, mailing it off to the personnel director. At first Colin was furious. Then he was frantic. Finally he called the personnel director to explain that a mistake had been made. Much to his surprise, the personnel director informed him that the materials he sent had been extremely impressive. "Best package I've seen in years," he said. "I just wish you had gotten it to me sooner. We filled the position the day before it arrived."

MARILYN

After five years as a full-time mom, thirty-two-year-old Marilyn was also job hunting, but her troubles did not begin until the day of her first interview. The expensive, conservative, designer suit she had purchased for the occasion "just didn't look right," and Marilyn was determined to make the best possible impression on her prospective employers. She feverishly went through her clothes closet, trying on dozens of outfits before settling on one that would suffice. Regrettably what Marilyn would later describe as her "nightmare" did not end there. She chipped a nail. Found a run in her panty hose. Couldn't decide which shoes to wear.

"By the time I was dressed, I was perspiring and my makeup was running," Marilyn recalled. She washed her face and reapplied it. By then, she was running late. When Marilyn heard over the car radio that there had been an accident on the freeway, she panicked, tried to take a shortcut, and got lost. Finally she arrived at her destination—fifteen minutes late. The interviewer kept her waiting fifteen more minutes—which Marilyn convinced herself was his way of punishing her for not being punctual.

"If you can believe it, things got even worse once the interview started," Marilyn claimed. "Every time I opened my mouth, something stupid came out of it. I just knew that man was thinking, 'Who is this idiot? She looks awful. She can't get to an interview on time, and she doesn't have enough smarts to sharpen my pencils much less run my product-testing department.' I kept trying to salvage the situation and I suppose I made a few fairly intelligent remarks, but all in all I was sure the interviewer wouldn't hire me if I was the last job applicant on earth."

Thoroughly disgusted with herself, Marilyn picked up her kids from school, dropped them off at her mother's, and went home, where she proceeded to eat a pint of ice cream, take three Valiums, and go to sleep. She was too depressed to get out of bed the next day or the day after that. It's difficult to say how long Marilyn might have walked around in her zombielike state of despair if the interviewer hadn't called on Monday to offer her the job she had been so sure she'd never get.

ALEX

During his job search Alex, a twenty-four-year-old MBA fresh out of graduate school, encountered none of the problems that plagued Colin and Marilyn. His résumé was fine—although he could *not* believe how hostile his girlfriend had been while she was typing it. "So I made a few suggestions, gave her some constructive criticism. Big deal. She's too sensitive," he said. Alex didn't worry about his appearance either. He knew he was handsome and looked terrific in his custom-made suit. "I've got to admit the tailor was a real pain in the butt," Alex commented. "I had to take the suit back three times before he got it right." And Alex definitely did not worry about the interviewer's opinion of him. He was too busy criticizing everything from the company's neighborhood to the number of times the interviewer checked his watch.

According to Alex, the offices were cramped and shabby. The receptionist was a "bimbo" who cracked her chewing gum while talking on the phone. The secretaries looked like they were "moonlighting as hookers during their lunch hour." And the interviewer? "He was a real bozo," Alex said. "I had to correct him *six* times before he could pronounce my name right. And by the time he was halfway through the basic corporate-philosophy rap, I knew the company was in trouble. They were doing *everything* wrong." He tried to tell the interviewer that. "But he was one of those 'by the book' type guys, not open to innovative ideas at all. I'm telling you, I wouldn't work for that company if my life depended on it"—which was just as well since the interviewer had no intention of offering the job to Alex, whom he pegged as an abrasive, overbearing, know-it-all.

BETSY

Although like Colin, Marilyn, and Alex, Betsy could use a job, she will not apply for one with any company that pollutes the environment, accepts government contracts, has a lower percentage of women or minorities in management than the percentage in the general population, or is affiliated with other companies that do any of those things. Consequently, she is unlikely to agonize over a cover letter the way Colin did—she rarely sends out résumés. She doesn't worry about her appearance like Marilyn. She does not wear makeup ("They use animals to test it") and won't dress for success ("I refuse to be a slave to fashion"). And unlike Alex, she doesn't waste time in interviews criticizing the offices or the secretaries. She simply states, at the outset, "I want to serve humanity," and proceeds to expound on her philosophy. If she elicits views from the interviewer that differ from her own—as she invariably does—then she knows the job will require her to compromise her values and decides she is not interested in it. With her high moral character intact, Betsy heads back to her parents' home, where she has been living ever since her unemployment money ran out.

Although Colin, Marilyn, Alex, and Betsy are quite different from one another and may or may not bear any resemblance to you, all four are perfectionists. You or someone close to you may be one too. Perfectionists:

- Set unrealistic, unreasonable, and thus unattainable goals and standards for themselves or others, but believe they *can* attain them if they try hard enough (or keep at it long enough)
- Strive to achieve their goals and measure up to their standards *counterproductively*—in a way that makes any task more difficult or nerveracking than it needs to be—or *neurotically*—in an anxious, obsessive, or compulsive manner
- Frequently neglect, avoid, or postpone the aspects of their lives that are not the focus of their intense striving and down-

play or denigrate their actual accomplishments (which may in fact be quite remarkable)

Performance perfectionists like Colin are scrupulous about any task they try to accomplish. Usually overachievers and sometimes workaholics as well, they must not only reach their goals but surpass them. There is always one more mountain to climb, always some way to improve upon their last effort.

Appearance perfectionists like Marilyn are concerned with the impression they make and are determined to present themselves in a positive light at all times. Some want perfect bodies and constantly diet, exercise, even resort to plastic surgery. Others want their clothing and makeup to be perfect, their homes to be showcases worthy of a full-color layout in *Better Homes and Gardens*, and everything they say or do to be judged favorably by everyone they meet.

Interpersonal perfectionists like Alex are harsh critics and demanding taskmasters who insist that others submit to *their* way of doing things, blame others when their meticulously laid plans unravel, and find working in groups a nightmarish experience. Trying to please interpersonal perfectionists is a thankless task: Nothing others do ever satisfies them.

Moral perfectionists like Betsy are unwilling to deviate in any way from the religious or political beliefs and values they've acquired over the years. As far as they are concerned, violating their strict moral code is a "sin" under any circumstances, and they have little tolerance for people whose standards are less rigid (or simply different) from their own.

Regardless of the area on which it is focused, perfectionism is both a behavior pattern—a way of operating in the world—and a thought pattern—a way of looking at yourself, other people, and the world at large and interpreting your experiences. In this chapter we will examine perfectionism from both of these angles and give you an opportunity to determine if you are a perfectionist yourself or if you have perfectionistic tendencies that may be limiting you in various ways.

Before each cluster of signs and symptoms of perfectionism we describe in this chapter you will find a self-test. Read each question carefully, decide whether you *almost always* (5), *often* (4), *sometimes* (3), *rarely* (2), or *almost never* (1) think, feel, or do what the question describes, and place the appropriate number in the space we have provided. Try to be fearlessly honest and try NOT to base your answers on what you think is the proper or best way to be (as most perfectionists are inclined to do) but on how you *really* are.

SELF-TEST 1

_____ Do you believe that anything worth doing must be done well—or at least as well as, and preferably better than, other people would do it?

_____ Are you reluctant to acknowledge your own or a given situation's limitations and lower your standards or revise your goals accordingly?

_____ Do you believe that NOT accomplishing what you set out to do in the way you hoped to do it counts as a failure?

_____ Do you feel that your high standards and willingness to go all out to live up to them are all that save you from a life of mediocrity or prevent you from settling for second best?

_____ As soon as you reach a goal, do you immediately set and start striving to achieve another one?

_____ Do you tell yourself that you'll be happy (slow down, take a vacation, find a relationship, etc.) as soon as you (get a promotion, lose ten pounds, etc.) or reach some other long-awaited level of success?

_____ Subtotal

Lofty Goals and Sky-High Standards

According to psychologist Alfred Adler, our goals are an integral part of who we are. Each and every one of us have and follow our own individual "life line," he claims. We use our goals to define ourselves, to guide us when we have decisions to make, and to keep us on track as we go about the business of daily living. In fact, were we not oriented toward some goal, our lives would be so disorganized and devoid of meaning that we literally would not know what to do with ourselves. Simply having goals is not what gets perfectionists into trouble, and there is nothing inherently wrong with setting *high* standards either. Many people who do so selectively are happy and productive. Achieving their goals and progressing step-by-step toward success as they define it provides them with a sense of satisfaction and accomplishment or wealth, power, and other tangible rewards that bring them pleasure, comfort, or a certain amount of security. But that is not the case for perfectionists, as you well know if you assigned ratings of 4 or 5 to one or more of the questions in Self-test 1.

If you are a perfectionist, you confuse doing the best you can in a given situation with doing the best there is every time. You may not apply that standard to all areas of your life, but in the areas you do, your expectations are *unrealistic*. You do not take into account the realities of your immediate circumstances, your present capabilities, or other very real limitations. For instance, when Colin, with the help of his impressive résumé and cover letter, did get a new job, he came home depressed and disgusted with himself every day for a week. "I felt like such a dunce," he told us. "Every time I turned around, I was asking someone to show me how to do something, and if I tried to figure it out myself, nine times out of ten, I'd be wrong." Night after night he complained to his wife, telling her that he never should have taken the job, that he'd never get the hang of it. "Finally she got fed up with me," Colin recalled. " 'For Pete's sake,' she said, 'You've only had the job a week. How can you possibly expect to know everything and do everything right without asking people to show you the ropes or making a few mistakes?'"

Naturally none of that had occurred to Colin, just as such practicalities as time or monetary constraints, the possibility that other people might not agree with you, or your need to learn new skills or accumulate additional information are not taken into consideration by you. Your expectations are apt to be *unreasonable* as well. They may be extremely strict and inflexible, leaving no room for human error or unforeseen circumstances (traffic jams, inclement weather, illness). They may be excessive, outrageously demanding, or just plain too high to be considered sensible by anyone—including you if you were thinking clearly about the matter. You do more than challenge yourself. You set up tests of endurance that can be passed only through superhuman striving. And you may not limit your standards to yourself. You may expect other people to live up to them too.

If you are a perfectionist, you raise the ante even further by making your goals—both long-range and immediate ones—your number-one, and all too often your *only*, priority. Landing a contract, closing more deals than your fellow real estate brokers, losing ten pounds, or getting your son into the best preschool is not just a part of your life. It *is* your life. You put everything else on hold (or pay the bare minimum of attention to it) until that glorious day when you are finally exactly where you want to be. Unfortunately while you are out pursuing perfection, time marches on. Life passes you by. Or as one perfectionist we interviewed put it, "I spend a lot of time fantasizing about how things will be rather than taking note of how things actually are. My attention is always wandering, to things I did earlier or things I still need to do. It seems like my life is out there—somewhere in the future, and the future keeps getting farther away." Having postponed your life, existing in a kind of pleasureless vacuum while striving to fulfill your ambitions, closing the gap between your dreams and reality becomes all the more important to you, and you feel all the more miserable as each day passes without

27

bringing the success you have been envisioning for so long. Many such days will pass because, as a perfectionist, you set things up so that you can never *really* succeed.

Consequently the very fact that you have to struggle to meet expectations that are unrealistic and unreasonable to begin with robs you of satisfaction when you actually do accomplish the things you set out to do. While a first-rate craftsman or any other pursuer of excellence will take pride in and celebrate his achievements, if you are a perfectionist, when you perform equally well (or even better), you immediately focus on doing it again, doing it faster, or with less effort. You literally turn your successes into failures by constantly reminding yourself that there is "always room for improvement" and going over every accomplishment with a magnifying glass that only picks out mistakes and proof of your own inadequacies. Complimentary and encouraging thoughts, though well deserved, never reach your conscious mind. They are drowned out by an inner voice that shouts, "You could have done better. You'll have to try harder."

When you do meet all of your criteria for "the best there is," another, even more perverse inner voice convinces you that your standards must have been too low. "Anyone could have done that," it says, and you respond by setting another goal, establishing a higher standard and rededicating yourself to reaching it. Of course all of that pales in comparison to the agony you experience when you actually miss the mark, come in second best, or fail to live up to your expectations. You bitterly blame your failure on others or bombard yourself with self-criticism, telling yourself that you are bad, lazy, stupid, careless, you name it. You have not just made a mistake or failed in a specific situation. You *are* a failure, a grossly inadequate, inherently flawed, thoroughly unacceptable, quite possibly worthless person— which is apt to be exactly what you had feared all along.

SELF-TEST 2

_____ Do you feel like an imposter and tell yourself that if people knew the real you, they would reject, dislike, or disapprove of you?

_____ Do you scold and criticize yourself when you make even minor mistakes?

_____ Will you go to almost any length to avoid looking weak, foolish, stupid, or flustered?

In situations that are not your strong suit or ones that might distract you from a more serious or "worthy" pursuit, do you:

_____ Think or talk about what you should be doing instead?

_____ Underestimate yourself, thinking "I can't" or "I'll never be able to" do what the situation requires?

_____ Predict disaster, assuming that you will fail, get hurt, or make a fool of yourself?

_____ Do you devalue yourself ("I'm just a teacher" or "I only have a bachelor's degree") or downplay your accomplishments ("It was nothing" or "I could have gotten an even better deal if I'd tried harder")?

_____ Do you feel extremely anxious or uncomfortable in unpredictable situations or ones you can't control?

_____ Subtotal

Low Self-Esteem

Low self-esteem afflicts virtually every perfectionist. Of course plenty of other people suffer from it too. However, if you are a perfectionist, you have your own unique way of compensating for your less-than-glowing sense of self-worth and your fundamental belief that you are not good enough the way you are. You try to prove you are worth something *by being the best there is at something*. If you can perform or look better than other people, get them to do things your way, or lead a more righteous life than theirs, then maybe, just maybe you won't have to feel like a loser anymore.

Judy, a thirty-nine-year-old wife, mother, church secretary, PTA president, hospital volunteer, AND competitive bowler, described it this way: "I think I'm so busy, constantly running, constantly doing because I'm afraid to stop. When I do, even when I just slow down a little bit, I have to look at myself and there's nothing there. Or nothing good anyway."

Unfortunately perfectionism is also the petri dish in which your negative opinion of yourself grows. Each and every time you fail to live up to standards that no one (no matter how competent and confident they are) can meet, you confirm what you believed all along: that you are not good enough, should be better, and thus must try harder to be the best.

If you assigned 4 or 5 ratings to several of the questions in Self-test 2, then you may share with Judy and most other perfectionists an inner emptiness, a pervasive sense of worthlessness, an acute awareness of your own flaws, and an ever-present fear that other people will discover that you are not nearly as calm, cool, confident, and accomplished as you appear to be. You may be saddled with an overactive conscience, damning inner voices that rise up to taunt and nag you whenever you make the slightest mistake. You may feel guilty or ashamed of yourself a great deal of the time, find it difficult to laugh at yourself (or much else for that matter), and in fact feel compelled to keep all of your emotions in check. Being in control is apt to be extremely important to you. As long as you are in the driver's seat, you can minimize the odds that you'll encounter situations you can't handle and opportunities to fail or look bad.

You may be plagued by a deep and abiding sense that you are an imposter, a fraud. Through your superhuman efforts to achieve, improve your appearance, or otherwise attain perfection, you have managed to fool plenty of people thus far. But you could be "found out" at any moment, and the prospect terrifies you. With every failure, error, or loss you run the risk that other people will see you the way you see yourself, be bitterly disappointed or thoroughly disgusted, and end up hating, rejecting, firing, or abandoning you. To prevent such a calamity, you devote a great deal of your time and energy to what experts in the field of addictions call impression management. You'll go to any lengths to look good, to appear confident and knowledgeable, or to accommodate people whose love or acceptance is important to you. One woman we know actually went to the library and researched any topics men mentioned during her first dates with them. "That way the next time I go out with them, I can show them I'm interested in the same things they are and they'll be more interested in me," she explained.

Although you may not go to such extremes, if you are a perfectionist, you are invariably an impression manager as well. You simply cannot risk losing other people's approval, acceptance, or admiration, which you use as a substitute for self-acceptance, self-approval, and self-esteem. Lacking an internal sense of your own value, you use other people's opinions of you and other external rewards as a yardstick for measuring your worth.

SELF-TEST 3

_____ Do you believe more is better and take mental inventories of the tangible trappings of success you've accumulated over the years?

_____ Do you find yourself competing even in noncompetitive situations or comparing yourself with other people even though your circumstances are quite different?

_____ Do feel that you have to work twice as hard as "truly successful" people in order to succeed yourself?

_____ Before making a decision or stating an opinion, do you try to figure out how other people will react to it or what they would like you to say or do?

_____ Do you crave praise and positive recognition, but when you receive it, find that you can bask in it only momentarily or doubt its sincerity?

_____ Subtotal

The Numbers Game and Other Ways to Prove What You're Worth

Have you ever watched two ten-year-old boys count and recount their baseball cards, all the while bragging about how many "Babe Ruths" or "Hank Aarons" they have? Or have you heard an eight-year-old girl say to a friend, "I have three Barbies, two Kens, a Skipper, and four Cabbage Patch Kids. How many do *you* have?" They are playing a youthful version of "The Numbers Game." By counting and comparing possessions that they know their peers consider valuable, they reassure themselves or prove to others that they are at least equal and hopefully superior to them. "Since I have these things of value (and lots of them), I am obviously of value too," is the unspoken and often unconscious message of the numbers game. Most kids outgrow it. Perfectionists play it throughout their lives.

You may play it aloud, especially when you feel anxious or insecure. At a cocktail party or a business lunch, when your brother (whom Mom always loved best) comes home for the holidays, or when the recently hired "hotshot" joins you at the watercooler, you suddenly turn into a walking résumé, going on and on about your latest accomplishments and acquisitions.

More often, the numbers game is an amazingly complex series of silent maneuvering and mental inventory taking designed to convince you that, yes, you are still leading the pack, still holding a winning hand. For perfectionistic surgeons it may be the number of operations performed; for students their grade point average and number of extracurricular activities. Perfectionist athletes keep track of the trophies, medals, and ribbons they've won, while perfectionist writers maintain a running list of books, articles, and advances. And of course there's always the money you earn and the items you've purchased with it. Although quantity doesn't guarantee quality and having lots of anything doesn't necessarily bring happiness, you string tangible proofs of success like worry beads, to count and recount whenever you doubt that you're the best. And that is just one way that you may turn to external sources to make up for the internal sense of self-worth you lack.

Another is competition. Although competition can be healthy and constructive, giving everyone involved an opportunity to put their talents to the test and push themselves a little harder than they might otherwise, if you are a perfectionist, you go to extremes. You set up competitions in every imaginable area of your life. You compete with people who don't even know there's a competition in progress. "I remember the day my first article was published," a writer who has since been published many times told us. "It just happened to be the same day I heard that my aunt was planning to visit. The first thing that popped into my mind when I heard that was that her son—my cousin Bob— never published anything." Of course Bob was a plumber who had absolutely no interest in publishing anything, but for a moment our writer friend was able to feel like a winner nonetheless. And that's the point: You can say to that inner voice that keeps calling you a loser, "No, I'm not. I beat the pants off Cousin Bob."

The flip side of competition is comparison, in which you enter an imaginary race with other people and declare yourself the loser. Cousin Bob may not have published anything, but he made more money than the fledgling writer. Most plumbers do. Jay, whom we described in the Introduction, may have been the youngest division head in his company's history, but there were men his age who were corporate presidents or outrageously wealthy entrepreneurs. Each time he read about them in *The Wall Street Journal,* he felt like a failure. As depressing as losing these races can be, they become even more destructive when you assume that your competitor won effortlessly, when you convince yourself that someone who looks good on the outside has no insecurities, weaknesses, or skeletons in their closets. Since you do have those things, you can never really win—unless of course, you make it a point to uncover the other person's flaws, going all out to discredit others in hopes of boosting your own self-esteem.

In hopes of validating your worth you may also slavishly seek other people's praise, approval, or guidance. Too insecure to trust our own judgment, some of us constantly ask other people for their opinions, defer to their decisions, or try to figure out what will please someone else and do that rather than something else that might actually be more beneficial. Some of us constantly need to be recognized, rewarded, and favorably reviewed. We can't tell that we've done well. We have to hear it. Roy, a gifted yet extremely insecure graduate student, was one such "approval junkie." Much to his credit he had gotten into therapy, where he began learning to listen without criticizing, as well as other relationship skills. He would try them out with his girlfriend and then report back to his therapist, invariably asking her to tell him he had done well. Unfortunately when he behaved more sensitively toward his girlfriend, he also sought her praise. "Wasn't that good?" he'd interrupt her to ask, "I reflected your feelings and encouraged you to keep talking. Am I getting good at this or what?"

Although you may do it more appropriately than Roy, chances are that you, too, check and recheck to make sure you've done or said the right things. And because approval and recognition are so important to you, you quite understandably feel rotten when it is not forthcoming and mortally wounded when you are criticized. What is more difficult to understand is the way you tend to turn the praise you do get inside out. As much as you depend on compliments to boost your self-confidence, you simply can't accept them graciously. You disavow them ("Really, it was nothing.") or doubt their sincerity ("It's okay. You can tell me the truth. I won't hold it against you.") or discredit the person who gives them ("What do these small-town reviewers know? I'll bet a critic from the *Times* would have seen all the flaws in my performance."). Sometimes you put other people in mind-boggling double binds. If they say you're great, you act like they're lying, and if they give you so much as a smidgen of criticism, you act crushed, leaving them with absolutely nothing they can safely say.

Along similar lines, you may be one of the countless perfectionistic men and women who reject suitors the moment you sense that they are really interested in you. That old "not good enough" feeling returns quickly and you must collect more "trophies" to count, garner more praise. One psychologist likened this practice to drinking salt water to quench your thirst. The first sip works for an instant, but then the salt makes you thirstier so that you must drink more, then more still. So it is with perfectionism. When all is said and done, relying on external sources to fill the emptiness inside you or disprove your deeply ingrained belief that you have little worth never does the trick.

SELF-TEST 4

_____ Does your life seem like a never-ending series of crises and catastrophes?

_____ Do the tasks ahead seem monumental and the accomplishments of the past seem minuscule?

Do you:

_____ Magnify your faults and minimize your strongpoints?

_____ Make mountains out of molehills?

_____ Think one mistake ruins everything?

_____ Think most people don't feel as insecure as you do?

_____ Subtotal

Perfectionistic Thinking

Now and then everyone has a day like Marilyn's. Most adults have gotten tongue-tied or made a less-than-perfect impression during a job interview. Some have even felt certain they performed so poorly that they would not be offered the job. Yet few became so depressed that they wound up spending two days in bed. But then few people—other than fellow perfectionists—would have interpreted their experiences the way Marilyn did.

First you must realize that what might appear to be an anthill to other people generally looks like Mount Fuji to Marilyn. She perceives relatively minor incidents as major catastrophes and almost always decides that they have ruined her entire day. She is even more likely to blow her own flaws and failings out of proportion. All her life she has tried to make the right impression. From her point of view a sort of magic cloud surrounded and protected her so long as she dressed right, said the right things, and played by the rules (which naturally included being on time). When the suit she planned to wear did not "look right," Marilyn's cloud burst, and she thought, "Please, don't let this be an omen," but fully expected it to be. Fearing that things would go from bad to worse, Marilyn unwittingly made sure they did by getting extremely upset over every tiny glitch in her plans and by repeatedly saying to herself, "You idiot. You can't do anything right. Who'd want to hire someone as klutzy as you? Maybe you shouldn't be looking for a job at all."

She assigned arbitrary negative meaning to neutral events, such as concluding that the interviewer kept her waiting in order to punish her for being late. And on the way home from the interview she obsessively went over every word she'd uttered and every raised eyebrow or frown she thought she had noticed on the interviewer's face. The more she thought, the more humiliated she felt and the more horrifying consequences she imagined: Her husband would be disappointed. Her mother would rub salt in her wounds, saying something like, "I told you that you weren't cut out to be a working mother. You can barely keep up with your responsibilities as it is." Maybe her mother was right, Marilyn thought, as she pulled up in front of her children's school, maybe I'll never work again; maybe dishpan hands and dirty laundry are my lot in life and I'll turn into a frumpy hausfrau with a lumpy body whose kids won't respect her and whose husband will stop loving her. With this distressing image firmly rooted in her mind, it was hardly surprising that Marilyn drowned her sorrows with a pint of ice cream, soothed her nerves with a few Valiums, and sank into the depths of depression. She had defeated herself with perfectionistic thinking.

As we mentioned earlier, perfectionism is both a way of operating in the world and a way of viewing the world, a cluster of unrealistic, unreasonable behaviors and a pattern of distorted thinking. Marilyn displayed many of the mental habits that prevent perfectionists from ever really feeling successful and worthwhile. Based on your answers to our questions, you may have discovered you have some of those habits too.

If you are a perfectionist, perhaps the most obvious mental trap you set for yourself is *all-or-nothingism*. You reduce life to black-and-white polar opposites, so that either all is well in your world or nothing is. You must achieve complete success: a piece of work flawlessly executed, a relationship with no conflicts in it, your personal best in every race, an A on every test. If you do not, you are a total failure. There is victory, or there is abject defeat. No shades of gray make it through your mental filter.

Perfectionistic dieters are prime examples of this distorted thought pattern in action. They put themselves on the strictest of diets, reducing their caloric intake to near-starvation levels. Then if they deviate from their food plan, if they eat so much as a handful of forbidden raisins or one cracker too many, they consider their entire day of dieting destroyed. They consume whatever they feel like eating, all the while berating themselves about their lack of willpower. They start the process over again the next day, sometimes restricting themselves even further—

which is another curious quirk in a perfectionist's thinking: When they fail to achieve a goal, instead of lightening up and trying to succeed at something a little simpler first, they set a *higher, more difficult* standard.

If you are a perfectionist, you also tend to blow things out of proportion and to *globalize* them, making a single event seem much more significant, all-encompassing, and catastrophic than it actually was. As one perfectionist described it, "When something went wrong, I never saw it as just that thing. It was much bigger than that, a reflection of a much bigger picture. It meant that there was something wrong with me, something wrong with the way I was living my whole life." Globalizing is often given away by words like *always*, *never*, or *completely*, and is often accompanied by *crucializing*, that is, upping the ante by making situations seem more critical or serious than they may actually be. A bad day is the "worst" day of your life; a less-than-brilliant remark is the "dumbest" thing you ever said; a difficult choice is the "most important" decision you ever had to make. Your out-of-proportion thoughts need not be negative. However, telling yourself that you have a shot at the "best" job you've ever heard of, that your interview is with the "most prestigious" company in town, or that you just met the "most exciting, sensitive, gorgeous" man in five counties can be self-defeating too. Having invested so much positive energy, if anything goes wrong, you are apt to be devastated. Close relatives of globalizing and crucializing are *trend spotting*—worrying that the negative event which just occurred will repeat itself endlessly—and *fortune-telling*—arbitrarily assuming that the worst will happen even when there is no basis for thinking so.

Almost everyone magnifies certain experiences and minimizes others. However, if you are a perfectionist, you are apt to blow up things that definitely do not need to look larger than they already are while simultaneously shrinking the very things that could make you feel better and help you accomplish what you have set out to do. Your faults and the obstacles that you need to overcome in order to reach your goals seem gigantic and insurmountable. But your strengths and past accomplishments, which could be a source of encouragement and comfort, seem minuscule and inconsequential.

Other distorted thought patterns include the following:

- *Tunnel vision:* Concentrating exclusively on one set of self-imposed goals or standards and pushing almost everything else out of your mind, including many things that could actually bring you pleasure and restore your sense of self-worth.
- *Blaming:* Believing that someone must be at fault and be held accountable for anything that goes wrong. Whether the culprit is you or someone else, you appoint yourself judge, jury, and executioner, making sure that no misdeed goes unpunished.
- *Shoulds, musts, and have-tos:* They make your life one long obligation, stirring up feelings of guilt and shame whenever you fail to fulfill or try to refuse internal demands (as well as other people's requests).

And of course expecting perfection is itself a distortion, a self-defeating cognitive cocktail made up of two parts believing that perfection is attainable, three parts denying that your standards are unreasonable, and five parts inability to tolerate your own or other people's mistakes.

SELF-TEST 5

_____ Do you go to almost any length to avoid making mistakes?

_____ Do you critique your performance, reviewing every nuance, looking for mistakes or places where there is room for improvement?

_____ When you realize you have goofed (or think you may have), do you have a great deal of trouble getting your imperfect words or actions out of your mind?

_____ Do you wrack your brain for ways to undo or make ammends for what you have done?

_____ Do you do something—have a drink, run, clean your clothes closet, devour an entire bag of potato chips without thinking—in order to calm your nerves or get your mind off your latest "failure"?

_____ Do you postpone or avoid experiences that might lead to similar mistakes?

_____ Subtotal

The End of the World as You Know It: Making Mistakes

By setting your standards as high as you do, you decrease your chances for success. You are less likely to stick to an 800-calorie diet than a 1200-calorie one. The probability that your perfect cover letter and résumé submitted ten days after everyone else's will land you a job is lower than the probability of getting the job by submitting the imperfect cover letter in a timely fashion. And your chances of finding an employer, a mate, or a friend whose ethics and values are identical to your own falls somewhere between slim and none. By expecting so much you increase your opportunities to fail tenfold. And at some level you know it. You are acutely aware that your perfect plans could unravel at any moment, and that is why you, like most perfectionists, may be a chronic worrier.

You may worry about what you do while you are doing it. An ever-present, ever-doubtful voice incessantly inquires, "Am I doing this right? Could I be doing it better?" When your performance seems to be up to par, your thoughts may turn to the worthiness of what you are doing. "Is this a good thing to do?" you wonder. "Could I put my time and talent to better use?" Your self-evaluation rarely ceases, not even when you are engaged in activities that have no rightness or wrongness to them—everything gets scrutinized with the same faultfinding lens. And if you _do_ make a mistake, you do not recover from it easily or well. You examine your failure endlessly, playing it over and over in your mind, like a videotape that you can't turn off. Worse yet, you don't necessarily learn from your review. Instead you get caught up in round after round of nonproductive self-recriminations. Rather than reassess your standards or come up with an effective contingency plan for the future, by continuing to punish yourself you make yourself increasingly miserable and anxious.

Callie, a physical therapist covering a vacationing colleague's caseload, couldn't understand why an elderly patient was tiring so quickly. According to her chart, she had covered twice as much ground with her new walker the day before. Thinking that the patient might be trying to "pull one over" on her substitute therapist, Callie pushed and cajoled her along until she turned pale and sweaty. After a brief rest the patient seemed fine, and Callie had an orderly take her back to her room, but at the end of the day when she was updating charts, Callie discovered that she had misread the other therapist's orders and pushed the patient too hard. "I knew that things like that happen all the time," Callie said. "But I didn't let them happen to me." She could not get her mistake out of her mind. "Every time I turned around, I was thinking, 'What if I caused serious damage? What if she has a heart attack from overexertion? If I come in tomorrow and hear that she did, I'll never be able to live with myself.'" Nothing Callie could tell herself would make those thoughts go away, and by seven o'clock that night her heart was pounding wildly, her ears were ringing, and every time she stood up, she felt like she would faint. "I didn't want to call the hospital and ask the floor nurse if the patient had a heart attack," Callie said, "but I had to do something. I couldn't take it anymore." Callie called her supervisor at home and told her what had happened. Although her supervisor didn't tell her anything she hadn't told herself (or reduce the risk of her patient having a heart attack one iota), Callie felt better. "Maybe its just my Catholic upbringing," she quipped, "but I was okay as soon as I confessed my sin."

As was clearly true in Callie's case, sometimes your worries can take on all the trappings of an obsession: a recurrent, per-

41

sistent, preoccupying thought that invades your consciousness, distracting you from all else and stirring up a tremendous amount of anxiety. And just as Callie acted on a compelling urge to confess her sins, you may find yourself automatically engaging in any number of compulsive behaviors (from drinking or overeating to apologizing or going overboard to make things up to people) that do not actually solve the problem but seem to turn off your mental videotape or reduce your anxiety. Or you may use another common response to chronic worrying: making it a point to avoid situations in which you might once again "fail" or stir up the same unsettling emotions you've experienced in the past.

The anxiety, obsessions, compulsions, and avoidance that so often accompany perfectionism are reasons why we consider it a psychological condition, a neurosis. However, it is not currently classified as such and need not be for psychologists to agree that it is most definitely counterproductive. The inability to let go of past mistakes and the fear of making new ones causes perfectionists to view any upcoming task or goal—no matter how capable they are of performing it—with alarm. And the negative energy they invest in it leads to:

- *Indecisiveness:* You become so worried about making the wrong choice that you have trouble making any choice at all.
- *Playing it safe:* Although every risk brings with it the potential for success, it is also accompanied by the possibility of failure. More often than not you eliminate that possibility by not taking the risk at all, getting stuck in a rut, and missing out on a whole range of positive experiences.
- *Procrastination:* When not making mistakes is a priority, you'll put off a task for as long as you possibly can. After all, until you start something, there is no chance of failing at it.
- *Perseveration:* This is a convincingly disguised form of procrastination. You get stuck on one part of a task—writing the first paragraph of a cover letter, for instance—postponing

that which you truly fear—mailing it out and failing to be called for an interview.

In these and other ways, which we will elaborate on throughout this book, perfectionism, though well intended, makes it more difficult for you to reach your goals or costs you too much in the process.

Scoring Your Self-tests

Take a few moments to go back through this chapter and tally up the numbers you used to answer each question. If your total score falls between 120 and 160, chances are that you are a perfectionist. If it falls between 80 and 120, you have perfectionistic tendencies. If you examine your high-scoring questions, you can get a sense of the specific ways that your standards, self-image, external-reward seeking, or thought patterns are leading you astray. But regardless of your score a crucial and perhaps controversial question remains: Is perfectionism really a problem and is there really anything wrong with being as perfectionistic as you are?

Although only you know the exact toll perfectionism has taken on you, it has undoubtedly cost you something and may have you trapped in a cycle of self-defeat. That cycle—a downward spiral *away* from health, happiness, peace of mind, and your original goals—is the subject of the next chapter and our most convincing answer to the question "What's so bad about wanting to be good?"

Chapter Two

What's So Bad
About Being Good?

SHARON

Sharon, a forty-two-year-old single parent with an unfailingly sunny disposition, works in the purchasing department of a large county hospital. Friendly and thoughtful, Sharon always remembers her co-workers' birthdays and anniversaries, takes up collections for retirement presents and baby gifts, and regularly delivers her homemade cookies to offices and nursing stations throughout the building. If it were not for these kind gestures, Sharon's colleagues might have wrung her neck long ago. Time and time again they had been driven to distraction by Sharon's perfectionism.

Determined to be helpful, thorough, and efficient, when Sharon had major purchases to make, she conducted exhaustive "research studies," attempting to get as much input as possible from as many people as possible. "I want to make the right purchase," she explained. "I'd hate to waste the hospital's money or hear that I'd chosen an inferior product *after* the deed was done." That hardly sounds unreasonable. However, being a perfectionist, Sharon needed more than general ideas about people's preferences. She had to be absolutely certain that she was making the right choice.

When Sharon was assigned the task of obtaining new photocopying equipment for the hospital, she distributed a five-page questionnaire and made daily follow-up phone calls until every one who received one returned the completed survey to her. She talked to every sales rep in a hundred-mile radius and, still unable to make a choice, began leasing machines on a trial basis. "Every two months I brought in new equipment and asked people to evaluate it," Sharon told us, her voice conveying how pleased she was to have come up with such a novel, seemingly foolproof plan. "I even developed a sort of report card, so that everyone who used the machines could grade them on quality, speed, and a few other points." She never could understand why people seemed so reluctant to fill out those report cards. "It only took a minute," she continued. "And I was doing all this work for *their* benefit. I really shouldn't have had to call them every week to remind them to turn in their report cards." But call them she did, and when they stopped accepting her calls, she cornered them in the cafeteria or raced to catch up with them in the halls.

It never occurred to Sharon that *more* paperwork was the last thing anyone in the hospital needed or that each time she brought in new machines, everyone had to take up their valuable time learning how to use them. She was too focused on her goal—finding the perfect copy machine—for their grumbling to get through to her. After eight months and four sets of machines Sharon still could not make a decision and was hard at work compiling another questionnaire (asking the hospital staff to compare and contrast the machines she had leased thus far) when her boss took the entire matter out of her hands. "He just up and signed a long-term contract with the company that I happened to be leasing machines from at the time," Sharon said. A year later she was still upset about "all that effort going to waste" and worried about the copy machines themselves. "I'm just not sure we ended up with the best ones for us," she said with a sigh.

HOWARD

When Howard, a thirty-year-old industrial-arts teacher, inherited a substantial sum of money from his grandfather's estate, he bought a house. "A fixer-upper," he commented. "It needed lots of work, but I could see it had tons of potential." Long before he actually closed on the property, Howard had a meticulously detailed remodeling plan that would turn his "fixer-upper" into a showcase. He began implementing his plan immediately, devoting every spare moment (and every spare dime) to creating an environment that was perfect in every way. He looked over the interior designer's shoulder while he drew up blueprints. He checked in with contractors and other workmen several times a day. In the evening and on weekends he pored over design magazines or sweated and strained to complete the remodeling projects he'd assigned himself. All other activities were abandoned as he dedicated himself to the monumental task before him, and after two years of single-minded devotion and hard work, he was far from done.

In an effort to keep up with the latest design trends, Howard has redone his kitchen twice. He won't have friends over because he cannot bear for them to see his home in its incomplete condition. He rarely goes out with his friends either. "There's so much to do around here," he noted. "I just don't have time to socialize." Exhausted after staying up half the night painting, wallpapering, or planning the next phase of his remodeling, Howard's teaching has begun to suffer. Having used up his inheritance long ago, he recently took out a second home improvement loan.

Doing More but Getting Less

As an outside observer, it is not difficult to see that Sharon's attempt to be helpful, thorough, and efficient had backfired. Clearly her expectations were unreasonable, her behavior counterproductive. She tripped over her own perfectionistic standards and got in her own way, making it impossible to accomplish what she had set out to do.

Howard's perfectionism tripped him up too. Try as he might, he could not remodel fast enough to keep up with the latest interior design trends or well enough to meet his own exceedingly high standards. While he tried ever more valiantly to fulfill his ever-more-grandiose fantasies, his social life fell by the wayside and his debts mounted. To all onlookers the end result— should Howard ever attain it—hardly seemed worth the effort he was putting into it.

All of the perfectionists we've introduced thus far found themselves in similar binds. Whether they were going after perfect cover letters or perfectly typed proposals, perfect places of employment or perfectly producing employees, perfect outfits to wear on perfect occasions or perfect mates, they ran themselves ragged, made themselves miserable, and all too often suffered consequences they most definitely did not want as a direct result of their perfectionistic efforts to get *exactly* what they did want.

In her autobiography *Dancing on My Grave*, world-renowned prima ballerina Gelsey Kirkland offered many dramatic examples of just how destructive the pursuit of perfection can be. She described a never-ending struggle to achieve the lightness and emaciated look required of ballet stars: starvation dieting during her teenage years and later vomiting to keep her weight down. To conform to the aesthetic standards of the people molding her career, she had plastic surgery: implants added to her breasts, ankles, and lips. Rigorous rehearsal schedules and her drive to be the best demanded a limitless supply of energy. She bolstered her own reserves with amphetamines and cocaine. The literally life-threatening health risks she took eventually caught up with her, cutting short the dancing career her desperate measures were meant to prolong.

After counseling and interviewing many, many perfectionists (and spending a good many years pursuing perfection ourselves), there is no doubt in our minds that relentlessly striving for perfection, expecting to be perfect, and repeatedly falling short of that unattainable standard takes an enormous toll. In the long run the costs of perfectionism always outweigh its benefits. But perfectionists themselves rarely think so. In fact, if you are a perfectionist, it may be practically impossible for your therapist, friends, relatives, or co-workers to convince you that your perfectionism is a problem or that the problems in your life that you do recognize are side effects of your perfectionism.

Why Not Be the Best?

"I admit I get a little carried away now and then," Sharon said. "But isn't it better to err on the side of caution than to rush blindly into things and make a really big mistake?"

"If you're willing to settle for second best, that's what you'll get," Howard insisted. "I was raised to believe that. I tell my students that. When I start thinking about giving up, all I have to do is ask myself where we would be if Madame Curie or Louis Pasteur or the men who fought for this country's independence had quit before they got to their goals. What separates successful people from mediocre ones is knowing what you want, working hard, and sticking with it until you get it right."

"I know I worry too much," Colin admitted. "I know I get worked up over things that other people see as no big deal. But I'm not other people. I've always had to struggle and fight to get ahead, to get noticed—hell, just to keep my head above water. And if I hadn't done that, I wouldn't have half of what I've got now. I'd just be some average Joe working on some factory assembly line somewhere and not giving a damn about anything.

That may be enough for some people, but it wasn't what I wanted my life to be."

Perhaps you've made similar statements at one time or another. Like Sharon, Howard, and Colin you may subscribe to the widespread belief that perfectionism elevates people to higher levels of success and certainly prevents them from descending into the dreaded abyss of failure or mediocrity. You may admit that your standards can sometimes be unreasonable or unduly demanding. Yet you may be convinced that had you not set such high standards in the first place (and tried with all your might to live up to them), you would never have gotten so far in life and been able to do or be or have so much. Even the excess stress that is so often the by-product of perfectionism seems worthwhile. Anxiety keeps you on your toes. If you stopped worrying, you might really blow it.

There is an element of truth in those perceptions. Perfectionists and people with perfectionistic tendencies are often remarkably intelligent, talented, and creative. They develop character traits that can be valuable assets in many settings: self-discipline, analytical skills, attention to detail, and a "sixth sense" that enables them to spot potential problems from miles away.

In addition, although being complete and flawless in all respects is an unattainable goal, while you pursued it, you undoubtedly accomplished a great deal. You can point to many signs of success (promotions, bank statements, awards, trophies, expensive high-status possessions) and can, in all honesty, say that your high standards, drive, ambition, and stick-to-itiveness made it possible for you to obtain those things. If perfectionism had not enabled you to get at least some of what you wanted some of the time, you would probably have abandoned it long ago.

Research has even shown that anxiety and advance worrying sharpens the senses and enhances performance—to a point. However, the very things that make you a perfectionist—unrealistic expectations, low self-esteem, dependence on external sources to supply your self-worth, and so on—ultimately push

49

you past that point. Instead of carrying you to ever-higher levels of success, perfectionism eventually halts your progress and undermines your efforts to be the best.

This unwanted and certainly unintended outcome of perfectionism was dramatically demonstrated in a research study conducted by Dr. David D. Burns, author of *Feeling Good: The New Mood Therapy*, in 1980. Burns compared insurance agents who scored high on a perfectionism scale with those who did not and found that the perfectionists earned an average of $15,000 a year *less* than the nonperfectionists. They were more likely than their less-perfectionistic counterparts to engage in such self-defeating behaviors as putting off sales calls because they were afraid that people would hang up on them, telling themselves that their sales pitch wasn't working before they were halfway through it, and deciding not to push for a sale because they were convinced they would not get it anyway. Because these perfectionistic insurance agents linked their self-worth to their job achievement, they had more on the line during every sales call, more to lose if they failed to make the sale. Ultimately their fear of failure and the habits they developed to cope with it actually sabotaged them, severely limiting their ability to succeed.

Those insurance agents as well as the other perfectionists we have described thus far did not get into trouble because they wanted to be good at what they did. They wound up in hot water because *being good was not good enough*. They had crossed the line between the healthy quest for excellence and the neurotic pursuit of perfection. If your score on the self-test in the previous chapter was relatively high, chances are that you have too. You did not intend to cross that line or even realize that it existed. In fact you may be convinced that excellence is what you have been pursuing all along. This conviction is based on more than an understandable reluctance to admit that you have gone overboard. If you are a perfectionist or have a significant number of perfectionistic tendencies, you have been doing what you do and thinking the way you think for so long that your expectations seem reasonable to you and the methods you use to fulfill them seem like they should work. You have long since forgotten or may have never actually known what the healthy pursuit of excellence is.

Seeking Excellence Versus Pursuing Perfection

People who pursue excellence can be as careful, meticulous, and thorough as perfectionists. However, they enjoy their accomplishments. They derive genuine pleasure from striving to measure up to high standards, and those standards involve doing what is proper, correct, better than average, or the best they can do in a given situation—*not* the best there is under any and all circumstances.

Although pursuers of excellence have their fair share of fears and insecurities, they are willing to venture into unfamiliar territory and to take calculated risks. They realize that they may fail, sustain a few flesh wounds, or stand out like sore thumbs. They will take that chance, test their limits, attempt the difficult, and try to rise to the challenge they are facing. They also recognize when they have reached a point of diminishing returns. Rather than trying harder and hoping that the same behavior will somehow produce different results, they change their approach to the situation or modify their goals. This flexibility enables them to learn from their mistakes as well as feel encouraged and motivated by their successes. As they progress toward their goals, they increase their competence, confidence, and sense of self-worth. And that is the fundamental difference between pursuers of excellence and perfectionists, whose overall life-style locks them into a rigid way of doing things and of perceiving reality that in turn undermines their confidence, stunts their growth, and maintains their less-than-glowing opinion of their own worth.

EXCELLENCE SEEKERS:

- Are self-accepting. They are aware of their strengths and their limitations and know that both contribute to their unique personalities. They believe that they are basically worthwhile and inherently valuable, albeit necessarily fallible human beings. They can lose and still have a positive self-image.

- Set goals and standards that take into account both their strengths and their limitations, increasing the likelihood of achieving their goals.

- When facing a challenge, focus on their strengths and on how to do well.

- Try new ventures, take risks, and learn from their experiences and mistakes.

PERFECTIONISTS:

- Are self-absorbed. Acutely aware of their flaws and deficiencies, they minimize their virtues and work hard to conceal their inadequacies. Because everything is a potential threat to their carefully constructed facade, they are constantly on the defensive. They must win and be infallible in order to believe they have any worth or value at all.

- Demand a higher level of performance than is humanly possible for them to achieve. Naturally this reduces their chance of success.

- When facing a challenge (which they usually see as a problem), focus on their deficiencies and concentrate on how not to do poorly or make any mistakes.

- Avoid new experiences and rarely take risks for fear of looking foolish or incompetent. Rather than trying to figure out how not to make the same mistakes again, they try to stay out of situations where the possibility for making those mistakes will arise.

EXCELLENCE SEEKERS:

- Are relaxed and careful when tackling new tasks and feel excited, clear about what needs to be done, and emotionally charged when entering unfamiliar territory.

- Are open to direction and constructive criticism.

- Derive a sense of satisfaction and enhanced self-esteem from their efforts. They appreciate a job well done and, in various situations, feel free to be less painstaking or results oriented.

- Lead balanced lives. They are able to relax, have satisfying personal relationships, participate in activities that are not even remotely related to their goals, and have fun. They can indulge in and thoroughly enjoy pursuits at which they do not excel.

PERFECTIONISTS:

- Are tense and deliberate in new, unfamiliar, and therefore unpredictable situations. They may devote so much energy to worrying about new tasks ahead of time that they feel anxious, confused, or exhausted before they even begin.

- Take criticism as a personal attack and tend to think that people would not make suggestions unless they doubted their competence in the first place.

- Rarely if ever see their efforts—including their best ones—as good enough. Believing that they could and should do even better, they derive little satisfaction from their accomplishments, even truly remarkable ones.

- Are single-mindedly devoted to certain areas of their lives to the exclusion of all else and rarely engage in any activity just for the heck of it or if they think they will not perform well at it. Their lives tend to be unbalanced and distinctly lacking in close personal relationships, relaxation, or purely pleasurable pursuits.

If the descriptions in the right-hand column are a better fit for you today than the ones on the left, you are apt to feel disheartened, perhaps even a bit disgusted with yourself. And if the life of an excellence seeker was what you wanted all along, but you ended up with many of the less-than-desirable traits of a perfectionist, you are probably being pretty hard on yourself right now. Please try not to be. The healthy pursuit of excellence is still within your grasp. The habits of perfectionism can be broken. The goal of this book is to help you do that, and you wouldn't have picked it up if you already knew how. You have a way to go yet, and you'll get there, but not by doing things the way you've always done them. Striving to live up to unreasonably high expectations, failing, trying for the same goal again, failing, and trying even harder has not helped you move forward to a truly fulfilling, truly successful life. Instead it has compelled you to travel the same bumpy roads repeatedly, moving in vicious circles, and ultimately getting trapped in a cycle of self-defeat.

DESMOND

Desmond, at twenty-five, is a bright, handsome, articulate, sensitive young man who does not believe that he is bright, handsome, articulate, or sensitive at all. In fact Desmond holds an exceptionally low opinion of himself—which was one of the reasons he started psychotherapy.

When asked to list any positive attributes he *could* think of, he said halfheartedly, "I guess I'm a hard worker. But then I have to be because it takes me twice as long as anyone else to get my work done." At first we assumed that Desmond was exaggerating, but as it turned out, he was not.

Desmond, an accountant, did not like to make mistakes. In fact he was so driven to perform his job flawlessly that he felt compelled to recheck his work not once or even twice, but always a bare minimum of three times. This of course meant that he could not finish eight hours worth of work in eight hours time. Each day he arrived at work an hour before the other accountants and stayed behind for several hours after they left. At first his superiors mistook his long hours for ambition. "But now they know I'm not doing extra work, just taking more time to do my regular work," he said with a sigh.

Desmond's perfectionism was not restricted to the workplace. "I'm really backward with people," he claimed. "I want to make a good impression, but basically I make no impression at all." Again Desmond was not overstating the facts. In social situations Desmond constantly felt that he was about to say or do "the wrong thing," and the mere thought of sticking his foot in his mouth, offending someone, spilling a drink, or "looking spastic" on the dance floor made him extremely anxious. Consequently even though he was terribly lonely and longed to be in an intimate relationship, he avoided socializing. When he could not "get out of" going to a social event, Desmond arrived late and left early, sometimes without uttering more than a few words to anyone.

Not oblivious to his problems, Desmond did make a number of dubious attempts to solve them. For instance, in what he called "a last-ditch attempt to get involved with people and hopefully build my self-confidence," he "forced" himself to attend church services every Sunday and joined a Bible-study discussion group that met one evening each week. "It hasn't really helped," he reported. But how could it? After a dozen meetings he had yet to discuss anything.

Like Sharon, Howard, and virtually every other bona fide perfectionist, Desmond's determination to be perfect and, even more so, his fear of displaying a single imperfection were defeating him. Perfectionism was preventing him from getting what he said he wanted: to be competent at his job, have a social life, get involved in a relationship, build his confidence, and overcome what he calls his "doing-the-wrong-thing thing." Yet he found it virtually impossible to conduct himself differently. This was particularly true of his checking and rechecking habit. "It's worse than quiting smoking," he groaned. "I'll promise myself to cut down to checking my work twice instead of three times, and sometimes I'll make it all the way through the day. But then right before I'm supposed to leave the office, I'll take out all the work I did that day and check it one more time."

Desmond was trapped. Self-doubt and a relentless internal voice that constantly reminded him to be careful triggered his exhausting, anxiety-provoking effort to make no mistakes whatsoever. His means to that end (compulsively checking his work and anxiously censoring himself in social situations) created negative side effects (a dim appraisal of his work habits by his superiors and an isolated existence devoid of companionship and intimacy), which left Desmond feeling more insecure and disgusted with himself. This stirred up more anxiety and triggered more perfectionistic behavior, which led to new failures, new doubts, and new counterproductive behaviors ad infinitum. And that is the cycle of self-defeat in a nutshell.

The Cycle of Self-defeat

Self-test

Using the rating scale provided in the previous chapter (*almost always* [5], *often* [4], *sometimes* [3], *rarely* [2], *almost never* [1]), answer the following:

_____ If you think that by attempting something you might appear foolish or make a mistake, do you put it off for as long as possible or talk yourself out of trying it at all?

_____ Would you rather do nothing than do an average job?

_____ When you fall short of your goals, is "I didn't try hard enough" one of the first things you tell yourself?

_____ Do you feel more exhilarated and sure of yourself while you are striving toward a goal than you do after you've actually achieved it?

_____ When you are having a bad day or things are going poorly in other areas of your life, do you focus more attention

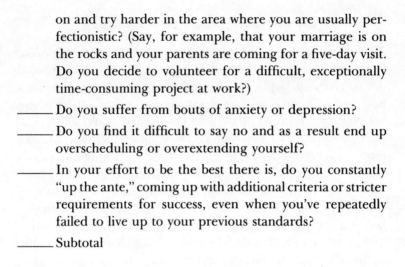

on and try harder in the area where you are usually perfectionistic? (Say, for example, that your marriage is on
the rocks and your parents are coming for a five-day visit.
Do you decide to volunteer for a difficult, exceptionally
time-consuming project at work?)

_____ Do you suffer from bouts of anxiety or depression?

_____ Do you find it difficult to say no and as a result end up
overscheduling or overextending yourself?

_____ In your effort to be the best there is, do you constantly
"up the ante," coming up with additional criteria or stricter
requirements for success, even when you've repeatedly
failed to live up to your previous standards?

_____ Subtotal

High ratings in one or more of those areas is a good indication
that your efforts to cope with your fears and compensate for
your failings are leading to more fear and failure, which compel
you to try harder to be the best there is, drawing you into your
own personal cycle of self-defeat.

There are countless variations on the basic cycle. You can get
caught in one while attempting to complete a specific task, as
Colin did while composing his cover letter. Or you may find
yourself in one that permeates all areas of your life, the way
Desmond did. Some self-defeating cycles are primarily mental—
Marilyn's ability to think herself into the pits of depression, for
example. Others, like Howard's round-the-clock effort to remodel his home, are mostly behavioral. Performance perfectionists, appearance perfectionists, interpersonal perfectionists, and
moral perfectionists each have their own versions of it (which
we will explore in later chapters). But regardless of how different
they may look on the outside, all cycles of self-defeat are downward spirals that lead perfectionists farther and farther away
from health, happiness, peace of mind, and their original goals.
All cycles also stem from the same source: the fundamental belief
that you are not good enough the way you are.

The Problem: "Oh, No! I'm Not Perfect"

As we pointed out in the last chapter, if you are a perfectionist, you decided long ago that you were not as good as you should be. You came to doubt your overall worth and, more often than not, homed in on one or several aspects of yourself that you believed were especially flawed and presumed would one day be your downfall. The inherent deficiency on which you blamed most if not all of your problems may have been something striking and important for functioning in your world: your intelligence or your temper, for instance. It may have been something with only minor significance in the overall scheme of things—keeping your room tidy or having neat handwriting—or something no one else thought was flawed—the shape of your nose or the pitch of your voice. It was frequently something that other people criticized you for or warned you about: being careless or sloppy or letting people take advantage of you or not saying your prayers. But no matter what it happened to be, you perceived that aspect of yourself as bad, wrong, sinful, foolish, unattractive, inadequate, or in some other way not as it should be. You came to believe that trait was intolerable, inexcusable, indeed completely unacceptable, and condemned yourself for being that way.

The Solution: "I Must Fix Myself"

I'm such a dope, such a klutz, so lazy, fat, gawky, or selfish, you told yourself over and over again. Everything would be okay and I would be happy if only I was smarter or funnier or prettier or had nicer clothes, you thought. I *should* be more careful. I *could* be kinder. I *must* study more. I *have to* make sure never to say anything offensive. Day in and day out you listened to this mantra of "shoulds, musts, and have-tos," which psychiatrist Karen Horney refers to as the "tyranny of oughts," and you found it virtually impossible to say no to those internal demands.

Painfully aware of your flaws, ashamed of and disgusted with yourself for being less than you assumed you should be, you began to pressure yourself to improve, alter, compensate for, and conceal your presumably fatal flaws. The standard you chose to measure your success in this regard was perfection. After all, if you were always careful and never made mistakes, got an A in every course, won every hockey game, or never allowed a speck of dust to rest for more than a second on any surface in your home, there would be no doubt in your mind that you had overcome your unspeakable deficiency.

The Conclusion: Perfectionism "Cures" Imperfections

As we will explain in more detail in the next chapter, you generally came to the conclusion that perfectionism "cures" imperfections at an early age and with more than a little help from your parents or other significant people in your life. Your decision to perfect yourself was an immature one, made at a time in your life when you lacked the knowledge, skill, and resources to appraise yourself or your circumstances accurately. It was usually an unconscious choice as well. However, once it was reached, the conclusion that you could cure your internal imperfections by striving for and attaining perfection in the world around you immediately began to show itself in your behavior.

Whether you came upon it by accident, observed other people doing it, or were actually told how to behave, you had found a method for coping with your sense of inadequacy and proving that you were good enough after all. For Desmond the behavior was checking for mistakes and choosing his words with extreme caution. For Sharon it was trying to figure out what would please everyone else and acting accordingly. Howard tried to keep his surroundings tidy and organized at all times, while Barbara, whom we described in the introduction, and Marilyn devoted themselves to staying in shape and dressing themselves exquisitely. You may have pursued a similar or completely different course of action. But no matter what that course of action was, it worked to your advantage at least once (and probably many times over). It brought you some sort of reward: praise, recognition, relief, a distraction, a sense of being in control, or an avenue for avoiding criticism or ridicule. It helped you cope with circumstances that were beyond your control or keep unsettling emotions at bay.

For instance, Desmond started "checking" when he was eight and his parents separated. "My mother was very depressed after my dad left," he recalled. "She was taking tranquilizers and crying a lot, wringing her hands and saying she wasn't sure she could go on living. She really scared me when she talked like that." Indeed the thought that his mother might actually try suicide terrified Desmond, so much so that he would awaken during the night convinced that she had ended her life while he was sleeping. "I'd get out of bed, tiptoe into her room, and check to make sure she was breathing," Desmond explained. "I still remember how relieved I felt when I saw that she was okay." At one point Desmond was checking on his mother a half dozen times a night. After a few months the need to check disappeared, only to reappear again when Desmond was sixteen and got into a car accident.

"My tire blew out, and I lost control of the car," he said, "I was sure it never would have happened if I had checked the tires." So check them he did, circling the car three times before getting behind the wheel. Again he felt relieved and soon afterward found himself checking test answers three times, checking door and window locks three times before retiring, checking phone numbers three times before dialing, and so on. In fact whenever he was worried that a mistake could have been or could be made, he went over his words and actions three times.

Similarly, as a young boy Howard took particular comfort in arranging things: his toys according to size, his crayons according to color, the food in the kitchen cabinets according to brand name. "I was always putting things in order," he said. "Or coming up with some new method of arranging them. One summer I got a set of Civil War soldiers and spent practically every free minute setting them up according to different Civil War battle strategies I read about in library books." That also happened to be the same summer his father lost his job and his whole family moved in with his grandparents. "Everyone was at each other's throats constantly," Howard recalled. "Sometimes the fights got so loud that the neighbors called the police. It just got worse and worse." And Howard spent more and more time in the corner of his room arranging and rearranging his soldiers. Unlike his family, they were something he could control. Moreover while poring over Civil War books and planning new battle positions, he was able to escape mentally, shutting out the chaos and conflict going on around him. "I know it doesn't make sense," Howard commented, "but once I had the soldiers the way I wanted them, I felt okay and as if everything that was happening would work out okay too."

While striving for your own brand of perfection or after accomplishing some task you had assigned yourself, for a fleeting moment you, too, felt okay. Your fatal flaw had been eliminated for the time being. Your past mistakes and your fear of making new ones were forgotten temporarily and your demise postponed. The feeling did not last for long. Your fundamental belief about yourself did not change. Your method failed as often or more often than it succeeded. But none of that really registered in your mind. You had come to believe that your way of doing things would bring the desired result if you just did it well enough and kept at it long enough. If you just tried hard enough, you would be good enough and life would be perfect.

The Hitch: Perfection Is an Illusion

Your ingenious plan for overcoming your inadequacies and coping with your difficulties had a hitch in it from the start. Perfection is unattainable. Making mistakes now and then is unavoidable. Countless circumstances are uncontrollable. Because you had neglected to factor these realities into the equation, each time you were confronted with them, you felt like a failure, confirming your original beliefs and dealing yet another blow to your self-esteem. You had unwittingly purchased a ticket for an

61

endless roller coaster ride of high hopes followed by bitter disappointments, leading to renewed ambition followed by new failures.

The best part of the trip is the striving. When you are heading
uphill in pursuit of your goal, you feel charged up, full of energy,
and as if you are on the verge of some incredible breakthrough.
Of course a good deal of that energy is cold, raw fear and anxiety,
but it is familiar and, at least in the beginning, not particularly
uncomfortable. Trying is something you know how to do well
and, as long as you are trying, perfection still seems possible and
magical. It will cure all your ills—an illusion that quickly fades
once you accomplish a goal. As we've mentioned, you do accomplish a great deal along the way. But when you reach a peak,
you feel no glow of achievement. You have only done what you
expected yourself to do. Conversely when you plummet downhill—after making a mistake, being criticized, or assuring yourself that you could and should do better—you are overwhelmed
with feelings of guilt and shame. You have failed to live up to
your expectations and frequently feel that you have disappointed
everyone else in your world as well. You continue your emotional
nosedive for as long as you can endure the pain and anxiety,
which isn't very long for most perfectionists. Propelled by those
old familiar "shoulds, musts, and have-tos," you immediately start
striving (and riding the roller coaster) again.

The Descent: Trying Too Hard

Over the years perfectionism brings you fewer rewards and more
self-punishment. Naturally matters are not helped by your tendency to magnify your flaws and failings. No setback is just a
setback. It is instead a complete rejection of who you have tried
so hard to become. You must come face-to-face with the negative
image of yourself you so desperately want to be rid of. Feeling
unworthy and inadequate, fearing that you've blown your last
chance at happiness, you are convinced that even worse disasters

are just around the bend. Blind to what you have done right and overlooking how far you've already come, you fall into the gap between what is and what you still hope could be. To close that ever-widening gap, you do more of what you've always done— more strenuously, more single-mindedly, and unfortunately more counterproductively.

It does not occur to you to lower your standards or to step back and take some time to experience joy or relaxation in other areas of your life. You just keep striving, trying harder not to make mistakes, and fighting more tenaciously to overcome and cover up your inadequacies. And trying so hard, trying *too* hard begins to take its toll.

The Cost: Self-defeat

When you reach this point in the cycle, your perfectionistic thought patterns and your perfectionistic behavior actually prevent you from achieving your goals or cost you so much in the process that your striving hardly seems worth the effort.

You work more hours but accomplish less. Like Sharon, you come up with such elaborate schemes to guarantee that you make the right decision that you never get around to making a decision at all. Like Desmond, you develop time-consuming rituals and routines. You want a relationship but reject all likely candidates or make a terrific first impression but won't let anyone get close enough to be a friend. At home, at work, with lovers, family, and friends, on the racquetball court and in pottery class, you are determined to "go for the gold" and be the very best. Wanting it all and willing to settle for nothing less, far too often you end up with nothing.

The strain of your relentless struggle may exact a physical toll—ulcers, skin rashes, headaches, chronic back pain—or a psychological one. You may begin having panic attacks, turn to tranquilizers or alcohol to calm your nerves, or use amphetamines or cocaine to give you an energy boost and a shot of false confidence. Your intimate relationships may buckle under the pressure of your constant nit-picking. Even your sex life can suffer.

Fearing failure and riddled with self-doubt, you begin to question your competence at every turn: Can I do it? What if I blow it? Where could I make a mistake? You get yourself so worked up and worried that resistance sets in. You postpone any task that you might complete imperfectly. Drawing upon the old adage "If you can't do something right, don't do it at all," you avoid situations that might lead to failure—even though they might also lead to pleasure and success. And some of you throw in the towel altogether, turning your predictions of failure into self-fulfilling prophecies.

Bernie, a National Merit Scholarship student, became so overwhelmed with anxiety during a science exam that he "went blank" and did so poorly on the test that he began to think his entire academic life might soon be over. After he went blank during a history test several weeks later, Bernie proved himself right—by quitting school. Five years later he still labels himself a loser and makes sure that label sticks by passing on every opportunity to return to school. We have heard similar stories from women who walked out on their families after years of pushing themselves to the limit in order to be perfect wives and mothers and from high-level executives who decided they'd never make it to the top and so left the corporate world altogether.

In these and other ways the cost of perfectionism can be astronomical. Although you may not have paid all that much yet, you will if you allow the cycle of self-defeat to continue long enough. Fortunately that is not necessary. You can break the cycle at any time and in a number of different ways, which we will be discussing later in the book. But first let's take a look at how the cycle began—with the "shoulds, musts, and have-tos" other people conveyed to you as well as the past experiences that convinced you that you were not good enough but could be if you tried hard enough.

Chapter Three

From "You Should"
to "I Should":
The Making of a Perfectionist

Before he turned two, Jay, the marketing division chief you read about in the Introduction, was talking in complete, complex sentences. He was reading at age three and showing signs of perfectionism by the time he entered kindergarten. If, for any reason, he did not immediately understand his teacher's instructions and could not figure out how to do exactly as she asked, he would become nervous to the point of hyperventilating. Coloring outside the lines was enough to send him off to the nearest corner to cry, and writing letters or numbers was sheer torture. Determined to form each one flawlessly and space them perfectly on the page, Jay would erase his mistakes so feverishly that he ripped his paper (and threw a tantrum if his teacher wouldn't supply a new sheet so that he could redo the entire assignment). Twenty-five years after the fact, Jay still recalls the bitter disappointment he felt when he was "fired" from his job of painting the face on a Halloween pumpkin. "We need this done before

Christmas," he remembers his teacher saying. "There's such a thing as being too careful, you know."

At eight Sharon, the hospital purchasing agent we introduced in the last chapter, would assign herself intricate "extra credit" projects in order to impress her hard-to-please third-grade teacher. Unfortunately she would stay up until one or two in the morning to complete them and then fall asleep during class the next day, incurring her teacher's wrath instead of garnering his praise. By about the same age Marty, the exercise physiologist and college hockey player, had already earned a reputation as a sore loser. He never played to play, only to win, and would begin badgering and bullying his teammates as soon as it became apparent that his team was on its way to defeat. Sometimes he would storm off the field in the middle of a game, race home, and lock himself in his room, where he sulked for hours.

And Barbara, the office manager whose quest for the perfect outfit and the perfect occasion to wear it left her with a closetful of unworn clothing, a mountain of debts, and a marriage rife with conflict, had been obsessed with her appearance for as long as she could remember. "I don't know how my mother put up with me," she commented. "I'd pitch a fit whenever I found the tiniest smudge of dirt on my shoes or if my barrettes didn't match my dress perfectly. And if those barrettes weren't exactly right, if they weren't clasped just tight enough or in just the right spot, I'd scream at the top of my lungs until my mother fixed them." Barbara was not quite three at the time.

Tracing the Path of Perfectionism

Like Jay, Sharon, Marty, and Barbara, if you are a perfectionist today, you have probably been one for quite some time. And like our patients and students, you may find that writing a history of your own perfectionism will provide you with valuable insights about the behaviors and thought patterns that are currently defeating you.

1. Take out a notebook or several sheets of paper and start your chronology by jotting down your earliest memories of trying to be the best, extreme reactions to changes in routine, mistakes you made that seemed particularly upsetting, any versions of the "numbers game" you recall playing, circumstances you tried to avoid, or opportunities you could have taken advantage of but didn't for fear of failing or looking like a fool.

2. Then after reading each of the following sections on perfectionism at various stages of development, stop and list any incidents of perfectionistic thinking or behavior that you remember occurring during that stage in your life.

EARLY CHILDHOOD. Your finicky behavior and fussiness as an infant or toddler may be legendary, vividly recalled, and frequently recounted by the members of your immediate family. Your mother may still talk about your refusal to take a nap until all of your stuffed animals were lined up on your bed in a specific order. Your dad may still tease you about correcting him whenever he altered a bedtime story in any way. Or your siblings still may not have forgiven you for the outings you ruined by throwing tantrums because you wanted a pink balloon instead of a green one or for the times you tattled on them because they wouldn't do exactly as you asked.

SCHOOL AGE. If the writing wasn't on the wall before you started school, your perfectionistic behaviors and thought patterns may have become apparent soon afterward. Like Jay, you may have been determined to follow every instruction to the letter and never make a single mistake. Or like Sharon, you may have been willing to go to any length to win your teachers' praise and approval. As a result of your difficulty handling challenges, frustration, or failure, perhaps you developed school phobia, coming down with real or feigned illnesses or crying hysterically and begging your parents to let you stay home. You may have played hooky when tests were scheduled or became disruptive and had to be removed from class just before it was your turn to read aloud.

By the time you were ten or eleven, many of your perfectionistic tendencies may have been in full bloom. Convinced that you were not doing well enough, you may have engaged in aggressively competitive behavior, accumulated and counted awards, A grades, baseball cards, or comic books to measure your worth. Or perhaps you were excessively concerned with following rules and making sure that your siblings and playmates followed them as well.

ADOLESCENCE. This is a time of extremes for one and all, and for you, it may have been the time when your perfectionistic behaviors and thought patterns were being etched in stone. Peer pressure was at its most intense. Your physical appearance and athletic ability took on enormous importance. Dating began, and having good grades was essential for getting into a good college (or getting into one at all). Consequently even if you were already getting terrific grades, wowing them on the football field, or soloing with the high school orchestra, you may have pushed yourself even harder, driving yourself unmercifully and living in a near-constant state of stress and tension. What with early-morning team practices, classes, extracurricular activities, after-school jobs, and homework, your schedule may have been jam-packed, leaving you no time for relaxation. As a budding perfectionist, even dating could seem like a competitive sport. And dissatisfaction with your body may have led to extremes in dieting and exercise, even eating disorders such as anorexia and bulimia or steroid abuse.

LATE ADOLESCENCE AND EARLY ADULTHOOD. Entering college can be a nightmare for anyone with perfectionistic tendencies and if you were a high achiever who had grown accustomed to being the best, it may have been extremely disconcerting to discover how much stiffer the competition was at the college level. It may have been difficult to accept that so many other people were as intelligent as you were—

or, worse yet, more intelligent—and to prevent the foundation for your self-worth from crumbling, you may have devoted yourself to disproving that fact: pulling all-nighters; writing extra-long, meticulously annotated term papers; volunteering to conduct research for professors; or doing anything else you could think of to outperform your fellow students.

By this time you may have had your entire future planned and layed out in front of you like the yellow-brick road to Oz. Because you would have to go on to earn a higher degree at a prestigous graduate school in order to give yourself an edge in the ever-more-competitive job market, getting good grades was of the utmost importance, an all-consuming task on which the rest of your life depended. Viewing every move you made as a step toward future success or failure, mistakes were unthinkable. You may have dropped any class in which you might not earn an A, making up credits by carrying a heavier classload the next semester. Naturally this not only increased the pressure you were under but also left you feeling like a failure for having to drop a course in the first place—undermining your confidence and making it more difficult to achieve the perfect grade point average you so desperately wanted. The cycle of self-defeat had begun and was apt to accelerate as you made the transition into adulthood: facing such new challenges as living on your own, entering the work world, marrying, beginning a family, and so on.

3. Complete your chronology by asking old friends or family members for additional evidence of past perfectionism. Because your behavior seemed natural (and not the least bit unusual) to you at the time, they may have clearer memories of that behavior than you do.

4. Once your history is complete, go back over it, paying particular attention to any time periods when you seemed especially driven. Try to determine whether anything out of the ordinary was going on in your life during those times.

Underline the items that are most like the perfectionistic thoughts and actions that are causing you trouble today and try to recall the ideas that might have been behind those past actions ("Dad gets angry when I'm not careful, so I'd better mow the lawn and trim the hedges perfectly—even if the lawn mower is too heavy for me to push and the hedge clippers are too big for me to handle." Or "Boys would like me if only I were thinner.")

5. Make a mental note of any other patterns you find, as well as the areas in which your perfectionism seemed most pronounced (schoolwork, athletics, dieting, dealing with the opposite sex, etc.).

The Roots of Perfectionism

No matter when it first became noticeable, the seeds of your perfectionism were sown at a surprisingly early age. The soil in which they grow, according to psychologist Alfred Adler, is the inherent sense of inferiority that accompanies our arrival in the world as tiny, helpless infants with needs we are totally dependent on others to fulfill. From the moment we are born, Adler theorizes, we are striving for superiority, trying to rise above our feelings of helplessness and dependency. We do this by developing behaviors that enable us to have a certain amount of control over ourselves and others. As infants we cry when we are hungry, wet, or uncomfortable, and if our caretakers appear in a timely fashion to address our needs, our inherent feeling of inferiority is temporarily replaced by a sense of superiority. We recognize that we have the power to get our needs met and feel safe, trusting, confident.

We repeat that process endlessly because the feeling of inferiority never departs completely. Our sense of self-worth and ability to set and achieve realistic goals rises each time we succeed in exercising control at various stages of development—when we learn to control our bodily functions, master new skills, reassure ourselves that caretakers who leave the scene will return, are able to obtain the praise, acceptance, and affection we desire, and so on. If, for reasons we will be getting to momentarily, our efforts to overcome our sense of inferiority (in whatever form they take) repeatedly fail to bring about the desired results, we become frustrated, fearful, and insecure, paving the way for an ever-more-desperate struggle to compensate for our inferiority and prove our superiority—in other words, perfectionism.

Karen Horney, another pioneer in the field of psychology, describes the same basic struggle in her book *Our Inner Conflicts*. She asserts that children come to terms with their own powerlessness, dependency on others, and fear that their basic needs will go unmet by modeling themselves after the powerful person on whom they depend—usually a parent. "If I can be like this person, who holds my very survival in the palm of her hand, then I will not feel afraid or need to worry about being deprived of the things that are important to me," is the unconscious premise that leads children to create standards for and images of the person they *should* try to be. Of course children do not see their parents or other adults in a realistic light. As far as they are concerned, Dad can do no wrong and Mom knows everything about everything. As a result the standards for their future self, the image of the person they ought to be, are an idealized image, an illusion that is and will always be beyond their grasp.

If youngsters simply attempt to be *like* mom or dad, recognizing their own limitations and incorporating into their self-image traits they observe in others or discover in themselves, then the modeling process achieves its purpose: enabling them to manage their basic anxiety, trust other people, and trust their own judgments and ability to get along in the world. However, if they actually expect and try to *become* their model and live up to the superhuman attributes they have assigned to their model, the discrepancies between the idealized image of the self and their real self lead to a loss of self-respect, feelings of self-contempt, and increased anxiety. They become victims of what Horney calls the tyranny of the ought: endlessly, obsessively, compulsively, and more often than not destructively trying to comply with internal edicts regarding what they ought to do in

71

order to become the person they ought to be.

To a greater or lesser extent all of us experience the internal conflict Adler and Horney describe. Our desire to resolve that conflict and relieve the anxiety it creates is thought to be one of the most powerful driving forces in our lives, motivating many of our actions, both positive and negative. In this light, striving for perfection in one or more areas of your life can be seen as a coping mechanism, an automatic response to a psychological tug-of-war that you do not even realize is taking place within yourself.

But why did you develop perfectionism and not some other behavior pattern, you may wonder? Why didn't you become depressed and unmotivated, for example, or develop psychosomatic illnesses, instead of setting impossibly high standards for yourself and relentlessly trying to live up to them? And where did you get the idea that perfection was attainable and that anything less was unacceptable? Social-learning theorists and psychologists subscribing to various schools of thought would tell you that you *psychologically inherited* that belief along with other attitudes and behaviors that were passed down to you by your parents and other influential people in your life. Because those people played a crucial role in your life, because you were young and unprepared to do anything else, and because you were not consciously aware of what you *were* doing, you adopted your role models' "rules" unexamined and used them to organize and interpret your unique life experiences in a way that *predisposed* you to perfectionism.

Learning to Be Perfect

"My grandmother was a real neatnik," Howard said while describing the turbulent summer when his family lived with his grandparents. "I think half the fights between my mom and my grandmother started over some mess one of us kids made. 'Didn't I teach you anything?' my grandmother would ask and then go on and on about the importance of developing good habits early in life and how we were all going to grow up to be losers like everyone on my dad's side of the family. She gave me the same lecture hundreds of times." Howard's grandmother drove home her point by inspecting his bed to make sure it had perfect hospital corners, tearing off the sheets and forcing him to remake it if he failed the inspection. She had him scrub bathroom tiles with a toothbrush. He had to polish her extensive collection of knickknacks every single day and return each item to the exact spot from which he removed it. Howard did not protest. In fact he volunteered to do more. As he explained, "Looking back on it now, it seems like I thought the fighting might stop if I did everything she told me just the way she liked it."

"During most of my childhood, my parents were missing in action," said Judy, the constantly-on-the-run wife, mother, and much more whom we mentioned briefly in Chapter One. Her parents owned a restaurant and were at work from the crack of dawn until late into the night. "We lived above the restaurant," Judy continued, "so we could see them if we went downstairs. But they were always so busy that you couldn't help feeling that you were in the way. I hated when they yelled at me for bugging them and I hated it even more when they yelled at one of my brothers for the same thing, because that meant I had screwed up. It was my responsibility to take care of them and to keep them from getting in my parents' hair." In fact at the tender age of nine, almost all the responsibility for raising her brothers and running the household fell on Judy's shoulders. Her parents were simply too busy (or too tired when they were not working) to attend to such things and they expected their oldest child and only daughter to handle everything but dire emergencies. Of course a child's concept of a "dire emergency" is different from an adult's, and disconcerting memories of seeking her parents' help with matters that they deemed less than urgent still linger in Judy's mind. "My dad would yell, but my mom's tired sigh was even worse," Judy said. "Either way I knew I'd let them down. When they said, 'You know, you could have handled that yourself,' I felt like a complete failure."

"If I heard it once, I heard it a million times," Linda, the single attorney who finds fatal flaws in every man she dates, commented. "'Don't make the same mistakes I did,' that's what my mom would say whenever she was depressed, which was most of the time." Linda's mother had married young. Madly in love, she had been devastated when her first husband walked out on her. She married a second time "for security" and put up with her physician husband's philandering for the same reason. "My dad always had someone else," Linda said. "He didn't even try to keep it a secret, but my mom pretended it wasn't happening or that it didn't mean anything or who knows what, but she seemed absolutely convinced that no matter what he did outside the house, he would always come home to his family." That proved not to be the case, and when Linda's father asked for a divorce, Linda's mother was not only shocked but completely unprepared for life without him. "She was a mess," Linda continued. "A basket case. She didn't have a single marketable skill, not a clue about making it in the real world. She wound up babysitting to make ends meet since my dad's support checks didn't exactly support us. Our home was a madhouse, and she was the maddest, most miserable part of the picture." Taking all this in, Linda did not need to be warned not to make the same mistakes her mother had. She vowed never to be in the same position. "I was going to be completely independent," Linda explained. "And I wasn't going to get married until I was absolutely certain that I'd found the right man—not some jerk who'd walk out on me the first chance he got."

By themselves the circumstances Howard, Judy, and Linda described did not guarantee that they would grow up to be perfectionists. Many nonperfectionists have similar backgrounds, and many perfectionists have different ones. However, in conjunction with other things that happened to them, other behaviors they observed, and messages about themselves that they received from people who were important to them, those circumstances set Howard, Judy, and Linda on the road to perfectionism or kept them moving along it. Their perception of the circumstances they had encountered and the meaning they assigned to their experiences became part of a mental picture of themselves, other people, and the world that paved the way for the perfectionism that would defeat them at a later date. If you are a perfectionist today, you have pieced together a similar mental picture: a perfectionistic mind-set composed of attitudes and beliefs you have been accumulating since the day you were born.

The Importance of Birth Order

According to Dr. Kevin Leman, author of *The Birth Order Book: Why You Are the Way You Are,* and other psychologists who have studied family structure, birth order plays a significant role in the development of any child's personality. If you happen to be a firstborn or only child, for example, you are apt to be more goal-oriented, critical, conscientious, and reliant on authority than middle or youngest children. You tend to have higher IQs and do better on tests as well. You are also the most likely to develop perfectionistic tendencies during childhood and to grow up to be bona fide perfectionists.

On the plus side, as a firstborn child you received more attention and stimulation from your parents than your siblings did. Your parents spent more time with you. But you were also the child they "practiced on," so to speak. Nervous and untested, your parents were likely to be overly cautious and determined not to make any mistakes while raising you. Although they were not necessarily trying to mold you into a perfect child, because childrearing was new to them, they made a fuss over everything you did, fretted over every problem you had, and tended to have unrealistic expectations about your abilities. They encouraged you to do more and sometimes to do those things before you were developmentally ready to do them. Because your parents seemed so pleased when you accomplished the tasks they set up for you, you tried hard to achieve them, basking in their approval when you succeeded, and when you failed, getting your first taste of the pressure to perform and frustration that would haunt you for the rest of your life. In addition if you spent the lion's share of your early years with adults, you may have taken on an adult-like seriousness or willingly assumed more responsibility than children your age were typically expected to handle.

That tendency is even more pronounced in only children. If you are one, during your formative years you quickly became accustomed to receiving a great deal of attention and got into the habit of relying on other people's reassurance and approval. Without siblings around to compare yourself to, you were likely to develop the "idealized image of the self" we mentioned earlier and to try but never quite manage to measure up to the only standard of comparison available to you—your parents' capabilities, which were clearly beyond your reach.

Frequently treated like a little adult and considered your parents' pal as well as their offspring, as an only child you tried to play the role in which you were cast: to fill shoes that were too big to fit or move around in without stumbling. Stumble you did. Tripped up by the limitations of age, size, maturity, and life experience, you may have been quite young when that "not good enough" feeling emerged. In addition, because you were in fact advanced for your age, you may have had a harder time coping with the demands or shortcomings of your peers and as a result became a loner.

Although middle children can also become perfectionists, they are less likely to and are often the exact opposite of their firstborn sibling. By the time they are born, their parents have usually developed a more realistic attitude about parenting and have learned through experience that mistakes are inevitable and hardly catastrophic. Because they know what to expect and can distinguish between normal behaviors and problematic ones, their approach to parenting is much more relaxed, even laissez-faire. Consequently middle children generally get the least amount of attention and tend to keep to themselves, taking themselves out of the competition for their parents' approval and affection. If you are a perfectionist and a middle child, either circumstances like those we will soon be describing intervened or you did not "drop out" of the race. Instead you did everything you could think of to be viewed as favorably as the firstborn apple of your parents' eyes.

Youngest children tend to be indulged rather than driven and are probably the least likely to develop perfectionistic tendencies. However, they may play a significant role in furthering the perfectionism of their firstborn brother or sister.

Sibling Rivalry

The eldest of three children, Alex, the interpersonal perfectionist we introduced in Chapter One, was quiet and serious during his early years. He rarely misbehaved, but recalls that when he did, his mother read him the riot act. "She'd ream me out but good," he explained, "send me to my room, and if I'd really gotten out of line, not let me watch TV for a week. But that wasn't the worst part. The part I really hated was when my dad got home and my mom told him what I'd done. He'd sit me down for a little father-son chat and tell me how much I had disppointed him. I felt about two inches tall." Horrified by the idea of disappointing his father, whom he, like most boys, idolized, young Alex tried very hard to behave himself and by age six was a model child. "But then Michael was born, and all hell broke loose," Alex said.

Although Alex had not had much trouble adjusting to the arrival of his younger sister, Michael's appearance on the scene was another story entirely. "He was a terror," Alex claimed. "And my mom let him get away with murder." Not only did she put up with misbehavior that she never would have tolerated from Alex, but she expected Alex to put up with that behavior too. Although he no longer thinks so, during his youth Alex was convinced that Michael lay awake at night thinking up new ways to torture him. As Alex remembers it, "One day Michael would destroy my model airplanes. The next he'd get into my paints, and I'd get in trouble for the mess *he* made. And when he was going through his biting stage, I wanted to kill him." During the stage Alex referred to, Michael's favorite pastime seemed to be biting Alex's arm. "My mom knew what he was doing but didn't try to stop him. And she wouldn't let me fight back," Alex recalled. "I was supposed to understand and be patient and wait for him to grow out of it." But that periodically proved to be too much to ask. "Naturally when I had enough and slugged him, he went crying to Mom, and I got punished," Alex said.

Although the foregoing is a fairly typical scene in any household with more than one child, it had added meaning for a perfectionist in training like Alex. For one thing Alex was painfully aware that unlike himself Michael was loved and accepted without having to "earn it" by behaving perfectly. Worse yet, Michael's presence made Alex's unreasonable goal of never misbehaving or disappointing his father even more difficult to achieve. He tried harder but still failed more often than he had before his brother was born.

When he was a few years older, Alex tried to make up for the ground he had lost by becoming his family's self-appointed policeman and reporting all of Michael's transgressions to one or both of his parents. He even "spied" on Michael, taking note of his misbehavior in school, at the mall, or on the playground. Although he sabotaged himself in the process—disappointing his father, who repeatedly told him that "nobody likes a tattletale," Alex felt vindicated each time he got his brother into trouble and developed the habit you saw in action during his ill-fated job interview: finding fault with others when his own self-esteem needed a boost.

Although you may not have coped in the same way, you, too, may have found yourself in the unenviable position of not only striving to obtain your parents' attention and approval but also competing with one or more of your siblings to keep whatever you had already managed to get from being taken away. In fact if you check your chronology, you may notice a rise in perfectionistic behavior during those times when sibling rivalry was most intense.

78

Special Status

Sometimes it is not your place in the birth order, but your gender or some other special characteristic that sets the stage for perfectionism. For instance Jay was the only male child in a family of six. His very traditional, "Old World" parents pinned all their hopes and aspirations on him, and throughout his life Jay, a youngest child, heard his father say, "We kept trying until we got it right." Apparently news of the women's liberation movement never reached Jay's household, where it was generally accepted that his sisters were *only* going to be wives and mothers. He, on the other hand, was expected to do great things and bring honor to the family name.

Similarly Marty was the third child of four and the second son but was elevated to special status and pressured to live up to it because of his natural athletic abilities. "The best years in my dad's life were during high school and college, when he was this legendary superjock," Marty said. "They still have his picture in the trophy case at his old high school and his record for most passes completed in a season still stands. After his playing days ended, I think his number-one goal was to have a son to carry on the winning tradition he started." Since Marty's older brother was small and uncoordinated, Marty became his father's legacy-to-be, a status that left Marty relentlessly striving to match his father's accomplishments and living in fear of letting him down.

Gifted children (those whose IQs are in the exceptional range, usually 130 and above, or who display exceptional talent in music, art, science, or other areas) are often awarded special status in their families as well as in the world outside their homes. Their high potential for achievement, the high expectations of their parents, teachers, and peers, and their own hypersensitivity to criticism or disapproval make them prime candidates for perfectionism. Because other people expect only the best from them and seem not just disappointed but also bewildered when they perform less than magnificently, gifted children come to expect magnificence from themselves and push themselves to extremes.

79

They frequently face misunderstanding and hostility from their less-than-"exceptional" peers and as a result lead lonely existences, hiding their hurt feelings because everyone seems to think that their exceptional abilities should enable them to rise above human emotions. As one gifted perfectionist put it, "Whenever I said I was depressed or angry or if I started to cry, someone would say, 'Come on, now. You're too smart to feel that way.'"

With all other avenues cut off, gifted children are left with only their achievements to measure their self-worth, paving the way for performance perfectionism. In addition they may cultivate a feeling of omnipotence and come to believe that their ability to achieve is limited only by the barriers other, less competent individuals construct. That attitude often gets translated into interpersonal perfectionism later in life.

Conditional Love and Acceptance

Circumstances such as birth order, sibling rivalry, and special status put you in a position to learn the attitudes and beliefs that make up your perfectionistic mind-set. However, the lessons themselves are found in your interactions with other family members: how your parents treated you, the messages about yourself that you received from them and others, and also the behavior you observed.

One of the most powerful positive lessons your family can teach you is that you are *unconditionally* loved and accepted—that you are recognized and valued for who you are and that you will not be emotionally abandoned no matter what you do. Unconditional love is freely given. You don't have to earn it. You are not required to pay for it after the fact. It is there even when you make mistakes, and it is not *only* there when you do something to please or impress the person whose love and acceptance is important to you. When you are unconditionally loved, you feel secure. As you attempt new tasks and venture out into the world, you know that there is a safety net to catch you should you stumble and fall. With it you develop confidence.

You are willing to take risks. More important still, you come to believe that you are a lovable, capable person whose flaws are not fatal and whose failings can be forgiven. In other words you learn to love *yourself* unconditionally.

Regrettably that is a lesson that you, like most of the perfectionists we have counseled or interviewed, may never have learned. In your family, love and acceptance may have come with strings attached. "I love you because you are you," was not the message you received. Instead you came to believe that your parents (or others) loved, approved of, and valued you if and only if you lived up to their expectations for you.

Judy, for example, grew up believing that in order to be loved and accepted, she had to earn her keep. "I know it sounds crazy," Judy said. "But I always had this feeling that I could be replaced, that my parents liked having me around because I handled all the things they were too busy to get around to and because I never asked for much from them in return. I was a good deal. I thought that if I stopped being one and didn't assume all those responsibilities, they wouldn't need me anymore. They'd have no use for me. I'd be nothing, a nonentity in their lives." Judy also believed that if she had the audacity to ask for time for herself or comfort when she was feeling upset, she would be rejected completely.

As you may have noticed, the most frightening aspect of being *conditionally* loved is not necessarily the fact that you have to live up to your parents' expectations in order to be accepted by them but rather the possible repercussions of failing to do that. You could anger or disappoint your parents, be forced to withstand an onslaught of criticism, the silent treatment, even physical abuse. You would feel rejected, emotionally abandoned, humiliated, horribly ashamed—all terrifying prospects for any child and more than ample motivation for trying harder to measure up to your parents' standards. Unfortunately as you struggled to do that, you came to believe that your worth as a person rested solely on those things you had to do to earn (or avoid losing) your parents' love and acceptance. Eventually you could love and accept yourself if and only if you achieved the goals and lived up to the lofty standards you set for yourself.

Parental Pressure

Jay had high standards to live up to on all counts. As we mentioned, his parents' expectations for their only son were very steep. And as Holocaust survivors, their desire for him to carry on and bring honor to the family name was intense. "My dad and his brother were the only ones in their family who got out of the camps alive," Jay explained. "They were left to keep the family alive, to make sure there was a family after they died. We never compared notes, but based on how driven my cousins are, I'm guessing my uncle pushed them as hard as my dad pushed me." And Jay's dad definitely pushed. Despite arriving in the United States practically penniless, with a language barrier and no formal education beyond the sixth grade, Jay's father had worked hard and gotten ahead, making a comfortable living as a mid-level executive with a utilities company. After striving all his life he wanted bigger and better things for Jay and, like Marty's father, began steering his son toward *his* goals at the first available opportunity.

Education was the key to success, Jay's father believed, and soon after Jay began talking, his dad began teaching him the alphabet, showing him how to sound out words in storybooks and drilling him with flash cards at the dinner table. "He taught me algebra when I was in the third grade," Jay recalled. "And at any given moment he could reach for the dictionary, pick a word at random, and ask me to spell it. I can still close my eyes and see the way he looked at me when I couldn't do it. He'd get this pained expression on his face, like I'd stabbed him, then he'd shake his head and walk away, or he'd look up and say to God, 'Tell me, please, what to do with this boy so he won't be such a dummkopf?'"

Despite a superhuman effort to always supply the right answers and never make mistakes, Jay would hear those words and witness that pained expression many, many times. He was a bright child with an above-average IQ, but not the "genius" his father expected him to be. Moreover, because he had not yet learned the basic skills and thought processes they required, he was rarely ready to tackle the intellectual challenges his father put before him. Although his father's expectations and demands were unreasonable, Jay was too young to know that, and his father seemed not to realize it. He kept pushing, Jay kept trying, and each time he fell short of his father's standards, he felt guilty, ashamed, and terrified that he would never be able to satisfy and therefore be accepted by his dad. Considering this parental pressure and Jay's response to it—trying harder and trying not to make mistakes—it did not surprise us that Jay was already showing signs of perfectionism by the time he entered kindergarten.

Parental pressure takes many forms, from physical punishment to extremely subtle signs of disapproval: disappointed looks, sad sighs, frowns, pursed lips, or eye contact between your parent and another person that seems to say, "Can you believe how dumb he is?" Impatient attempts to step in and take over a task you are trying to complete or negative predictions and warnings ("That's too much for you, let me do it," or "I'm telling you now that you're getting in over your head, so don't come running to me when things don't work out") conveyed your parents' lack of confidence in you, which you were apt to see as a dare to do better and try harder. And words like "I expected more from you" or "You know better than that" cut like a knife. But your parents did not have to say they were mad or disappointed to get their message across. In fact, saying nothing is a particularly powerful form of parental pressure. By refusing to discuss the misdeed, walking away, or giving you the silent treatment, your parents reinforced the very belief their conditional love and acceptance originally planted in your mind: that making mistakes or doing anything less than is expected of you means you will lose the attention and affection you so desperately need.

If your parents' expectations were unrealistic or impossibly high to begin with, their pressure put you in a real bind. You wanted to please them, but you were literally incapable of meeting their standards. Your striving habit began at that point and may have been exacerbated by parents who seemed to take for granted the successes you did achieve. (Of course you got straight A's again. They expected nothing less. Yes, you looked "fine" on prom night. You were taught how to dress and groom yourself, weren't you?) Your past track record of success meant that you failed to get the approval you were seeking. Your successes had become so commonplace that your parents forgot that achieving them was still a struggle and that your effort still deserved to be rewarded. When the prize at the end of the race was not forthcoming, you were left with only the struggle and an inevitable sense of letdown. As you have seen, that pattern can persist within your own mind indefinitely.

Even more detrimental are parents who raised the stakes each time their child did manage to live up to their expectations. As Jay put it, "I know my dad only wanted what he thought was best for me, but he was impossible to please. When I did something well, even when I did exactly what he said he wanted, he never said, 'Good job, kid. I'm proud of you.' It was always, 'Okay, let's see you do it again. Only this time I want you to do this, that, and this other thing too.' I'd get straight A's, and he'd tell me about an essay contest he wanted me to enter. Or I'd win the regional debating competition, and he'd ask how my science-fair project was coming. No matter what I did, there was something else I had to do to make him happy. He was always *going to be* proud of me, but never once, not once in my entire life, did he say he actually was."

Because it resembles the "motivational" strategy used to get donkeys to pull carts (tying a carrot to a string and hanging it just beyond the donkey's reach), this form of parental "encouragement" is often referred to as carrot dangling. Its implicit message—which no child can miss—is that the child will be loved if he achieves a specific goal, will be accepted when he meets a specific standard, or will be valued once he learns how to conduct himself in a certain way. However, once he lives up to that expectation, instead of getting the "reward" he was promised, he gets another goal to achieve, another standard to meet, or another lesson to learn—and another promise. If there was a single surefire way to turn a child into a relentlessly striving, frequently frustrated, never quite satisfied perfectionist, carrot dangling would be it. Not surprisingly parents who are most likely to use this form of pressure tend to be perfectionists themselves.

Perfectionist Parents

If one or both of your parents were perfectionists, you definitely knew it. Not only did they demonstrate most of the characteristics we described in earlier chapters, but they also set unrealistic, unreasonable standards for you. They seemed unable to accept the fact that, like any child, you occasionally misbehaved or made a mistake.

"My mother was a perfectionist, all right," Barbara said, "She kept our house spotless, dressed to the nines just to go to the grocery store, and flew into a rage if my dad was late coming home for dinner, because the meals she prepared were perfectly timed. Everything would be ready at six o'clock on the dot, and you darn well better be at the dinner table with your hands washed and your napkin on your lap ready to eat. As far as she was concerned, having to wait until five minutes past six meant the entire meal was ruined and all of her hard work had gone to waste."

Barbara's mother also dressed Barbara like a "little porcelain doll," in starched pinafores and immaculate white dresses. Then she would send Barbara, who was no more than two and half at the time, out to play and warn her not to get dirty. But being a normal, active toddler, Barbara did get dirty. "My mother would take one look at me and start to scream," Barbara recalled. "She'd drag me into the house, yank off my clothes, give me a bath, and dress me all over again. I don't remember exactly what she

85

said, but I do know she would lecture me the whole time, and I got the feeling that she thought I was really rotten and that I had gotten dirty on purpose just to make her miserable." As you may recall, by the age of three Barbara had taken on the job of making sure she looked perfect herself and could be heard saying to herself, "You're a bad, bad girl," whenever she noticed so much as a speck of dirt on her clothing or body.

If your parents were perfectionists, they were apt to view your accomplishments the same way they viewed their own: with an eye on how you could do even better. Every bit of praise you did receive was apt to be followed by a few "helpful" suggestions or bits of "constructive" criticism. Marilyn, the appearance perfectionist who talked herself into a depression after her job interview, still recalls how her perfectionist mother could build her up and shoot her down practically in the same breath. "I'd come home from school with a drawing I felt relatively proud of, and the moment my mother saw it, she would start to gush. 'Oh, darling, isn't that *wonderful*! You're so *talented*. I'll bet you'll grow up to be a great artist.' Then she'd head toward the refrigerator and I would be sure she was going to hang it up for my dad and everyone else to see. Only she almost never did. Instead she'd turn back and start pointing out things that were wrong with my picture. She'd say, 'Of course it's a *lovely* drawing, sweetheart, but don't you think that this line is wrong? And it would look even prettier if you used a different shade of blue on this part. And what's that supposed to be over here? Why don't you sit down and draw it over?' She always pulled the rug out from under me that way."

Every perfectionist knows that "there's always room for improvement," and your perfectionist parent was no exception. Like Marilyn, just when you thought you had gotten something right, you were told about something you did wrong or could do better. You expected praise and got criticism or another push toward perfection and, like Barbara, you eventually began pushing yourself in that direction too.

Perfectionist parents try to "create" perfect children—children who present no disciplinary problems, who always do as they are told, and who are, in short, the best children they can possibly be. Their children's accomplishments are yet another external measure of their worth, and their children's failures (even if they aren't really failures at all) are invariably seen as evidence of their own failure as parents. This perception makes it virtually impossible for them to reassure and guide children who are struggling in any way—as you well know if you have ever turned to your perfectionist parent for emotional support and received an impatient, irritated response instead.

Finally, your perfectionist parent taught you perfectionism by example. Like all children, you naturally assumed that the perfectionistic behavior you observed was "good" behavior, the sort of behavior that was normal and preferable for members of your family to engage in. Without ever realizing you were doing it, you began mimicking your role models and, more important, *identifying* with them: incorporating their actions and attitudes into your personal blueprint for the person you should try to be. You are apt to be following that same blueprint to this day and, ironically, doing and saying to yourself many of the things you absolutely hated having done or said to you by your parents during childhood.

Parents Who Don't Push

"My parents never pressured me," Sharon claimed. "They didn't even know I was alive." Of course that was not true, but there was no denying that Sharon's parents largely ignored her. Her mother's time and attention went to caring for and encouraging Sharon's severely handicapped brother. "If he got a spoonful of food into his mouth, Mom would pop open the champagne, but when I had the lead in a school play, she didn't even show up. I know taking care of my brother was tough on her, but she didn't have to act like I didn't exist. She could have tried to be a little bit interested in what I did." Although Sharon's father payed a bit more attention to her, it wasn't enough. "He was out

87

of town on business most of the time," Sharon explained. "He was gone so much that he couldn't really keep up with what was happening to me. If I wanted his advice, I had to explain all the background information to him and he didn't really have the patience to sit through the whole story."

Without feedback about the things she did or guidance to help her make decisions about what to do in the future, Sharon was plagued by self-doubt and uncertainty. She did not know how good "good" was, and even though she was fairly certain that no one would even notice if she did something wrong, she did not want to be "bad." So Sharon decided to be perfect. Not consciously of course, but within the confines of her own young psyche, it seemed safest to try to do everything right and nothing wrong. That way she could be sure that she would never harm anyone and might even please someone enough to finally be noticed, accepted, and loved. This line of thinking is one of the reasons why children whose parents don't push or take much interest in them at all can still grow up to be perfectionists.

A second reason is *negative modeling*, which was definitely at play in Linda's case. Her mother selected the wrong man to marry, not once but twice, and as a result she was miserable and her life was a mess. Or that's how Linda saw it anyway, and she promised herself that she would NOT be that way herself. Her mother had no marketable skills, no drive, no ambition, and again, from Linda's point of view, those deficiencies explained why her mother was so dependent on men in the first place and could not "get her act together" after her divorce. Linda vowed to be completely independent, self-sufficient, and successful. The fear that she would end up like her mother was a powerful one, and the only way Linda knew to make sure it did not become a reality was to set very high standards for herself and others and never, under any circumstances, settle for less than the best. That was how she became a perfectionist.

You, too, may have had a negative role model, a parent whose habits you found so unacceptable that you promised yourself you would never be that way yourself. Your childhood home may have been chaotic, disorganized, and messy. Today your home is immaculate. There is a place for everything, everything is in its place, and you will go to any length to keep it that way. Or your parents may have been embarrassingly uneducated. Having vowed never to sound as unsophisticated as they did, you may have become a walking encyclopedia who reads five newspapers a day to keep up on current events, only watches the all-news and public-broadcasting stations on TV, and feels terribly guilty for harboring a single negative thought.

Dysfunctional Families

A dysfunctional family is:

- One that revolves around a parent's alcoholism, addiction, compulsive behavior, mental illness, or some other problem
- One in which parents are emotionally unavailable to their children and too overwhelmed, overworked, or concerned with their own problems to meet their children's needs
- One in which family members routinely break promises, keep secrets from "outsiders" and from one another, and act like the perfect family in front of others
- One that has strict, unspoken rules that everyone adheres to whether they make sense to them or not
- One in which the open expression of feelings and direct discussion of personal or family problems is discouraged.

If your family fit that description, your home life was apt to be confusing, inconsistent, and unpredictable. Receiving little nurturing or guidance, you were forced to find a way to survive in the midst of chaos and, if you were lucky, to restore some order to your own life. Stifling your real self and developing habits that you would carry with you into your adult life, perfectionism may have been part of the coping strategy you chose, especially if you took on the role of family hero the way Judy did.

Once referred to as "parentified" children, family heroes are hyperresponsible "little adults," who feel pressured to grow up quickly and assign themselves the impossible task of holding their fractured families together. They believe that if they just try hard enough, they can keep everyone happy, prevent crises from occurring, even control the dysfunctional family member's dysfunctional behavior. There are few expectations more unrealistic, unreasonable, and impossible to attain than these, but that fact does not prevent the family hero from trying to live up to them or from feeling horribly guilty and inadequate when she fails to do so.

The lack of consistency, honesty, and emotional expression in dysfunctional families can also contribute to perfectionism. It prevents you from trusting your own judgment or other people's positive comments about you. The universal tendency of dysfunctional-family members to blame themselves for their family's problems also did its part in creating your perfectionistic mind-set. It was practically impossible not to conclude that "if only" you were smarter, kinder, less of a bother, or otherwise better, your family might be "normal." If you were perfect, then your family would be too.

Other "Teachers"

Your lessons in perfectionism did not end at your family's doorstep. Teachers who were stingy with praise or who encouraged intense competition among their students promoted your "try harder" mentality. Learning disabilities that were not diagnosed until after you had encountered numerous failures despite your very best effort may have instigated your striving habit. Peers who formed cliques and excluded you or who teased you for being different in any way certainly stirred up a caldron full of "not good enough" feelings. So did the media. Television in particular bombarded you with images of perfect families, men and women with perfect bodies, people who could go through all sorts of trials and tribulations without smudging their makeup, much less losing their cool, and of course products that were "guaranteed" to make you as perfect as the people who pitched them.

Throughout your life you encountered rejection, ridicule, failures, and disappointments that may not have been particularly traumatic in and of themselves. Yet they seemed to confirm the attitudes and beliefs that were already beginning to come together in your mind. They seemed to require the same sort of striving and approval-seeking behaviors you had learned earlier in your life and had been practicing for years. As time passed, you had more and more experiences that appeared to be consistent with what you already believed. As a result more and more pieces of your perfectionistic mind-set fell into place. You encountered more and more opportunities to try your hand at being the best and to try harder if you fell short of the goal. As a result more and more of the perfectionistic behaviors you learned and practiced became habits—automatic responses that you relied on, whether they actually worked to your advantage or not. And the messages that were conveyed to you by others— "You've disappointed me," "I expected more from you," "You're too smart to feel that way," "You should have known better," "You could have tried harder," "There's always room for improvement," "Okay, so do it again, only better"—became the internal demands and self-critical, self-punishing statements you heaped upon yourself. The pressure others once placed upon you now comes from within, and the resulting sense of inadequacy and self-doubt keeps the cycle of self-defeat going strong.

Part Two

FOUR

PERFECTIONISTIC

PATHS

AND WHERE THEY

CAN TAKE YOU

A s you no doubt know, once adopted, a perfectionistic mind-set easily perpetuates itself, taking you down the same path repeatedly, although not necessarily the same path other perfectionists take. In the next four chapters we will be describing the four most common areas in which perfectionism flourishes: performance, appearance, interpersonal relationships, and moral codes. There is a considerable amount of overlap among the categories. So don't be surprised if you have perfectionistic tendencies in more than one area. Most perfectionists do. We have tried to provide enough information in each of the four chapters for you to create a composite picture of your own perfectionism in whatever form it takes. Finally, we have followed the course of perfectionism in each area farther than it may have taken you yet, but not any farther than some of you will go if you allow your perfectionistic behaviors and thought patterns to go unchecked.

Chapter Four

Performance Perfectionism: *"I Am What I Do— Perfectly"*

Performance Perfectionism in a Nutshell

· Performance perfectionists define themselves in terms of what they *achieve, accomplish, or produce*. They prove their worth by *winning:* outperforming all competitors, making the most money, receiving the most recognition, collecting the most awards. Their lives revolve around *doing* things that are complete and flawless in all respects and, even more so, around *not* doing things that are incomplete or flawed in any way.

Marty, who acted as if his entire future could be assured or destroyed by several typographical errors in a proposal, was a performance perfectionist. So was Jay, who climbed the corporate ladder at breakneck pace but, instead of basking in his success (or even enjoying it for so much as a moment), lived in fear of "screwing up somehow." Unable to trust other people to do things the way he knew they should be done, he tried to do them all himself, staying late every night, working every weekend, unintentionally undermining his staff's morale, and actually decreasing their productivity.

Colin was a performance perfectionist too. As was evident during the job-hunting misadventure we described in Chapter One, Colin believed that preparation was the key to success and invariably assigned himself a dozen steps to accomplish before he could actually embark upon the task at hand. He would list each step and the time he estimated it would take to complete it, all too often talking himself out of doing anything until he had enough time to do everything. Performance perfectionists can be world-class procrastinators.

They also tend to be dissatisfied with themselves—no matter how much they do or how well they do it. Judy, yet another performance perfectionist, felt that way. After a day jam-packed with obligations and responsibilities—a job, housework, child care, volunteer activities, and more—Judy would lie in bed berating herself for all the things she did not get to do and all the things she could have done better.

If you are a performance perfectionist, you yoke yourself to an unbelievably full agenda of daily tasks and expect to complete them all without feeling tense or exhausted. When you cannot achieve that impossible goal, you assume that your deficiencies—rather than the unrealistic nature of your goal—are at fault. "If only I wasn't so disorganized, so scatterbrained and inefficient, so lazy and incompetent," you think, "I would have gotten those things done today." Completely ignoring what you did accomplish in order to dwell on the things you missed, naturally you vow to try harder tomorrow. All too often you end up trying too hard and paying too high a price for the success and self-esteem you were seeking.

According to recent studies and surveys conducted by sports psychologists, athletes are particularly susceptible to performance perfectionism. Some struggle and sacrifice to reach top levels of competition, only to self-destruct, quit their sport, descend into a prolonged depression, turn to alcohol and drugs, even attempt suicide after turning in less than their best performance in a long-awaited event or coming in second instead of first. They are incapable of consoling themselves with the fact that they had attained a level of success other people can only dream of or that they did the very best they could under the circumstances. Seen through the mental filter of all-or-nothing thinking, being the second-best runner, skater, gymnast, or weight lifter is not an accomplishment but a failure. From their perfectionistic point of view, all the years of hard work and self-discipline had been completely wasted and all their dreams for the future had been destroyed.

Highly competitive and acutely aware that there can be only one winner in any event, athletes at any level can and do cross the line between the pursuit of excellence and the quest for perfection: berating themselves unmercifully for every less-than-perfect performance and driving themselves to the limit of their endurance and beyond. They obsessively worry about their weight and body fat, speculate that every twinge of pain is the first sign of a career-ending injury, ignore actual warning signs of illness and injury, train harder than is necessary for peak performances, even take steroids to give themselves that competitive edge. They push themselves too hard, and their bodies rebel, leading to poorer showings rather than better ones. They respond by pushing themselves harder, eventually burning themselves out.

Of course athletes haven't cornered the market on performance perfectionism. There are performance-perfectionist actors, who delay productions by arguing with directors over every line in a script; writers, who revise their work so many times that they miss deadlines; and dancers, who take a hundred rave reviews in stride but can repeat verbatim every critical word written about their work. In fact there are performance perfectionists clinging to their rung on the career ladder in every imaginable profession. Some literally work themselves to death.

If you are a performance perfectionist, you have many of the same traits and habits as overachievers in general and people with type-A personalities. They, too, are driven to achieve more

99

and more in less and less time. Suffering from "hurry sickness," they overdo, overschedule, rush from place to place, and urge everyone else to get a move on too. Overachievers and type-A men and women have high expectations and stressful life-styles. However, your perfectionistic behaviors and thought patterns increase the pressure you feel.

Because you concentrate on your deficiencies and on your potential to fail instead of focusing on your strengths and your chances for success, you suffer from worry sickness as well as hurry sickness. Your life is not a challenging climb up a mountain of your own making but rather a perilous journey through a jungle of self-doubt and uncertainty. When you do reach your destination, at best, you feel relieved to have survived the trip.

Thanks to your perfectionistic mind-set, you don't take pride or pleasure in the process of attaining your goals *or* in the outcome of your superhuman striving. Hooked on the praise, applause, recognition, or other tangible rewards, "playing the game" is no more than an inconvenience on the way to victory. Yet each time you emerge victorious, your thoughts immediately turn to sustaining your success, surpassing it, or finding fault with the way you played the game. You have become your own carrot dangler, both the donkey pursuing the carrot and the driver holding that reward just beyond your own grasp. Disappointment and dissatisfaction are virtually guaranteed.

Performance perfectionists frequently focus their energy on perfecting a single aspect of their life, neglecting their family, friends, health, and anything else that is not directly related to the goals they have established for themselves. However, the most anxious and guilt-ridden performance perfectionists tend to be those who expect to perform perfectly in a variety of roles.

Judy fit that description. She ran herself ragged trying to live up to the idealized image of herself as a superwoman: an indispensable and perfect employee, wife, mother, household manager, family finance officer, and community member. At work Judy felt compelled to be "most valuable employee" all day, every day. At home she tried to be patient and understanding at all times. No matter how tired she was, she forced herself to get actively and enthusiastically involved in her children's activities. She cooked, cleaned, entertained, rarely turned down her husband's sexual overtures, and always found time to help out a friend or relative. It was not uncommon to find her organizing a fund-raising drive over the telephone while cooking dinner, keeping an eye on the kids playing in her yard, and following the evening news on TV. Nor was it unusual for her mind to be elsewhere when she was supposed to be concentrating on a single task. In the midst of typing a letter she wondered whether her job was taking too much time away from her kids. While getting her kids ready for bed she thought about how distant her husband seemed during dinner and wondered if she'd been neglecting him. During lovemaking she suddenly remembered a PTA meeting she needed to reschedule. Like any performance perfectionist who spreads herself too thin and can't seem to let up in any tension-filled department, no matter what Judy was doing at any given moment, she worried and felt guilty about other things she could be doing more of or should be doing better.

Performance perfectionists are:

- Highly competitive
- Achievement oriented
- Impatient
- Easily frustrated
- Time pressured and preoccupied with deadlines, constantly rushing from one task or activity to the next

Performance perfectionists also:

- Have ultra-high standards for what constitutes success and work hard to live up to them, more often than not to the exclusion of everything else in their lives
- Tend to do two or more things at once: driving and talking on the car phone, jogging while listening to the all-news radio

station and exercising the dog, cooking dinner, and helping the kids with their homework

- Expect to perform tasks flawlessly, and when they fear they will not, put tasks off for as long as they can
- Tightly pack every available moment with "productive" activities and feel guilty or tense when they take time to relax or have fun
- Tell themselves, "If you want something done right, you'd better do it yourself," and find it difficult to delegate work or to allow others to do the jobs they've delegated without interfering
- Have difficulty accepting criticism and react negatively to suggestions

Performance perfectionists are repeatedly told:

- "You're too hard on yourself. Everyone makes mistakes."
- "Lighten up. How about taking some time to enjoy the fruits of your labor?"
- "You're killing yourself. If you don't slow down, you're going to end up in the coronary care unit or the psych ward."
- "Anybody else would be thrilled with that performance."
- "Working hard is one thing, but working all the time is ridiculous. If you don't start paying attention to your friends and family, you're going to end up counting all that money you're making all by yourself."

Sound familiar? If so, performance—achieving, accomplishing, and producing—is an area in which your perfectionistic behaviors and thought patterns are apt to be most noticeable and, regrettably, most counterproductive as well. Having found an external source to supply you with self-esteem (your accomplishments and the recognition that comes with them), you may go back to the well again and again and again, staying on the same course *even when your never-ending quest for tangible proof of your worth actually jeopardizes your health and chances for happiness.*

The Making of a Performance Perfectionist
•
ADELE

At six Adele was "creative, inquisitive, and highly motivated to learn, a bright, imaginative child, an excellent student, and a very talented little artist." We knew that because Adele, now forty-six and the head of her own graphic design company, had shown us the first-grade report card on which those words were written. "That was the first nice thing anyone ever said about me," Adele informed us. "And I never would have known it if a neighbor wasn't visiting when I brought that report card home. She read it out loud. My mother never said a word about it."

According to Adele, "Being bright and imaginative meant nothing in my family. In my family you did what you were told and never questioned authority. All I got from my mother were orders. 'Clean your room.' 'Set the table.' 'Watch the baby.' and 'Leave me alone. Can't you see I'm busy?'" Adele's father, a long-distance truck driver, had even less to say. "He was hardly ever home," Adele explained. "And when he was, I swear all he did was grunt or pick on my mother. He was always criticizing her and bossing her around. He was so mean to her that I must have assumed he would be mean to me and stayed out of his way."

Getting so little attention or nurturing at home, the praise and encouragement Adele received once she started school were like water offered to a man who had been wandering in the desert. She cherished every smile, every nod of approval, every gold star and positive comment placed on her papers. Her thirst for these rewards and reassurances was insatiable. She still had every report card and every other tangible sign of success she had ever accumulated filed away in hand-painted "memento" boxes neatly stacked in her home library.

At eight Adele decided to become a great artist and was moving full speed ahead toward her dream by age fourteen when she was admitted to her city's Fine Arts High School. Although the competition among her equally talented and ambitious peers

103

was intense, Adele continued to excel. Naturally she had a box full of ribbons, awards, and copies of drawings that had been printed in her school magazine to prove that.

At sixteen Adele realized her parents had no intention of sending her to college. She was "bound and determined to make it in spite of them." Or perhaps to spite them. "They were stupid, unsophisticated people. Completely unaware of anything beyond their back door and not the least bit curious about it either," she commented bitterly. Already driven to use external rewards as measures of her worth, Adele's resentment provided an extra push toward perfectionism. Her relentless striving began in earnest. She won a scholarship to the Rhode Island School of Design and worked two jobs to cover her living expenses and the cost of art supplies.

During those extremely lean years Adele realized that "the life of a starving artist wasn't all it was cracked up to be" and put her original dream of being a great artist on hold. First she would make lots of money. She changed her major and, upon graduation, began her assault on the advertising world, making a name for herself and winning numerous awards for her product designs and print advertising artwork. She also developed a reputation for being difficult.

"It never ceases to amaze me how low people's standards are," Adele continued. "Everywhere I worked, people settled for mediocrity just to make the quickest buck. They made it seem like a sin to care about quality." Of course to Adele, who was by then a full-blown perfectionist, quality meant perfection. Her work had to be complete and flawless in all respects before she would allow anyone to see it and, in a field that required collaboration, bouncing ideas off one another, and taking cues from one's colleagues in order to come up with a coordinated, cohesive advertising campaign, Adele's approach was clearly counterproductive. Countless deadlines were missed because she had refused to let copywriters see her "unfinished" designs. In addition Adele's caustic comebacks to the slightest hint of criticism made working with her about as pleasant as walking through a mine-field. No one knew when she would explode.

To make matters worse, Adele hated to "waste" her time and talent on small-fry accounts or, for that matter, anything that wouldn't get a great deal of recognition or better yet be nominated for some sort of award. She went all out to persuade her superiors to assign big accounts to her and sulked for days when they did not. "It only stood to reason that if I was the best artist, I should have gotten the best projects to work on," she commented. "What's the point of being good at what you do if you can't strut your stuff?"

For more than a decade Adele moved from advertising agency to advertising agency, invariably leaving each one on a sour note, always feeling as unappreciated as she did in her childhood home. Finally she started her own company. She'd show them, she thought, and worked sixteen hours a day, seven days a week, to do just that. Although individuals and companies were clamoring for her designs and she had filled several more "memento" boxes with awards and favorable reviews, Adele's marriage (to an equally driven and perfectionistic banker) had long ago died of neglect. Her mood swings—from the pits of depression when anything, no matter how small, went wrong, to the heights of euphoria each time her work was praised or rewarded—made working for her a nightmare, and few employees stayed with her for more than six months. In addition, thanks to a diet of greasy fast food and candy bars eaten on the run or while working, when we met her, Adele weighed well over two hundred pounds. Her blood pressure and cholesterol levels were sky-high and she had an ulcer. Although she still dreamed of the day when she could "leave the rat race behind, live at the beach, and work on true works of art," between her desire to achieve even greater success in the graphic design business and her decidedly unhealthy life-style, it was less likely than ever that she would see that dream come true.

The Performance Perfectionist's Predicament

The Driving Force Behind Performance Perfectionism

Like all perfectionists, performance perfectionists are driven by a powerful need to prove to themselves and others that they are valuable, lovable, capable people. Like all perfectionists, when they look inside themselves, they see someone who is *not* as valuable, lovable, or capable as they should be. And like all perfectionists, they turn to external sources to supply them with the sense of self-worth they cannot generate internally. If you are a performance perfectionist, achieving, accomplishing, or producing things and the resulting rewards, recognition, praise, and approval are that external source.

Because ours is by and large a competitive, externally focused, performance-oriented society, many, many people derive a sense of identity and enhance their self-esteem based on what they accomplish, achieve, or produce. We believe, "I am what I do. Consequently the more I do and the better I do it, the better I am." And *anyone* who thinks that way has a personal investment in reaching his goals and finds even professional defeats personally painful. The inability to accomplish tasks as well or as quickly as he hoped stirs up self-doubt and insecurity. He spends a few hours or a few days worrying that he might not be as good or as smart or as competent as he thought he was. That line of thinking and the distress it creates is magnified tenfold if you are a performance perfectionist, who tends to consider any source of self-esteem other than your accomplishments meaningless and who has an unrealistic, unreasonable definition of what constitutes success in the first place. *You* believe, "I am what I do *perfectly* and I am diminished by anything I accomplish, achieve, or produce that is less than complete and flawless in all respects."

With this belief fueling your perfectionistic behavior and keeping your perfectionistic thought patterns going, at best you place more value on your achievements than on any other aspect of your life. At worst you live your life as if your achievements and your self are one and the same. Or as Judy put it, "You know how Descartes said, 'I think, therefore I am'? Well, for me it was, 'I do, therefore I am.' My whole life I've gotten things done to prove I existed. At the end of the day I'd say, 'See, you did this and this and this,' and because I had done something, I knew I was someone, that my life had some meaning and some value to the people I had done things for."

In addition, the things Judy failed to do became her goals for the following day, assuring her that she would still "be someone" when she awoke the next morning. Although you may not think that your accomplishments are the only things that verify *your* existence, chances are that you do keep yourself so busy and try to do so much because all that activity makes you feel important, indispensable, and more worthwhile than you would feel if you slowed down and did less. Moreover there is a certain exhilaration, an adrenaline rush that accompanies your race toward your goals, and it can be downright addicting. In fact, you may feel depressed, lethargic, and disoriented when you are not straining and striving to reach new levels of success. That is one reason you may have gotten into the habit of coming up with new goals as soon as you've achieved the old ones, planning tomorrow's tasks as soon as (and sometimes before) you complete today's or worrying about losing the ground you've gained without ever stopping to feel good about what you've already accomplished.

In addition, because your deeply ingrained assumption that you are not good enough the way you are can prevent you from internally generating positive self-esteem, you may become dependent on external measures of your worth and need more and more tangible proof of success in order to feel good about yourself. You may turn into an approval "junkie"; a praise addict; a frenetic, fanatic numbers-game player who counts everything and compares your "totals" with everyone else's. Unable to see that you are more than your "trophies," you are endlessly driven to get, have, or do more.

107

The Hitch: Fear of Failure

Defining yourself based on what you achieve, accomplish, or produce is unquestionably a double-edged sword. If you are what you do perfectly, then you also are what you fail to do perfectly. If you prove that you are a valuable, lovable, capable, worthwhile person by being the best there is at the things you do, then each time you turn in a performance that is less than complete and flawless, you have proven that you are not valuable, lovable, capable, and worthwhile after all. If you are a winner when you outperform all real and imaginary competitors, you are a loser if anyone has or does anything better than you. You approach each goal you set for yourself with your entire identity on the line. If you succeed, you are a hero. If you fail, you are the lowest life-form on the planet. Unfortunately, because your standards for success are so high and because deep down inside you believe you do not have what it takes to succeed, the potential to fail seems to lurk around every corner and with it the prospect of feeling utterly powerless and completely inadequate. Consequently if you are a performance perfectionist, avoiding failure and the emotional uproar it creates is apt to be an even more powerful motivating force in your life than your desire to succeed.

An awareness of the possibility of failure can be beneficial. It can keep you on your toes and help you plot a course of action that maximizes the potential for success and minimizes the risks involved in various undertakings. However, if you are a performance perfectionist, you are not just aware of the potential for failure. You are obsessed with it. You assume that failure is virtually guaranteed and view potential mishaps, no matter how unlikely they may be, as if they were catastrophic certainties. At any moment the house of cards you have devoted so many years to building could come tumbling down around you. One wrong move, one hasty decision, one imperfect performance, and you could lose everything you have worked so feverishly to obtain. Merely thinking about such disastrous consequences fills you with anxiety and dread. Preventing the worst-case scenarios you envision from becoming realities eventually takes precedence over all else—including the logical steps you would take to accomplish tasks, achieve your goals, and be productive.

Tormented by your drive for perfection and your nightmare visions of what might happen if you failed to perform perfectly, you may ward off your fears by putting off projects that stir up those fears. Preoccupied with your own deficiencies, you stew instead of do, often magnifying your fears in the process and making the task at hand seem much larger, more difficult, or more crucial than it really is.

Waiting for the perfect moment and the perfect conditions for getting the job done perfectly, you tell yourself that you will get around to making that sales call, filling out that graduate-school application, or tackling that year-end report when you are in a better frame of mind or have enough uninterrupted time to complete the whole project at one sitting. Unfortunately long before that mythical perfect moment arrives or those perfect conditions are met, you are confronted with real deadlines, demands, and the need to make clear-cut decisions.

Sometimes you know what you must do but procrastinate by doing something else instead—the way Colin did when he spent a week looking for sample letters, straightening his office, and revising his résumé before sitting down to write his cover letter. Sharon also avoided failure by prolonging the "preparation" stage. In an elaborate effort not to purchase the wrong photocopying equipment, she spent months surveying the hospital staff and testing out different machines. Similarly students who can't bear the thought of turning in a less-than-perfect paper often spend so much time researching their topic that they don't get around to writing their papers until the day before they're due. What's more, they consult so many sources and accumulate so many note cards that they find it virtually impossible to organize the mountain of facts they've found.

Perseveration—repeating one activity to the exclusion of others—is yet another form of procrastination. You start the task at hand but get stuck somewhere along the line: writing and rewriting the first sentence of a report, for instance, organizing and reorganizing your desk, listing and relisting the pros and cons of any decision before making it, or checking and rechecking your work before you turn it in, the way Desmond did. Although you are convinced that you are just being careful or thorough, you are also delaying the completion (and possible rejection) of a project you consciously or unconsciously fear will come off badly.

In whatever form it takes, procrastination is always self-defeating, and especially so for performance perfectionists, who measure their own worth based on how much they accomplish. For one thing, putting off anxiety-provoking tasks until the last possible moment invariably increases anxiety. In a state of sheer panic, procrastinating performance perfectionists race to complete whatever they have postponed. Their haste leads to carelessness and mistakes. Their frenzy leads to self-criticism. "This shouldn't be so hard," they think. "What's the matter with me? I should be able to do this with one hand tied behind my back." They dillydally and delay until they truly do not have enough time to complete tasks to their satisfaction and must settle for a less-than-perfect showing or miss their deadlines, angering and aggravating anyone they were hoping to please.

If you are a performance perfectionist, making sure that you don't fail eventually becomes more important than doing what it takes to succeed and you

- Don't explore new paths, even the ones that could bring you the joy, success, and peace of mind you are seeking
- Are reluctant to take risks, even the ones that are necessary for getting where you want to go
- Are determined to avoid every imaginable situation in which you could lose, make a mistake, or fail to measure up to your own expectations.
- Are constantly on the lookout for potentially dangerous cir-

cumstances and always waiting for the ax to fall, literally worrying yourself sick
• Are so afraid of turning in a less-than-perfect performance that you are too anxious to think clearly, making any goal harder (and all too often, impossible) to achieve

Therein lies the performance perfectionist's predicament and a prescription for self-defeat: a compelling urge to prove your worth by accomplishing, achieving, or producing things perfectly stirs up fears of failing, which prompt you to do whatever you can to avoid failure. Unfortunately your avoidance behaviors make it more difficult to achieve your goals and can even bring about the very failures you were trying to avoid, reinforcing your fears, motivating you to try harder to avoid failure, and further reducing your chances for success.

The Way Out for Performance Perfectionists

The key to overcoming performance perfectionism and breaking its cycle of self-defeat is learning to lead a balanced life: *keeping* your drive, ambition, and the performance-related skills that can work to your advantage, but *modifying* them and *making room in your life* for relaxation, fun, activities that feel good even though you may not do them well and pursuits or relationships that won't necessarily "get you anywhere" but will enrich your life. As difficult as it may be for you to believe right now, by doing *less* in the areas where you've always strived so hard to succeed and doing *more* to replenish your energy and appreciate the joys of *not* achieving, you will actually experience more success as well as more satisfaction when you do achieve a goal.

Obviously such a transformation will not occur overnight and in fact is a matter of making incremental changes in your lifestyle one step at a time. We describe those steps in Chapters Nine and Ten and recommend that performance perfectionists, in particular, take a look at and try the following:

Chapter Five

Appearance Perfectionism:

"I Am the Image

I Create "

Appearance Perfectionism in a Nutshell

Appearance perfectionists define themselves by the *image* they present to the world. Because they believe the aspects of themselves that matter most are the ones other people see, appearance perfectionists are obsessively concerned with the way things *look*. They derive a sense of self-worth from *controlling* that which is visible to the naked eye: their weight and the size of their thighs or biceps; the clothes they wear; the environment in which they live; the way their desks, drawers, even the condiments in their refrigerators are arranged; and most of all the impression they make on other people. Compliments, appreciative looks, and other signs of approval are the rewards they seek. Criticism, rejection, offending people, and hating what they see in the mirror are the consequences they are determined to avoid.

For appearance perfectionists, life is one long "beauty" pageant with every move they make and every word they utter scrutinized by a panel of judges composed of everyone they meet and also the harshest critic of them all—themselves. If appearance perfectionists could just pass their own inspections, they would finally feel safe, secure, and self-confident. They would finally rid themselves of that distressing "not good enough" feeling. But unfortunately like all perfectionists they set their standards too high for that to happen. Try as they might, they can't seem to make their bodies, wardrobes, homes, glib repartee, or any other external reflection of themselves complete and flawless in all respects. Yet they are compelled to keep trying, to keep striving for that outward appearance of perfection and that mirror image of flawlessness that may one day satisfy them and that will hopefully conceal their flaws from others in the meantime. There are few fates more dreaded by appearance perfectionists than having people think that they are less than perfect.

Of the perfectionists you've met so far, Howard was most definitely an appearance perfectionist. Long before he purchased the house he was practically going into bankruptcy to remodel perfectly, Howard paid meticulous attention to his surroundings. He would not start teaching a shop class until he and his students had all the tools and materials they needed arranged on their workbenches in the exact order they would be using them. Nor would he leave his house to pick up a date before every dish was washed, every book and record was shelved, and every surface was sparkling clean. He was convinced that any woman worth bringing home would think less of him, maybe even refuse to go out with him again, if he brought her back to an apartment that was not spotless. Of course his efforts to make his place look perfect often made him as much as an hour late for his dates, a fact that did not exactly endear him to the women he was hoping to impress.

Barbara, of the perfectly-put-together outfits that hung in her perfectly organized closets awaiting the perfect occasion to be worn, was an appearance perfectionist too. "When I know I'm going someplace special, I'll decide what to wear at least a week in advance," Barbara said. "That way I can be sure everything is clean and I have all the accessories I need." Even with her advance planning, it will take Barbara several hours to get dressed, made up, coiffed, and perfumed. If something goes wrong—if her hair does not fall "just right" or her eyeliner seems a bit too thick—she cannot "let it go." She must not only fix but completely redo the flawed aspect of her appearance: sticking her head under the spigot so that she can rewet, reset, dry, and restyle her hair because one curl would not stay in place, or removing all of her makeup and starting over because her mascara was "clumpy." As you might expect, Barbara comes completely unglued when an unexpected change in the weather makes the outfit she planned to wear inappropriate. Forced at the last minute to come up with an alternative, Barbara is apt to feel ill at ease for the rest of the evening and to have a rotten time.

According to Ralph, a fifty-two-year-old lawyer, a crooked picture hanging on the wall, dust on a mantle, or so much as one cigarette butt left in an ashtray drives him crazy. Even when it is not his picture, mantle, or ashtray, Ralph feels compelled to "set things right," as he puts it. His more tolerant friends joke about his "neatness fetish" and playfully offer to pay him to do their spring cleaning. But many of his associates as well as several important potential clients have been offended by his uninvited straightening of their offices or embarrassed when he brought out a "crumb collector" to clean off their table between courses at a fancy restaurant.

Amelia, a twenty-eight-year-old divorced interior designer, has taken appearance perfectionism even further. In the two years since her divorce she has had her breasts enlarged, her nose fixed, her thighs liposuctioned, and silicone injected into her lips to make them look fuller and, she hoped, sexier. "It's a jungle out there," she said, referring to the singles scene. "When you're competing with all those nubile nineteen-year-olds, you need all the help you can get."

Some appearance perfectionists create a facade of sublime independence. Showing that they need anything from anyone is a sign of weakness that will ultimately lead to rejection, they believe, so they present themselves to the world as completely self-sufficient and unflappable. They are unwilling to drop their facade under any circumstances, not even to be in an intimate relationship, which by definition requires that two people share their real selves and turn to each other to fulfill various needs that neither one can meet as well on his or her own.

Other appearance perfectionists have masks for all occasions, changing them to please and create the best possible impression on the person with whom they are interacting at any given moment. For instance, when Amelia meets a man who seems interested in her, she tailors her behavior to his expectations. "When I'm with a guy, I'm always trying to figure out what he likes," she says, "If he's a down-to-earth sort of guy, then I act very natural and earth-mothery. If he's an ambitious, professional man who likes his women smart and aggressive, that's the woman I try to be. If he likes to go sailing, we go sailing. I just make sure to take plenty of seasickness pills ahead of time. The way I see it, when you're sixteen, dating's fun, but when you're twenty-eight, it's serious business. If you want a guy to like you, you've got to work at it." And if you're an appearance perfectionist, you're going to work very hard. In fact whether you're a neatnik, a diet and exercise fanatic, a compulsive organizer, or someone who tries to appear strong, capable, and confident at all times, creating and maintaining an outward appearance of perfection can be a twenty-four-hour-a-day job.

Ironically, because of the extremes they go to in order to make things look perfect, appearance perfectionists—who so desperately want to be viewed in a positive light—are often seen as quirky, odd, finicky, rigid, stilted, "too good to be true," and difficult to be around for any length of time. Rather than gaining acceptance, they engineer their own rejection. What's more, because they engage in numerous counterproductive behaviors—from spending more than they earn in order to remodel their homes, to revamp their wardrobes, or to improve their physical features or fasting away precious vitamins and minerals while dieting to obtain the perfect body—appearance perfectionists are often defeated by the very measures they turned to in order to improve and perfect themselves.

Appearance perfectionists:

- "Fish" for compliments but have trouble accepting them; discounting or disbelieving the positive comments people make about them, they seek second, third, or fourth opinions, and doubt their credibility as well
- Are extremely sensitive to criticism and often perceive the absence of praise as a sign of disapproval
- Assume that other people will judge them as harshly as they judge themselves and feel that they are being judged by others almost all of the time
- Have a place for everything and tend to feel extremely ill at ease when everything is not in its place
- Have fixed, ritualistic ways of doing things (e.g., using the equipment at the gym, putting on makeup, or cleaning the kitchen in a certain order or preparing meals, eating, making phone calls, and so on at specific times and for specific lengths of time) and can become extremely anxious or irritable when those routines are disrupted
- Avoid situations where they might appear foolish in front of others
- Forgo potentially pleasurable activities because they have "nothing" to wear, feel fat, have their schedules made and don't want to change them, or for other relatively unconvincing reasons
- Become more perfectionistic whenever things are not going well in other areas of their life

Appearance perfectionists find it difficult to:

- Be spontaneous or let down their guard for so much as a minute
- Laugh at themselves or "get" the humor in most humorous situations

- Use, enjoy, or allow other people to see the very things they have worked so hard to perfect
- Let anything that does not look just right to them stay that way for more than a minute or two
- Get anywhere on time (because they invariably find something about their clothes, hair, makeup, homes, or offices that aren't "just right" and feel compelled to fix them right there and then)

On a fairly regular basis, appearance perfectionists are told:

- "You're trying too hard. Just relax and be yourself."
- "Would you *please* stop fussing? You look fine."
- "Don't you think you're going overboard?"

If a number of those statements describe you, then creating positive impressions and keeping up flawless appearances is probably the primary area on which you focus your perfectionism. Unfortunately your relentless striving in this area may be backfiring.

The Making of an Appearance Perfectionist
•
MARILYN

Marilyn, whose reentry into the work force we described in Chapter One, claims to have been concerned about appearances all her life. "When I was a little girl, I wouldn't go to sleep at night until all of my dolls and toys were in their proper places," she recalled. "Everything had its own spot, and if my mother wouldn't arrange them the way I wanted, I'd get out of bed after she turned out the lights and put them where they belonged. I just couldn't sleep unless everything was where it was supposed to be. There was something comforting about that"—especially when young Marilyn woke up after midnight to hear her father,

118

drunk and more often than not a big loser at the racetrack, crashing into furniture as he stumbled through their apartment and then, a few minutes later, fighting with her mother. On those nights Marilyn would "block out" the sounds that upset her by taking an inventory. "Where's Barbie?" she'd say to herself. "Where's Teddy? Where's my red ball and my green bean bag?" Each time she found an object exactly where it was supposed to be, Marilyn somehow felt better.

By ten Marilyn was a full-fledged "impression manager," choosing her words carefully, monitoring all of her actions, watching her father to see if he'd been drinking or her mother to see if she looked irritated. She adapted her behavior accordingly. "I never wanted to upset anyone," Marilyn recalled. "I wanted to be good so my dad wouldn't go out and get really drunk and so my mom wouldn't pick on me, which was what she generally did while my dad was off somewhere drinking and gambling." Somewhere along the line Marilyn had gotten it into her head that by controlling what she said and did she could control events going on around her and restore some order to the chaos in her family home.

Of course Marilyn's father drank and gambled no matter what Marilyn did. His reasons for engaging in those behaviors had nothing to do with her. In addition, Marilyn's mother criticized and lectured her on everything from proper bed making to good manners, both to vent her frustration about circumstances she could not control and because she was a perfectionist herself. Nothing anybody did satisfied Marilyn's mother. She was quite literally impossible to please. But Marilyn did not know that at the time. She did not know that her basic premise ("If I show Mom and Dad how good I am, everything will be okay around here.") was inaccurate. She kept trying to be sweet and considerate and tidy and orderly enough to make her dysfunctional family functional. She kept failing and feeling "horribly ashamed" of herself for "not being good enough."

Young Marilyn was so painfully aware of how "abnormal"

her family was because she was an avid television viewer. She watched *Leave It to Beaver* and *Father Knows Best*, *Lassie*, *Donna Reed*, and *The Brady Bunch*. She thought the mothers and fathers on those shows were "perfect" and she knew all too well that her mother and father were not. But maybe she still could be, Marilyn thought. If she watched those TV parents carefully and made sure she looked and acted like them, when she grew up, maybe she could be a perfect mother and have a perfect family too. Of course she would also have to make sure she was nothing like her own parents—especially her mother. You see, when Marilyn wasn't blaming herself for everything that was wrong with her family, she blamed her mother.

"I was pretty sure that my mother drove my dad to drink," Marilyn said. "She never had a kind word to say to him and she didn't even try to make herself attractive for him. She was always overweight and she just kept getting bigger and bigger." Her mother's weight problem may have been the reason that Marilyn, beginning in her teens, channeled her appearance perfectionism (and her determination to be different from other members of her family) into obsessive dieting.

By her own admission Marilyn was "absolutely paranoid" about gaining weight and, at fourteen, became convinced that she was getting fat. Even though her weight was well within normal range, Marilyn put herself on a strict diet and exercise regime. She lost weight rapidly and felt "terrific" about it. "Finally I found something I could do right," she said. Within weeks she was a diet expert. She could quote the calorie count and fat content of any imaginable food item and calculate the number of calories burned per minute by every imaginable form of exercise. Within months people began warning her that she was getting too thin, but she ignored them. The girl Marilyn saw in the mirror still needed to lose a few pounds. She might have starved herself to death had she not overheard a boy she liked saying, "Marilyn's okay, I guess, but who wants to go out with a bag of bones?" Marilyn immediately stopped dieting and gained back her weight as rapidly as she had lost it, became alarmed when she reached the upper limit of her normal weight range, and started dieting again.

After several trips through that cycle she started having trouble sticking to her diets and discovered the weight-control properties of laxatives and vomiting. By her early twenties Marilyn was a bulimic, forcing herself to vomit after almost every meal as well as bingeing on mind-boggling quantities of food when she was particularly upset with herself and then "purging" by vomiting, taking laxatives, and exercising fanatically. Although Marilyn abandoned this dangerous practice during both of her pregnancies, she went back to it soon after her children were born. By then she had also developed dozens of other appearance-perfectionism habits.

Marilyn kept her home spotless and her two daughters "adorably" dressed. She hovered over them, reminding them not to get dirty, urging them to behave themselves, and feeling mortified whenever they acted up in public or, heaven forbid, threw a tantrum in the supermarket. No matter what else she had on her schedule, Marilyn went through the motions of June Cleaver and Donna Reed's lives, cooking her family a hot breakfast every morning; having a gourmet meal waiting for her husband when he got home each evening; always dressing, fixing her hair, and putting on her makeup by no later than 8 A.M., even on weekends, unless, of course, she was too depressed to get out of bed. In recent years she often was.

Sadly (and typically for appearance perfectionists), Marilyn's endless effort to make everything perfect on the outside never made her feel good on the inside. In fact she described herself as "being on one long emotional roller coaster ride." As she did with the job interview we described earlier, Marilyn would anxiously anticipate upcoming events (even relatively minor ones such as trips to the mall or lunch with a friend) and worry about making a good impression. During those events she would nervously look for signs to tell her what sort of impression she was making. Afterward she would review the entire event, seeking and more often than not finding several things that had not looked or sounded just right. Then, dwelling on those flaws (which she was certain everyone saw and judged as harshly as she did), Marilyn criticized, badgered, and berated herself into a depressed mood. If she was really disgusted with herself, she would binge, purge, take some tranquilizers, and confine herself to her bed. Clearly her life wasn't working out like an episode of *The Brady Bunch* after all.

The Appearance Perfectionist's Predicament

The Driving Force Behind Appearance Perfectionism

Although your background and behavior may be somewhat different from Marilyn's, if you are an appearance perfectionist, you, too, embarked upon a crusade to improve yourself or your surroundings because you sincerely believed that perfecting the aspects of yourself and your life that were visible to the naked eye would make you happier, more self-confident, and more acceptable to other people. As a result of growing up in a dysfunctional family, being raised by extremely critical parents, or being ridiculed and rejected by your peers because you were chubby, had a big nose, or dressed in secondhand clothes, you came to believe the following:

> My flaws and deficiencies are to blame for all the chaos, confusion, and unhappiness in my life. When those flaws become visible, criticism, ridicule, rejection, and many other horrors inevitably follow. Therefore to prevent those catastrophic consequences, to maintain some semblance of control over my life and the events that go on around me, and to be loved, accepted, and rewarded, I must conceal my flaws and control the impression I make on other people. By doing that, by making things perfect on the outside, I will prove that I am a worthwhile person once and for all and never have to feel anxious or unhappy ever again.

Although you never recited that "credo" aloud and are probably not consciously aware that you live by it, that belief system is the driving force behind your appearance perfectionism.

You came to those conclusions at an early age and then promptly forgot about them. However, once adopted, those fundamental beliefs were repeatedly reinforced. Praise, approval, a day without cruel teasing from your peers, or a week of relative peace and quiet on the home front convinced you that your "self-improvement plan" was working. And rather than having the opposite effect, uproars, criticism, and rejection simply confirmed the premise behind your "plan," convincing you to try harder. But making the greatest impact of all was the fact that your early perfectionistic behaviors came with an extra added bonus: a way to distract yourself from the unsettling events going on around you, relieve anxiety, and feel in control of your own destiny.

When Marilyn said that having her toys in their proper places was "comforting" and that finding them right where they were supposed to be helped her "block out" the sound of her parents' arguments, she was describing this side effect of appearance perfectionism. Howard mentioned it too. As you may recall, after perfectly arranging his miniature Civil War soldiers on their mock battlefield, he had a sense that "things would work out okay" between his parents and grandparents as well. Helen, a recovering anorexic and exercise addict, put it this way: "Of course I didn't realize it until I had been in therapy for a while, but my obsession with dieting and working out started at a time when everything else in my life seemed completely out of control. I couldn't stop my parents from getting divorced. I couldn't make guys like me or adjust to my new school overnight or guarantee that I would get into the college of my choice. But what I put into my mouth and what I did with my body—those were things I *could* control. I focused all my energy on counting the calories I consumed and the calories I burned, comparing what I weighed when I got up to what I weighed before bed, finding ingenius ways to fool my mother into thinking I was eating more than I really was—you name it. Since my mind was so crammed with that stuff, there wasn't room for anything else. I was so sure that everything was going to be perfect when I reached a certain weight or looked a certain way that I didn't get upset about other things—even though those other things were just as bad, maybe worse, than ever."

There are few things in life that are more frightening and uncomfortable than the pulse racing, head spinning, stomach churning, and intrusive, unbidden thoughts that accompany anxiety or the sense of being utterly powerless and completely at the mercy of people or circumstances we cannot influence or control. Consequently when we stumble upon a way of squelching those feelings or diverting our attention from the events that provoke them, we wholeheartedly embrace the "cure-all" behavior we have discovered and we tend to engage in it over and over again. In fact psychological research has repeatedly shown that *anything* that reduces anxiety and enables us to feel "in control," no matter how "out of control" our circumstances actually may be, is extremely habit-forming.

Appearance-perfectionism behaviors and thought patterns are no exception, and chances are that:

- You practiced organizing, arranging, impression managing, and any other means of perfecting yourself or your surroundings until they became habits
- You continued to rely on those behaviors to comfort and distract you long after you had forgotten why you began behaving that way in the first place
- You now engage in them automatically whenever you feel anxious or insecure

If you are an appearance perfectionist, you feel that way most of the time.

You see, no amount of external change ever entirely eliminated *the imperfections you saw in your mind's eye* or permanently warded off your fear that those imperfections would ultimately bring about your demise.

The Hitch: You See What You Believe

Because the real source of your dissatisfaction, doubts, and fears was always your self-image and *not* your mirror image, from the moment you consciously or unconsciously concluded that looking good would make you feel happy, worthwhile, and in control, you unwittingly set yourself up for failure. No matter how drastically you alter your appearance or how deftly you maintain the image other people see, because your sense of self-worth is virtually nonexistent or mostly negative, you are chronically dissatisfied with yourself. At the very core of your being you still believe that you are dangerously flawed and inherently unacceptable. And as a result nothing you see in the mirror or find reflected in other people's eyes ever completely convinces you that you are finally good enough. Therein lies the appearance perfectionist's predicament: Driven to create an outward appearance of perfection, you can never achieve your goal because your perception of external reality is distorted by your deeply ingrained assumptions about yourself.

This distortion has been documented repeatedly by psychological research, including numerous studies on body image. Our mind's eye makes us bigger than we really are, those studies demonstrate. In fact up to 95 percent of all women overestimated the size of their bodies by an average of 25 percent. In addition, research has shown that the more we worry about the way our bodies look, the more we tend to "blow ourselves up." Obsessively preoccupied with their weight, women with eating disorders such as anorexia or bulimia thought they were *75 percent* bigger than they actually were. A similar phenomenon is widely reported by plastic surgeons. They have been tormented and even threatened with lawsuits by patients who still saw themselves as "ugly" even after cosmetic surgery was successfully performed to their exact specifications.

As an appearance perfectionist you may suffer from tunnel vision, which blinds you to everything but imperfections. You might spend a small fortune redecorating your living room, for instance, and hear from everyone you know that the results are absolutely dazzling. Yet every time you sit in or even walk past it, you feel anxious or depressed because all you notice is the tiny scratch at the base of your wall unit or the bubbles in the paint on the windowsill. Similarly if Barbara's necklace did not hang exactly the way she thought it should or her scarf was not the exact same shade of blue as the blue in the print of her dress, she was inconsolable. It did not matter that she looked terrific overall. She did not look perfect. She would even mention that to people who complimented her, brushing off their positive comments and pointing out the flawed elements of her outfit (which they would never have noticed on their own).

Thanks to your convoluted perfectionistic mind-set, like Barbara you may find ways of turning virtually any plus into a minus. When your impression management succeeds and you actually impress people, you are apt to decide that they are easily fooled, negating, minimizing, and thus receiving no real benefits from the praise, acceptance, or approval you tried so hard to obtain. In addition, you may resent anyone who already has the body, wardrobe, air of self-confidence, or immaculate home you are striving to attain. Not only do you compare these external attributes, but you generally assume other people were born with them or got them without putting in half as much effort as you do. That perception makes you more resentful—and more disgusted with yourself.

In these and other ways you see what you believe. Because you are convinced that you are too flat-chested or too plain, a sloppy dresser or a careless housekeeper, a boring conversationalist or a "chatterbox" who constantly puts her foot in her mouth, when you look in the mirror or try to read other people's reactions to you, those imperfections are what catch your eye, capture your attention, and remind you that you still are not good enough and so must try harder to be.

At the same time your perfectionistic habits are turning your original premise—"By looking good I can feel worthwhile and in control"—upside down. Whenever you do *not* feel worthwhile or in control, indeed whenever you feel the slightest twinge of anxiety, you start searching for something about your appearance, your environment, or the impression you are making that is not "just right," and you get busy trying to fix it. In fact your appearance perfectionism may increase tenfold whenever you are upset or worried about *anything*—even if your troubles have absolutely nothing to do with how you or your surroundings look.

For instance Rose, a lifelong appearance perfectionist and recent divorcée, told us how, during the months immediately following her divorce, making sure she looked perfect became "a full-time job." She said, "I couldn't think about anything else. I didn't *want* to think about anything else." Depressed and feeling sorry for herself, Rose became obsessed with the idea that everyone else felt sorry for her too. "I would picture my friends talking to each other on the phone and saying, 'Poor Rose. She's all alone and miserable,' and then deciding to invite me to dinner or the theater as if I was their favorite charity or something," Rose recalled. Even though it probably had no basis in reality, Rose was mortified by her fantasy and went "all out" to show her friends that she was doing fine.

"For days before we were due to go out, I would clean and organize my home. Once I rearranged my living room furniture four times to make sure it would look perfect when they came to pick me up. I'd even go out into the yard to rake leaves and trim the hedges, just to let them know that I didn't need a man around to take care of those things." Rose would get so caught up in doing these things that she didn't have time to feel depressed. As she put it, "I was too exhausted to worry about what would become of me, a forty-eight-year-old woman with no husband and a poorly paying part-time job." Of course every time Rose slowed down, her worries came rushing back and nagged at her until she got busy with something else.

Soon Rose's appearance perfectionism consumed almost all of her time and energy. Whenever she left the house, even if she was only going to the grocery store, Rose had to look perfect. She could agonize for hours over what to wear to the library, and if she had someplace special to go, she "just had to" purchase a new outfit that she could not really afford. She could spend several more hours getting ready, scrutinizing every nuance of her appearance, fixing and refixing her hair and her makeup or frantically rooting through her dresser drawers for the perfect accessories. Then she would straighten her entire house—"just in case I ran into someone I knew and invited them to stop in for coffee." By the time she finally got herself out the door, Rose was exhausted and ironically would try *not* to be spotted by anyone she knew because if a friend did want to stop by for coffee, she wouldn't be able to keep up her end of a cheerful conversation (and her friend might think she was depressed).

For months Rose went around and around in this vicious circle, devoting herself to creating an outward appearance of perfection so that she would not have to face her fears or solve some very real problems, such as how to make the mortgage payments on the house she kept so spotless. Reality kept coming back to haunt her, however, stirring up more self-loathing and self-doubt, prompting her to see more imperfections in herself and her surroundings and steering her down the same counterproductive, time-consuming, self-defeating path again and again and again.

Rose's appearance perfectionism had become self-perpetuating, and although yours may not have yet, it definitely could. Rather than helping you feel in control, your habitual behaviors may begin to control you and, instead of enabling you to feel safe, secure, and self-confident, they may lead to chronic dissatisfaction and numerous physical, financial, or psychological problems.

The Way Out for Appearance Perfectionists

After years of trying to feel good on the inside by looking good on the outside, it may come as no surprise that to kick the appearance-perfectionism habit, you must reverse that process: working from the inside out so that you can see yourself and your surroundings in a more realistic light, increase your tolerance for anxiety or other unsettling emotions, and come to appreciate who you are no matter how you look at any given moment. Replacing negative self-criticisms with positive self-affirmations, stopping to ask yourself what's really eating you when you start worrying about some external imperfection, both visualizing yourself and intentionally practicing not appearing perfect as well as specific anxiety-reduction techniques are just a few examples of "cognitive restructuring" strategies that will improve your self-image and get you off the appearance-perfectionism treadmill.

You will find those strategies in Chapters Nine and Ten, and as an appearance perfectionist will especially benefit from the following:

- Regaining your sense of humor (page 203)
- Relaxation (page 207)
- Visualizations and affirmations (page 209)
- Goal-trimming (page 217)
- Altering distorted thought patterns (page 224)
- Strategies to stop catastrophizing (page 230)
- Strategies to cope with obsessions and compulsions (page 234)

Chapter Six

Interpersonal Perfectionism:

"I'm Fine.

Everyone Else Is a Mess."

Interpersonal Perfectionism in a Nutshell

An interpersonal perfectionist defines himself by the company he keeps. He feels good about himself and in control of his own life when *other people* do things the way he thinks they should be done (flawlessly) and keep up the appearances he thinks should be kept up (perfect ones). An interpersonal perfectionist expects friends, lovers, spouses, children, co-workers, and just about anybody else he meets to live up to his lofty standards at all times, and he will nag, belittle, correct, coerce, or manipulate to make sure they do.

An interpersonal perfectionist boosts her self-esteem and verifies her worth by outdistancing all competitors in a race only she knows she is running. If she can't "win" on her own merits, she finds ways of declaring her opponent a "loser," usually by locating fatal flaws and glaring inadequacies in anyone who might prove to be superior to her in any way.

Interpersonal perfectionists are determined to protect themselves from the negative consequences they assume forming close relationships will bring: pain, self-doubt, or the scrutiny and rejection of their real, less-than-perfect selves. They don't want "messy," unpredictable people disrupting their neat, orderly lives or interfering with their meticulously laid plans. In the process of achieving these goals, they limit or eliminate their chances of finding or benefiting from supportive personal relationships or successful professional collaborations.

The Many Faces of Interpersonal Perfectionism

FAULTFINDERS. Alex, the twenty-four-year-old recent MBA-program graduate we introduced in Chapter One, was an interpersonal perfectionist with one of those arrogant, know-it-all attitudes that made almost everyone he encountered want to wring his neck. Listening to him tell cabdrivers how to navigate city streets, instruct a tailor with twenty years' experience how to fit a suit, or advise a personnel director on how his company should be run, you would hardly think of Alex as insecure. But he was. He may have acted as if God had retired and left him in charge of the universe, but when he wasn't pushing people around, telling them how to improve themselves, or summing them up in single scathing sentences, Alex was extremely unsure of himself. In fact Alex was so unconvinced of his own worth that he constantly tried to reassure himself by proving he was superior to others. To obtain his proof, Alex played an inverted version of the numbers game. He filled his "scorecard" with other people's faults and failings. Each time a receptionist cracked her gum, an interviewer mispronounced his last name, or anyone did anything that was less than complete and flawless in all respects, Alex made a mental note of it. I would never do that, Alex thought, and knew that he wasn't so bad after all.

INSPECT-AND-REJECTERS. Linda, the thirty-three-year-old attorney who described her relationship history as "dating and discarding," was an interpersonal perfectionist too. "I can tell in the first ten minutes if a guy has what I'm looking for in a man," she said. He usually didn't, and it generally took *less* that ten minutes for Linda to come to that conclusion. She frequently rejected men on sight because they were short, balding, less than impeccably dressed, had chosen professions she considered boring, or otherwise failed to match her fantasy of the ideal man perfectly. Although Linda was beginning to realize that she might never meet her "dream man," she was not ready to give up the quest. "There's nothing wrong with having high standards," she declared. "And there are definitely worse things in life than being single—like marrying the wrong guy and selling your soul to hang on to him only to end up getting dumped anyway, the way my mother did."

While there's nothing wrong with knowing what you want (or don't want) from a relationship or harboring detailed romantic fantasies of Ms. or Mr. Right, approaching relationships with a ten-page checklist of necessary attributes in hand and "discarding" people the instant you recognize that they lack one item on that list is not a sign of "high standards." It is a defense against intimacy, and interpersonal perfectionism is particularly effective in that regard.

By refusing to settle for anyone who is less than complete and flawless in all respects, interpersonal perfectionists never have to risk getting close enough to people to be hurt by them. They do not have to test themselves or their relationships and perhaps fail. Before the relationship gets off the ground or as soon as the going gets tough, they simply slip on their faultfinding glasses, hone in on the other person's inadequacies, and either sever their ties to that person immediately or criticize, nitpick, and distance themselves from that person until he or she leaves them. Although that may hurt less in the short run, it also destroys the possibility of falling in love and living happily with someone who may be a bit less than their ideal but is nonetheless wonderful and an excellent match for them.

CONTROLLERS. Unlike Linda, Peter, a thirty-eight-year-old cabinetmaker, had no qualms about being in a relationship—as long as it was on his terms. "I have my way of doing things,"

Peter explained. "Women know that when they get involved with me. So do my friends and the people I do business with." What the people in Peter's life didn't know and indeed could not know until they had been involved with him for a while were the lengths to which he would go to make sure things were done his way. Peter decided how much time he would spend with his friends, what they would do when they were together, where they sat in a movie theater, how to divvy up the bill in restaurants, even the topics of their conversations. With each of the six live-in girlfriends he had had over the past ten years, Peter had done all the cooking because he "had yet to find a woman who chops vegetables and measures seasonings properly." After his current girlfriend cleaned the kitchen, he would go in and clean it over again. And each time she turned on the TV, he would say, "Don't you think you watch too much television?" Sometimes he would turn off the set and hand her a book. In these and countless other ways Peter tried to *control* every aspect of his relationships because he, like most interpersonal perfectionists, had little tolerance for the *process* of relating to other people.

Interpersonal perfectionists don't like surprises, but relationships—both personal and professional ones—are full of them. They don't proceed in a logical, step-by-step manner from first meeting straight through to marriage (or business partnership). They aren't organized or predictable or ever a "sure thing." Yet interpersonal perfectionists want them to be. People in relationships argue and fuss, forget to take clothes out of the dryer, and number report pages in the upper-left-hand corner instead of the lower right. In fact they can be counted on to do exactly what we least expect at the most inopportune moments, stirring up emotions that interpersonal perfectionists prefer not to feel: confusion, frustration, anxiety, self-doubt. So they make "rules" for their relationships and expect the people in their lives to follow them to the letter. There is no room for dissent in their dictatorships. "If people don't like the way I do things, they don't have to hang around with me," they declare, and their friends, lovers, customers, and business associates frequently take their advice, spending as little time with them as possible or walking out of their lives altogether.

LONERS. "It's okay with me if people go out of their way to avoid me. In fact I'm glad they do," said Ellen, a thirty-two-year-old computer programmer and an interpersonal perfectionist who claimed to have lost interest in relating to people years ago. She viewed people as "inconsiderate, disruptive nuisances who charge into your life, turn it upside down, and charge right back out again," and she dealt with the discomfort relationships caused her by not involving herself in them at all. Ellen lived alone. She preferred to work alone. She rarely dated and couldn't spend more than an hour at a family gathering without "climbing the walls." Even people with whom she had never interacted irritated her to no end. Misshelved library books, parents who couldn't keep their toddlers from whining in public, and sales clerks who could not make change in two seconds flat were just more proof that the entire human race was dangerously inept and a threat to her health, happiness, and peace of mind. She tried to have as little contact with people as possible.

MIRROR POLISHERS. Of course not all interpersonal perfectionists take such a dim view of relationships. Many wouldn't know what to do or who they were without them. They are almost totally dependent on other people to supply them with a sense of self-worth. Some interpersonal perfectionists who fit that description are what we call mirror polishers. They judge themselves and believe other people judge them based on the accomplishments and appearances of their families, friends, coworkers, the men or women they date, even their casual acquaintances. The people in their lives are like mirrors, reflecting positively on them and boosting their self-esteem or reflecting negatively on them and reminding them that they are not good enough the way they are. To ensure that people add to their worth rather than detract from it, some mirror-polishing interpersonal perfectionists actually select friends and lovers for their image-enhancing qualities and rather ruthlessly replace them when someone more impressive comes along. Others constantly advise, instruct, and otherwise push the people in their lives to improve themselves, playing Henry Higgins to various and sundry Eliza Doolittles, the way Aaron, a forty-year-old concert promoter, did with his girlfriend Carolyn. In an endless effort to mold and shape Carolyn into the "perfect" woman, Aaron "taught" her how to dress and "advised" her on the amount of makeup to wear and how to fix her hair. When they went to restaurants, he held classes on choosing wine. When they had social functions to attend, he went over the guest list, telling her what to say to various "very important" people and conducting dozens of "pop quizzes" on the day of the event. He even insisted that Carolyn tell people she was "in medicine" so that they might assume she was a doctor and not "just" a nurse.

Many a mirror-polishing parent takes a similar approach to childrearing, pushing and prodding his or her youngsters to excel, dressing them impeccably, incessantly warning them not to get dirty, and enrolling them in a half dozen "enrichment" activities by the time they turn four. These interpersonal-perfectionist parents insist on perfect table manners while their children are still in high chairs and behavior they can be proud of at all times. A normal two-year-old's willful no, an active three-year-old's grass-stained overalls, or a first-grader who scores in less than the nintieth percentile on a national achievement test can mean only one thing: They are failing as parents. They push harder, unwittingly creating a new generation of perfectionists.

PLEASERS. The flip side of the mirror-polishing coin, "pleaser" interpersonal perfectionists go overboard trying to make their relationships perfect—no matter how far from perfect the people with whom they have those relationships may be. In fact pleasers frequently get involved with decidedly dysfunctional individuals: alcoholics, gamblers, men and women prone to violence or mental illness, people who can't hold down jobs or make commitments. As a result they can't help but feel dissatisfied with their relationships. Yet they feel so empty and worthless without a relationship that they will do just about anything to hang onto and perfect the ones they have.

Pleasers run themselves ragged trying to cover up their spouse's latest "screwups" in hopes of creating the impression that their relationships are complete and flawless in all respects. They make excuses for other people's misbehavior and are always on the lookout for future mishaps, which they believe they can somehow step in and prevent from happening. They constantly come up with ingenious schemes to take the pressure off their errant mates or floundering colleagues. But most of all, because they believe it will eliminate nerve-racking conflicts from their lives and turn their disastrous relationships into ones they can feel safe in and proud of, pleaser interpersonal perfectionists bend over backward to make everyone happy and meet the needs of everyone around them, even when that means sacrificing their own happiness and failing to meet their own needs.

In whatever form it takes, interpersonal perfectionism leads to chronic dissatisfaction, disappointment, frustration, and self-doubt. Interpersonal perfectionists may not recognize that their standards are unrealistic, unreasonable, and impossible to meet. They may be completely convinced that it is not their own but other people's inadequacies that "ruin everything." However, when people or relationships fail to live up to their expectations (as they invariably do), interpersonal perfectionists feel like failures themselves. And as any perfectionist would, they cope with failure by trying harder to succeed, using the very same methods that led them to fail in the first place. By now you know exactly where that vicious circle will take them: straight downhill to self-defeat.

Interpersonal perfectionists:

- Pick, pester, correct, nag, warn, and remind their children, employees, spouses, and others not to "mess up," frequently looking over their shoulders to make sure they don't
- Are quick to judge others and can often be heard griping about someone's specific faults and failings or delivering broad, global indictments of people in general (e.g., "No one

cares about quality anymore," or "I cannot believe how low most people's standards are")

- View other people as rivals and try to one-up them in various ways ("A Volvo? It's a good car, but personally I prefer my Mercedes." "I'm glad you enjoyed your week in Martinique. Did I ever tell you about the ten days I spent in the Orient?" "This pie is delicious, but you really must try my torte recipe. It will knock your socks off.")
- Feel uncomfortable in the presence of people who seem superior to them in any way
- Make sure they come out ahead by associating with people whom they see as less capable and accomplished than they are—then quickly get bored with them or decide they are "hopeless losers" and behave condescendingly toward them
- Have little tolerance for other people's "quirks" or habits and harp on things, such as the way their secretary sips her coffee or their spouse refolds the newspaper after reading it
- Assume that other people want to hear about everything they do wrong, believe that those people should change their behavior as soon as it is brought to their attention, and grow increasingly annoyed if they do not, sometimes flying into a rage and feeling justified in doing so because they have pointed out the problem at least a hundred times
- Have absolutely no idea how irritating (or downright infuriating) their behavior is and feel genuinely surprised when their "constructive" criticism or "helpful" advice is greeted with sullen silence or blatant hostility
- Complain that they have no "real" friends

Repeatedly, interpersonal perfectionists are apt to hear:

- "Get off my case!"
- "You're impossible to please."
- "Don't you *ever* have anything pleasant to say?"
- "Who asked you?"
- "What *now*?!"

If a number of those statements or our descriptions of inter-personal perfectionists resemble your own behavior or experi-ences, then other people may bear the brunt of your perfectionism and you as well as they are undoubtedly suffering because of that. Ultimately your need to perfect and control other people or your relationships with them will prevent you from fulfilling your equally and perhaps more powerful needs for love, accep-tance, intimacy, emotional support, a sense of belonging, or other people's practical help in achieving your personal and profes-sional goals.

The Making of an Interpersonal Perfectionist
•
PETER

Several months after Peter was born, his father died in an in-dustrial accident. "I never forgave him for it," Peter said. "I knew he didn't do it on purpose, but still, for most of my childhood, I hated him for dying because, if he had lived, my mother wouldn't have married my stepfather." According to Peter, his stepfather, a career military officer whom Peter refers to as the Colonel, made his youth a living hell. "The Colonel thought you raised kids the same way you turned new recruits into soldiers. Push them hard, teach them blind obedience, make lots of rules, and punish them every time they break one or make a mistake. The day he moved in, our house turned into a boot camp."

At first Peter was the only "grunt," and he vividly recalls his stepfather "getting right up in my face like a drill sergeant and shouting at me, calling me an idiot, a baby, a slob, a good-for-nothing loafer. I honestly can't remember all the names he called me, but I can assure you they were all bad." If Peter, who was no more than four at the time, started to cry, his stepfather "gave him something to cry about," slapping his face, smacking his hands with a spatula, or beating him with a belt. "Sometimes he'd skip the shouting and go straight to the beating," Peter recalled. "Or he'd send me to bed without supper, only first he'd make me sit there and watch him eat. Every other bite he'd tell me how delicious the food was. He'd keep asking me if I wanted some until I said yes, and then he'd say, 'Well, you should have thought about that before you misbehaved.'"

Most of the time Peter's "misbehavior" involved the scrapes, mistakes, and impulsive acts that are typical for growing boys, but that did not faze the Colonel. And where was Peter's mother while he was so obviously being abused? "At first she would try to stop him," Peter explained. "But they would end up fighting, and he would threaten to leave or actually walk out and not come back until she begged him to. So after a while she just made excuses for him, telling me that he meant well and only wanted me to do the right things. She made it sound like what he did was my fault." Young Peter believed his mother, and when she suggested that if he "tried a little harder," maybe his stepfather would not be so hard on him, Peter took her advice. In fact he devoted practically every waking moment to avoiding the Colonel's punishments, doing everything with extreme caution and making absolutely sure to follow the Colonel's rules.

By the time he turned seven, Peter's conscientiousness had begun to pay off. "Sometimes I'd actually go five or six days in a row without getting into trouble with the Colonel," he said. "Every once in a while he even acted like he liked me." Unfortunately the relative calm was broken once Peter's stepbrother and stepsister were born. "I was supposed to be the commanding officer, and the buck stopped with me," he explained. "So whenever they did anything wrong, I got slapped around or sent to my room—'confined to quarters,' the Colonel called it—or had my favorite possessions taken away." Peter was by then a fast learner and, in no time flat, was bossing his siblings around to make sure they didn't misbehave, and taking over their chores or redoing them so that the Colonel wouldn't find fault with them and punish him. As you could see from our previous description of him, Peter had carried those early interpersonal perfectionistic habits with him into adulthood. By age thirty-eight he had payed for them many times over, and they continued to take their toll.

As soon as he ventured outside the walls of his childhood home, Peter was shocked to discover that very few people were as conscientious as he and he instinctively tried to get them to be. He ordered his peers around like the miniature version of the Colonel he had unwittingly and out of self-defense become. Although his teachers lauded him for his leadership ability, Peter's classmates shunned him on the playground or beat him up when he got off the bus near his home. Because the powerful programming he'd received at home was impossible to shake, Peter couldn't "lighten up" and instead developed the "take me or leave me" attitude that would remain with him for years to come.

Peter never became a true loner, however. Like almost anyone who receives so little love (and so much punishment) early in life, Peter had a powerful unmet need to belong, to connect with and be accepted by people. After "dry spells" of varying lengths, Peter would feel himself being drawn to people, especially people who at first glance seemed to be as exacting as he and as intolerant of ineptitude. "Looking back over all of my relationships with women and most of my friendships with men, too, I realized our first conversations were almost always gripe sessions," Peter said. "We'd talk about how shallow other people were or how ticked off we got when people did certain things." Peter would invariably conclude that he had finally found someone who shared his outlook on life, someone who would finally understand him and not "punish" him by disagreeing with him or disrupting his routines or refusing to do things his way. He was always wrong, and no matter how blithely Peter said, "It's my way or the highway. If you don't like the way things are around here, move on," it hurt him each time a relationship crumbled under the weight of his excessively controlling behavior. After six live-in lovers had come and gone, even Peter was willing to admit that his perfectionism might be "causing a few problems."

Those problems were even more apparent in his cabinet-making business. For obvious reasons he could not afford to lose customers. Yet he constantly insulted them by telling them in no uncertain terms that their ideas were "stupid" or accusing them of wanting to cut corners and then blame the less-than-perfect results on his workmanship. His insistence on doing things his way "and everyone else be damned" had sent countless customers packing, which was why he decided to take on a business partner to handle sales and billing and customer relations. However, Peter's interpersonal perfectionism prevented him from letting his associate do his job. He had gone through three business partners in as many years, not to mention all the hassles and expense of dissolving those partnerships. And of course, left to his own resources, Peter continued to drive customers away. When we first met him, not only was Peter alone and lonely on the home front but he was on the verge of declaring bankruptcy as well.

The Interpersonal Perfectionist's Predicament

The Driving Force Behind Interpersonal Perfectionism

Although interpersonal perfectionists direct their perfectionism at other people, the driving force behind their habits and thought patterns is an internal one. They operate under the influence of a deeply ingrained assumption that they are not, and in all likelihood will never be, good enough to have the unconditionally loving, supportive, lasting relationships that they—like all human beings—crave.

Like Peter, many interpersonal perfectionists were raised in an atmosphere of nonacceptance, where failure and mistakes were taboo. They may have experienced constant criticism, punishments that were too severe to fit their "crimes," even physical abuse. Some were reared by perfectionist parents who may not have been particularly punitive but did just as much damage by carrot dangling and expecting more from them than they could possibly deliver. *"No one who matters to me can accept me as I am"* was the lesson they learned from their early experiences, and it became the fundamental belief on which their interpersonal perfectionism would one day be based.

Other interpersonal perfectionists lost a parent through death, divorce, or abandonment, and although those circumstances were beyond their control, they thought they were somehow to blame. Or later, during adolescence or young adulthood, relationships that were important and meaningful to them ended, contrary to their wishes and in spite of their best efforts to continue them. They were rejected and in the process badly hurt, perhaps humiliated as well. Again they blamed themselves. *"There is something about me that drives people away,"* they came to believe then and would continue to believe for years to come.

In other instances interpersonal perfectionists were only children and the center of their parents' universe or elevated to "special" status in their families, receiving the mixed blessing of preferential treatment accompanied by higher expectations. When they ventured out into the world, they realized they had been duped. Their peers in particular did not treat them in the "special" way they had grown accustomed to being treated. In fact they may have been taunted and ridiculed, called stuck up, nerdy, or a mama's boy, or simply ignored. "Maybe I'm not so special after all," they thought, and because the love, affection, and approval they had received in the past was linked to the idea that they *were* special, that thought terrified them. *"If I don't stand out in a crowd, if I'm not the star, then I am nothing,"* they assumed, and that assumption would stir up self-doubt and anxiety throughout their lives.

Although their fundamental and largely unconscious perceptions are nearly identical to the ones that drive performance and appearance perfectionists, interpersonal perfectionists responded to them differently. Instead of (and sometimes in addition to) striving to enhance their sense of self-worth by achieving or creating an outward appearance of perfection, they focused their attention on the external threat to their self-esteem—other people—and did so in one, two, or all three of the following ways:

PROJECTION. "I'm not the problem, you are" is the basic premise behind the psychological defense mechanism known as projection. Interpersonal perfectionists who rely on it take their own flaws, failings, and fears and "hang them" on other people: noticing in others, feeling irritated by, and trying to change traits and habits they would be mortified to acknowledge in themselves. The process is entirely unconscious, and trying to tell an interpersonal perfectionist that he is projecting and attributing his own imperfections to someone else is an exercise in futility. However, if you think you are an interpersonal perfectionist and the things that seem to annoy you the most tend to be the very things you were criticized or punished for in the past, then chances are that you are projecting.

Why do you do it? Because you have identified with and internalized the characteristics of someone who was once hard on you, becoming the critic instead of the criticized, the fault-finder instead of the faulty one, the powerful finger pointer rather than the powerless victim. In addition, finding flaws in others reassures you that you are not so bad (since everyone else is clearly so much worse) and distracts you from your own insecurities, self-doubts, and that nagging "not good enough" feeling. You are simply too busy scrutinizing and critiquing other people to spend much time inspecting yourself (and perhaps discovering that you don't measure up).

REJECTION. Because being accepted is inconceivable to many interpersonal perfectionists, they assume that at some point in any friendship or intimate relationship, they will be rejected. When that happens, they will be hurt. They may fall apart at the seams. They will have more unwanted proof that they are unlovable and destined to fail in the realm of relationships. Consequently they adopt "the best defense is a good defense" stance, home in on other people's flaws, and reject *before* they can be rejected.

Unfortunately the fact that they did the rejecting does not

alter the fact that they lost the relationship. Nor does it significantly diminish their disappointment or feelings of failure. Indeed the demise of their relationship, even at their own hand, confirms their original premise, making it more difficult to get close to someone or commit themselves to a relationship the next time around.

REFLECTION. Some interpersonal perfectionists, most notably those who need to feel special, expect the people in their lives to make them look good. They may cling to, cater to, and bask in the reflected glow of people they put on pedestals. They may play "King of the Hill," surrounding themselves with people to whom they feel superior and constantly confirming their superiority by bossing those people around. Or they may relentlessly struggle to make sure that the people in their lives don't make them look bad. Believing that every less-than-perfect utterance or action on the part of their friends, families, or colleagues says something negative about them, they coerce, cajole, correct, criticize, and try to control those people.

When their "reflections" don't shape up or their relationships buckle under the pressure of their perfectionism, interpersonal perfectionists who want their relationships to make them feel special instead feel worthless and compelled to seek out "replacements," starting the whole self-defeating process all over again.

The Hitch: Needing What You Fear, Fearing What You Need

No matter what interpersonal perfectionists say, they need people. They may sincerely believe that they would be infinitely happier and more successful if they didn't have to contend with messy, disruptive, unpredictable, and for the most part uncontrollable human beings. They may have learned to live without close relationships and even arranged their lives so that they have as little contact with people as possible. Yet no matter how they have coped with their concerns about relating to other people, they have not eliminated their needs for unconditional love, acceptance, a sense of belonging, emotional support, and intimacy, which can only be fulfilled by other people, imperfect though they may be.

Those needs can be ignored temporarily, but they cannot be erased permanently. We are first and foremost social beings, who learn from one another and turn to each other for things we cannot get as well (or at all) on our own. We need people in order to thrive and grow. It is through our relationships with other human beings that we initially learn to believe in ourselves and, throughout our lives, replenish and rediscover ourselves. Although some of us may be more geared toward relationships than others, all of us require a certain amount of fulfillment in this area as well as a certain amount of faith in our ability to get our interpersonal needs met.

Despite their protests to the contrary and because of the sorts of experiences we mentioned earlier, interpersonal perfectionists may actually crave unconditionally loving, nourishing, stable relationships *more* than people who were accepted, nurtured, and made to feel they belonged in the past. And regrettably, because of those same experiences as well as the dubious relationship track record that results from years of trying to one-up, correct, avoid, or control people, they have practically no faith in their ability to get their needs for love, affection, and closeness met. In fact they believe that trying to fulfill those needs will only lead to failure and disappointment. So they do everything in their power to protect themselves from the frustration, pain, and loss of self-esteem that their presumably inevitable failure will bring.

Therein lies the interpersonal perfectionist's predicament and their prescription for self-defeat: Although they—like all human beings—need to be unconditionally loved, accepted, and supported, because they assume they will not be (and indeed believe they are not good enough to be), interpersonal perfectionists engage in behaviors that drive away or distance them from people who could love, accept, and emotionally or practically support them. As a result (and as they predicted), they fail to have satisfying relationships or achieve other goals. This confirms their original premise, perpetuating their interpersonal perfectionism and leading to more interpersonal failures ad infinitum.

The Way Out for Interpersonal Perfectionists

Getting to the roots of interpersonal perfectionism, healing the wounds caused by past relationships, and rebuilding trust in oneself and others can be a lengthy process and may require professional help. However, if you think you are an interpersonal perfectionist, there are many things you can do immediately and on your own to reduce the conflict that undoubtedly exists in your relationships today and pave the way for more satisfying relationships in the future. In Chapters Nine and Ten you will find strategies and suggestions that can help you develop tolerance, share control, communicate more effectively, cut back on destructive negative criticism, and negotiate compromise solutions to interpersonal problems. You will want to pay particular attention to and take the time to try the following:

- Creating a well-balanced life-style (page 195)
- Suggestions for being with people (page 211); for developing tolerance (page 213) and being empathetic (page 214)
- Goal-trimming (page 217)
- Altering distorted thought patterns (page 224)
- Relationship repair (page 239)

Chapter Seven

Moral Perfectionism:
"I Play by the Rules.
All of Them. Always."

Moral Perfectionism in a Nutshell

Moral perfectionists define themselves in terms of their moral and ethical codes. Deriving a sense of self-worth from selflessly serving others, dedicating themselves to a worthy cause, or adhering to rigorous religious or political doctrines, moral perfectionists relentlessly strive to live "pure" lives or "meaningful" ones. They put themselves in a box labeled Christian, Jew, Feminist, Vegetarian, Animal-Rights Activist, Recovering Alcoholic, Pacifist, or simply Virtuous Person, and devote themselves to living up to the standards they believe they must meet in order to be worthy of that label.

Everyone does that to a certain extent. However, moral perfectionists take more than a realistic, well-meaning interest in pursuing their chosen path and are not satisfied with merely doing the best they can to be true to their beliefs in a given situation. Being perfectionists, they go to extremes, turning reasonable, potentially life- and self-esteem-enhancing value systems into oppressive sets of rigid rules and regulations that they expect themselves and others to follow to the letter at all times. Through the lens of their perfectionism they view every imaginable thought, feeling, or action as either good or evil, virtuous or sinful, a step on the stairway to heaven or a turning point that could lead them down the path to hell. In their mind's eye there are absolutely no shades of gray and absolutely no circumstances that justify breaking or even bending the "rules."

Moral perfectionists want to be morally and ethically complete and flawless in all respects: resisting *every* temptation, *never* harboring a negative thought or expressing a negative emotion, *always* putting their cause or calling above all else, or avoiding *all* situations that might require them to compromise their values in *any* way. Clearly those expectations are unrealistic, unreasonable, rarely if ever attainable, and the reason why most moral perfectionists go through life mired in doubt about their own virtue or obsessed with the virtue of the people around them.

Although moral perfectionists try to follow their moral and ethical codes of conduct religiously—that is, in a conscientiously exact and scrupulous manner—they are not necessarily religious. Some do devote themselves to "pleasing" God and perfectly embodying the teachings of a specific faith. However, others construct their lives around social or political causes, recovery programs such as Alcoholics Anonymous, and personal-growth philosophies such as est, or simply a broad, all-encompassing notion of "being good." Whether religious or secular, it is not the source of a value system or the values themselves but rather what moral perfectionists do with them that causes problems. They magnify them tenfold and then pursue them as if they were tangible goals. Like performance perfectionists, they rack up accomplishments and other external measures of their worth, keeping score of their good deeds, self-sacrifices, and ethical behaviors as if "doing the right thing" were an event in the Olympics. Like appearance perfectionists, they struggle to present themselves to the world in a positive light, wearing their beliefs on their sleeves, so to speak, and trying to look virtuous, devout, or committed to their causes at all times. And like all perfectionists, they repeatedly fail to live up to their own expectations. No matter how closely they adhere to their moral or ethical codes, they are never satisfied with their efforts. In fact judging their thoughts and feelings as well as their actions, moral perfectionists obsessively review and negatively evaluate their moral and ethical "performances" and, falling short of their impossibly high standards, end up feeling guilty or ashamed of themselves a great deal of the time.

As Felicia, a forty-three-year-old clergyman's wife and mother of four, put it, "I try so hard to be a good person, but I just can't pull it off." Giving no thought to the hours she spent visiting the elderly in a local nursing home, the cookies she made for a youth group bake sale, the typing she did without pay for a nearby clinic, or how she patiently counseled several distraught friends, Felicia lies awake at night haunted by her "misdeeds." "I shouldn't have reprimanded my son so harshly," she thinks. "Why did I leave the laundry until tomorrow?" she asks herself. "If I had put my mind to it, I could have gotten to it today." She remembers swearing when she stubbed her toe, being impatient with a salesclerk, and thinking "horrible thoughts" about the driver who cut her off on the highway. To anyone but a moral perfectionist these would seem like minor transgressions, but to Felicia they were glaring character defects and irrefutable proof that she was not a "good" person. Naturally they were an impetus for her to "try harder" as well.

Like other perfectionists, moral perfectionists minimize their moral and ethical plus-side and magnify their failings, finding huge gaps between their idealized image of a good person and the person they perceive themselves to be. That gap may have been as wide as the Grand Canyon to begin with, since many moral perfectionists judge themselves based on their ability to serve perfectly not only their immediate circle of friends and family but also the entire community in which they live, or humanity as a whole.

Sid, a fifty-two-year-old social worker, once owned his own

business and lived comfortably in the suburbs. "Back then every-thing was me, me, me," he said. "As long as my wife and kids had what they wanted and we were keeping up with the Joneses, more or less, I didn't worry about anything. I hardly ever read a newspaper, and when there was a depressing story on the TV news, I changed channels." When a lifelong penchant for "play-ing the ponies" and betting on sports began whittling away at his life savings and taking precedence over things such as making mortgage payments, Sid's perspective began to change. Thanks to the perfectionistic mind-set that had always compelled him to go to extremes, Sid became as feverishly involved in Gamblers Anonymous as he had once been involved in gambling and de-scribed his spiritual awakening as "opening my eyes to lots of things I'd been blind to before."

Having changed careers and taken a job in one of the worst neighborhoods of a nearby city, Sid now noticed every homeless person he passed, and if one asked for money, he would dig into his pockets and hand over a fistful of change. As anyone would, he realized that he had not made a significant difference in that individual's life or a dent in the larger problems of poverty and homelessness. But unlike anyone other than another moral per-fectionist, he viewed that as a personal failure. Hours later, when he sat down to eat lunch or stopped at the grocery store on the way home from work, he would be hit with a wave of guilt. "People are starving right under my nose and all I do is hand them a few coins," he would think, "I should be ashamed of myself." Sometimes Sid would wrap up his lunch and give it to the first homeless person he saw, or buy only the discounted, bruised fruit and day-old bread at the grocery store and put the money he saved into the "poor box" of the nearest church. Al-though his sacrifice had no greater impact than his spare change did, it assuaged his guilt, at least temporarily.

"My wife says I've become a very depressing person," Sid explained. "But I can't be happy-go-lucky when there's so much ugliness in the world today, so many problems. I have to do my part to solve them. If I didn't, I couldn't live with myself." Of course no matter how much he did to reduce the "ugliness in the world," he could never do enough. Sid was painfully aware of that and was having a hard time living with himself despite his best and, by almost anyone's standards, truly admirable efforts.

In addition Sid rarely if ever saw the actions he did take as admirable. Most moral perfectionists don't, and in fact cannot, allow themselves to. For instance, Beth, a staff lawyer with the NAACP, turned down far more lucrative positions to accept her current job and at twenty-seven, had already won several "landmark" cases that would improve the quality of life for minorities. Yet she is far more likely to belittle those accomplishments than pat herself on the back for a job well done. "Whenever I hear myself telling people about this politically correct, public-interest job I have and the good works I'm trying to do, it sounds like I'm bragging," Beth said, "and I get really disgusted with myself," sometimes so much so that she stops talking in mid-sentence and insists on changing the subject.

Even though they measure their worth by doing good, many moral perfectionists consider pride a character flaw. According to their moral and ethical code, giving themselves credit for the good deeds they try so hard to accomplish is taboo. Merely mentioning their positive attributes to others is bragging, and bragging is "against the rules." Since it is "bad" to feel good about being good, it is practically impossible for moral perfectionists to derive any satisfaction from striving to be morally and ethically perfect. Instead they constantly question their motives and engage in ethical nitpicking, searching their souls for imperfections and exceptions to their near-perfect conduct, which prove they are not good enough after all. As Beth put it, "The other night I was walking down the street when a black man stepped out of an alley and started walking toward me. I was petrified, but after he passed and nothing happened, I got really mad at myself because it dawned on me that I probably wouldn't have been that scared if he had been a white man. I thought I had risen above that sort of racist thinking a long time ago, and it really bothered me to see that I hadn't." In fact it bothered Beth so much that several days later she was still worrying about it. "I began to wonder if I even had a right to be in my job," Beth continued. "Should a white woman from an upper-middle-class background be representing minorities? Did I deserve my position when I still had prejudices myself?"

As you can see, moral perfectionists have a real talent for self-flagellation. They psychologically beat themselves up over the tiniest slipups. Any real or imagined failure to comply with their incredibly long list of "shoulds, musts, and have-tos" leads to an orgy of self-criticism, a distressing mental recounting of all their "sins."

When performance perfectionists fall short of their goals or fail to live up to their lofty standards and conclude that they must try harder, they can work longer hours, check their work more carefully, or gather more "expert" opinions before making a business decision. Appearance perfectionists can further restrict their diets, purchase new clothes, or reorganize their closets. Interpersonal perfectionists can always find someone to criticize or control. But how does someone try harder to be morally and ethically perfect? How do moral perfectionists counter self-doubt and relieve guilt feelings stirred up by something as intangible as their values or prejudices or commitment to a cause? More often than not, through an elaborate system of rituals, tests, and self-punishment.

"Sometimes I feel so ashamed of myself that I curl up in a ball and cry," Felicia acknowledged. And on those nights when her list of "misdeeds" seems especially long and horrifying, she gets out of bed and composes an equally long list of "amends" to make the next day. Some of the items on her list—for instance, apologizing to her son for harshly reprimanding him—are directly related to her "sins." But other items could only be described as penance. For example, to atone for her "horrible thoughts" about the driver who cut her off on the highway, Felicia might assign herself the distasteful task of washing and cleaning out the family car. Only after she has "come clean" in this manner can Felicia stop obsessing about her failings and fall asleep. Of course the following night any amends she failed to make are added to her daily list of misdeeds, and Felicia starts the entire process over again.

Similarly, Beth decided that she would not be worthy of her job until she had purged herself of all racist thoughts and feelings. She set up a test for herself: She would make eye contact with and say hello to a dozen black men a day every day for two weeks. If she failed that test, she would know that she was hopelessly prejudiced and submit her resignation to the NAACP. Fortunately Beth's test was not particularly difficult for her to pass and she managed to assuage her guilt temporarily and hang onto her job. Of course it didn't really eliminate all of her prejudices, which she realized the next time she started ethically nitpicking and discovered that most of her close female friends were white.

Moral perfectionists will go to almost any length to obtain tangible proof of intangibles like goodness, devotion, concern, compassion, and righteousness. They will curtail or completely abandon their social lives to make more time for prayer or volunteer work, protest marches or letter-writing campaigns. They will donate every spare dime to charity, skipping meals or postponing necessary purchases in order to have more money to give to others. They will say certain prayers in a specific order at the same time every day, refuse to associate with people who don't share their perspective on life, give away most of their worldly possessions to prove that they are not materialistic, and much, much more. They will take extreme measures to atone for their real or imagined sins as well, and between self-sacrifices to prove their worth and self-punishments to pay for their unworthiness, morally and ethically perfecting themselves can become a twenty-four-hour-a-day mission.

Describing herself as "an environmentally conscious animal-rights and antinuclear activist," Betsy, whom we introduced in Chapter One, was one such slave to her political-belief system. While certainly admirable in principle, in practice Betsy's causes ruled her life. They dictated her diet, her attire, her mode of transportation, and her employment options. She selected the few friends she had based on them and incessantly argued with everyone from her parents to total strangers because of them.

Betsy saw nothing wrong with being carted off to jail during antinuclear protests and nothing irresponsible about being thirty years old and still living in her parents' home, contributing next to nothing for room and board because she refused to take any job that fell the least bit short of her morally perfect standards. "People who don't take a stand are the irresponsible ones. Doing nothing while the government and big businesses destroy the planet, now, *that's* wrong," she declared, turning the tables and taking the heat off herself in the same way interpersonal perfectionists do.

Also like interpersonal perfectionists, moral perfectionists are quick to judge other people and harshly critical of anyone who does not subscribe to and live by the same value systems they do. On one level, by identifying "sinners" and comparing themselves to people who don't take the same stands with the same tenacity they do, moral perfectionists confirm their "goodness." Proselytizing and trying to "convert" people to their way of thinking is also another method of proving their commitment and devotion to a philosophy or cause. On a more fundamental level moral perfectionists may be trying to protect themselves from feelings of anxiety and self-doubt. By rejecting or distancing themselves from people whose points of view differ from or contradict their own, their belief system remains intact and unchallenged, which is of the utmost importance to moral perfectionists. Questioning their moral or ethical code shakes the very foundation on which their identities and sense of self-worth are built. In addition, merely entertaining the notion that their way might not be the one and only right way is considered an infraction of the "rules," perceived as a lack of commitment, or seen as a sign that their will to resist temptation is weakening— all of which makes moral perfectionists extremely uncomfortable. That was certainly the case for Paul, a twenty-five-year-old bookstore salesclerk and recently born-again Christian.

Paul had moved three times in the past year, each time motivated by his inability to tolerate his roommates' "thoroughly disgusting" behavior. Paul's first roommate was "rowdy": a beer drinker who shouted and swore while watching sporting events on TV. "Even on Sundays," Paul said. "It made me so nervous that I would sleep on the couch at the Christian Life Center on Saturday nights and not go home until all the games were over the next day."

Paul's next roommate "wasn't a believer. I tried to turn him on to God, but he just wasn't interested." In fact he articulately argued a case for God not existing at all, and that made Paul even more nervous than beer drinking and swearing had.

He then moved in with a minister's son, who didn't drink or seem particularly enthusiastic about sports. "But he talked about sex *constantly*," Paul explained. "Considering his upbringing, I couldn't believe my ears." Paul was "completely shocked" the first time his roommate brought a woman home to spend the night. The second time that happened (with a different woman, to boot), Paul "gave notice" and moved out by the end of the month.

Now Paul lives alone. "Financially I really can't afford to," he said. "But spiritually I can't afford not to. I don't want to take the chance that some other guy who looks nice and normal on the outside will be as morally bankrupt as my last three roommates turned out to be."

Moral perfectionists also:

- Appear tight, tense, overly serious, and in some instances robotlike in tone or demeanor. They may only "come to life" while discussing causes or value-laden issues they feel passionate about.
- Have difficulty dealing with their own or other people's emotions, especially anger but also excitement or unabashed affection.

- Become anxious and indecisive when confronted with questions that don't have clear-cut right or wrong answers and in situations where there isn't a right or wrong way to behave.
- Lack confidence in their internal sense of right and wrong. When asked for their opinion, they may consult and quote the Bible, the AA Big Book, the teachings of a political or religious leader, or some other "higher" authority.
- Tend to stereotype people (e.g., "All government officials are crooks." "Never trust a lawyer." "Today's college students aren't interested in learning. They just want a degree to get a better job when they graduate.") It is less threatening for moral perfectionists to categorize and label people in this manner than to grapple with individual differences and the idea that someone can behave "badly" and still be a "good" person.
- Are apt to have gaping holes in their moral and ethical codes that enable them to reconcile such inconsistencies as being patriotic Americans who spearhead book banning and other censorship campaigns; or constantly decrying the disintegration of traditional family values even though they are having extramarital affairs.

The Making of a Moral Perfectionist

Although their upbringing and early life experiences are similar to other perfectionists' backgrounds in most respects, moral perfectionists are more likely to have received strict religious training during childhood and to recall God being portrayed as an all-seeing, all-knowing judge capable of meting out swift and terrible punishment for any and all wrongdoing. Even though they may no longer practice the religion in which they were raised, many moral perfectionists report that they still feel as if they are being watched and think that they will not be allowed to "get away with" any misdeeds, even unintentional ones.

"Several years ago, I was flying from New York to Los Angeles and stopped in an airport gift shop to buy a magazine," one moral perfectionist told us. Halfway through her transcontinental flight she discovered that the salesclerk had apparently mistaken her ten-dollar bill for a twenty and given her too much change. "I got terribly upset about it," she continued. "My hands were shaking and my heart was beating a mile a minute. I could hardly breathe and I couldn't stop thinking that I shouldn't have that money, that not counting my change on the spot and giving back the extra ten dollars was the same as stealing, and *God knew it*. I was absolutely convinced that something was going to happen to the plane because I had stolen that money. I was actually in tears, thinking that all the other passengers, all those innocent people, were going to pay for my sin. I hadn't prayed in years, but I did for the rest of that flight and I promised God I'd find a way to repay the money if he'd just let us land safely in L.A." True to her word, when the plane landed, she rushed to the nearest gift shop, bought an envelope and a stamp and mailed a ten-dollar bill back to the shop in New York.

As much as many of us laugh about the religious dogma that was drilled into us during church or synagogue services or in parochial schools, those tenets—including the idea that we can avoid swift and terrible punishment by admitting and atoning for our sins—frequently come back to haunt us. They tend to run on endless tape loops in the minds of moral perfectionists, whose overly active consciences often echo the messages they received from overly conscientious parents. "My mother was always saying things like, 'You'll never go wrong if you put God first, other people second, and yourself last,'" Felicia said. "And whenever I was worried about anything, she accused me of being self-centered. 'Do you think the whole world revolves around *you?*' she'd say or she'd call me ungrateful and remind me about how much worse off other people were. In two seconds flat I'd feel like the most horrible, worthless person on the planet." Felicia still feels that way whenever she does anything that could in any way, shape, or form be considered selfish.

As a rule, moral perfectionists received more than their fair share of messages with moralistic overtones from influential people in their lives: grandparents, teachers, ministers, or rabbis, as well as their parents. However, the most powerful ingredient that goes into the making of a moral perfectionist appears to be *strict prohibitions against normal impulses*. Natural sexual curiosity may have been met with severe and humiliating punishments. The expression of negative emotions such as sadness or anger may have been surreptitiously frowned upon or blatantly criticized. Protesting unfair treatment or, in a moment of frustration, blurting out, "You never listen to anything I say," could lead to days of stone-cold silence that hurt more than any tongue lashing or physical beating ever would. Some moral perfectionists were even given the impression that the instinctive and inescapable need for nurturing was unacceptable.

By the time Callie, the physical therapist we mentioned in Chapter One, was born, her father had already been diagnosed with a rare neurological disease and told he had no more than two years to live. He would live six more years primarily because Callie's mother dedicated herself to keeping him alive as long as possible. Of course with so much of her time and energy devoted to her husband and her thoughts focused on him even when she was not physically caring for him, Callie's mother had very little to give to Callie. So her grandmother and other neighbors and relatives took turns caring for her, fitting her into their lives according to their needs and schedules rather than hers.

Naturally Callie longed for more nurturing and attention, especially from her mother. But every time she sought to satisfy this need, she, in one way or another, received a message that said, *"I cannot take care of you. And since Daddy is very sick and will die without my care, you must not expect me to."* Thanks to the "magical thinking" that is common in young children, Callie came to believe that wanting love and attention, or worse yet, resenting the fact that she was not getting it, could actually kill her father. By the time she was three, she had filed that message in her unconscious, twisting it around a bit so that, at the most fundamental level, she believed, *It is wrong and dangerous to need nurturing and bad to want to be taken care of.* At four Callie discovered that she could feel better about herself and be close to, if not cared for by, her mother by helping to take care of her dad. At five she could do everything from changing oxygen tanks to making her father's bed while he was lying in it. And when her dad finally died, six-year-old Callie comforted her severely depressed mother and did not expect anything in return. She had learned that *it was good (and safe) to take care of others.* Replacing her "bad" urge to be taken care of with a "good" one (wanting to take care of others), for years to come she would sincerely believe that she did not have needs for love, nurturing, or emotional support. She became the ultimate caretaker.

Callie took in stray animals, spent cold winter evenings bringing coffee and blankets to the homeless, sent money to dozens of charities even when it meant sacrificing something she wanted for herself. All of Callie's adolescent boyfriends and adult lovers were "wounded birds," drug users, men in allegedly loveless marriages, men who were so insecure that they required constant reassurance and adoration to get through the day without becoming depressed. Callie anticipated their every need and fulfilled it. Her friends and family could clearly see what Callie of course could not—that these men were "draining her dry" and were so self-centered that they would not so much as lift a finger to do anything for her.

In every job she ever held Callie, in addition to handling her own responsibilities, picked up the slack for everyone else. Rarely sharing information about her own life, Callie listened to her coworkers' and even her bosses' problems, and her typical response to *not* getting promotions or pay raises was simply to do *more* for the very people who had not rewarded her with the salary or status she deserved. Again others told her that she was being exploited. "If you'll do it for nothing, why should they give you anything?" her friends asked, but somehow Callie didn't see it that way. A certain amount of suffering and self-sacrifice was expected of a "good" person, she believed, and striving to be a good, selfless, caring person was the only thing she truly felt safe, secure, and worthwhile doing.

The Moral Perfectionist's Predicament

In religious circles it's called seeking a state of grace: living in accordance with God's laws, confessing and atoning for sins (including the original one committed by Adam and Eve in the Garden of Eden), so that you can die with as "clean" a record as possible. Psychoanalysts call it reaction formation: a psychological defense mechanism that unconsciously converts impulses you came to believe were bad or dangerous into their opposites *before* you become consciously aware of them. But whatever it's called, the need to squelch natural, instinctive, but supposedly unacceptable urges and replace them with altruistic or self-sacrificing behaviors or devout, sometimes ritualistic, religious practices is the driving force behind moral perfectionism.

Like Callie many moral perfectionists developed their habits and distorted thought patterns early in their lives. While the unintentional neglect of her caretakers prompted young Callie to transform her need to be nurtured into a desire to sacrifice herself for the good of others, some moral perfectionists had rigid codes of conduct passed down to them by members of their family through repetition, scare tactics, and physical punishment. Other moral perfectionists started seeking a state of grace later in life, often after years of being decidedly imperfect when it came to morality and ethics. Paul, who ran away from home at sixteen, is a case in point.

"There was nothing really awful about my family," he explained. "I wasn't being abused or anything like that. I just got tired of all their rules and took off." Paul described the next five years of his life as "living on the streets until I got sick or scared or the cops picked me up for vagrancy or disturbing the peace. Then crawling back home with my tail between my legs." But he always left again, and when he turned twenty-one, his parents kicked him out for good. "For the next three years I hustled," Paul said. "I sold drugs and I used them, lots of them. I ran scams on tourists. I shoplifted and slept with anyone who seemed the least bit interested. I partied all the time. I thought that was freedom. I thought it was fun. But to tell you the truth, I was scared to death most of the time. I was scared that some girl's boyfriend would beat me up. I was scared of getting arrested or getting robbed or coming down with some incurable disease." It was in fact a disease—hepatitis—that indirectly "saved" Paul. He collapsed on the steps of a homeless shelter operated by a Christian Life Center, and the man who got him to the hospital visited him there every day.

"He talked to me about God," Paul recalled. "He quoted Scripture and told me how he'd turned his life around. He just kept talking until I started hearing him and realized that what he was saying made sense. I *had* been filling up the emptiness inside me with everything I could get my hands on. But it was a spiritual emptiness that only God could fill, and he would if I let him into my life and followed the path he showed me." Paul did follow that path—with a single-minded devotion born of his fear that he had used up all his chances. "When I looked back over my life, I realized how close I had come to dying dozens of times," he said. "God's grace had saved me then, but it might not the next time. I'd be signing my death warrant if I didn't get things right on the first try." Of course getting things right meant striving for moral and ethical perfection, which Paul did, getting a job at a Christian bookstore, spending all his free time at the Christian Life Center, limiting his circle of friends to fellow Christians, and watching his every move like a hawk. He believed that "one slip meant it was all over."

Many a recovering alcoholic, addict, and compulsive gambler has echoed that sentiment. Convinced that they have one shot at recovery, at least initially and sometimes for years, they try to work the Twelve Steps perfectly, pushing themselves so hard that the added pressure may actually lead them away from true recovery and straight into a relapse.

Whether embarked upon at an early age or well into adulthood, the road to moral perfectionism is paved with fear: fear of failure, fear of falling from grace, fear of incurring the wrath of God or the disapproval of one's peers or parents. Moral perfectionists wholeheartedly believe that no misdeed goes unpunished, that every move they make, every word they utter, even every thought that crosses their mind is being scrutinized and could be found wanting. Even if they manage to get away with something now, they will have to pay later, they believe.

If life were fair and every aspect of it as black and white as moral perfectionists try to make it, they might suffer fewer repercussions. But unfortunately everything is not that clear-cut. Bad things can even happen to people who are very, very good, and when they do, moral perfectionists become confused about how to be morally and ethically good enough. Since they are also more determined than ever to be perfect, that confusion can lead to a near-constant state of anxiety, tormenting some moral perfectionists and prompting them to engage in all sorts of ritualistic, self-testing, and self-punishing behaviors. For others the anxiety never reaches the conscious level of their minds. Their habitual behaviors take care of it before they are even aware of it. Either way the motivation behind their thoughts and actions can be found in the following fundamental belief: "If I do everything in my power to live perfectly and in accordance with my value system, I will feel safe. I will feel secure. I will feel worthwhile."

Operating under that assumption can work in our best interest when we want to control a behavior that is truly dangerous or self-destructive. However, moral perfectionists apply it to a whole range of thoughts, feelings, and behaviors, stifling any urge or impulse that can in any way be construed as less than morally or ethically perfect. They are philosophical when being disappointed would make sense; or when they have every right to be jealous or angry with someone, they may show excessive friendliness and concern instead. This conversion of "bad" wishes into their opposites consumes an enormous amount of energy, makes moral perfectionists extremely rigid, and frequently convinces them that something horrible would happen if they were to experience any kind of pleasure or feel many other emotions that *human beings cannot help but feel*.

The Hitch: You're Only Human

Based on the messages and treatment they received from influential people in their lives, the behaviors they observed, the rigid codes of conduct they had to comply with, and other life experiences, moral perfectionists came to believe that huge portions of their basic makeup and entire sides of their personalities were unacceptable and destined to get them into trouble. If they wanted to gain acceptance and avoid punishment (and who doesn't), they realized that they had to stifle those less than morally and ethically perfect parts of themselves: their sexuality, their skepticism, their anger or frustration, their curiosity, their disappointment, any and all self-interest, even their need for nurturing. They had to control their behavior at all times, push all unthinkable thoughts out of their minds, squelch every unacceptable emotion. The "bad" parts of themselves simply could not be allowed to exist.

The impulses, urges, feelings, and ideas moral perfectionists try to eliminate exist in all of us and are rarely if ever as horrible or dangerous as they think. Many are basic human needs, drives, or instincts, and they live on in spite of our efforts to kill them off. Therein lies the moral perfectionist's predicament: To be morally and ethically perfect, they cannot allow themselves to acknowledge, feel, or act on a whole range of human needs, instincts, and emotions. But because they are human, they can never completely eliminate those unsettling yet nonetheless essential aspects of themselves. The best they can do is to bury them alive and constantly be on the lookout for signs that they are resurfacing so that they can quickly send them back underground again. As you might imagine, that is an endless, exhausting, and ultimately self-defeating task.

Countless times during any given day moral perfectionists encounter people or circumstances that stir up "forbidden" thoughts and feelings: A co-worker takes credit for their ideas and they want revenge; they cannot afford a new car but their obnoxious, gossipy neighbor can and they are jealous; they feel sexually attracted to their best friend's husband, who often seems to be flirting with them. Resentment constantly courses through moral perfectionists' veins. They tell waiters about errors made in their favor on a check, while their friends take advantage of major miscalculations on their tax returns. They work hard and even assume extra responsibilities, but a co-worker who sleeps with the boss gets promoted. Not only do these less virtuous individuals get away with their morally and ethically imperfect behaviors and profit from them to boot, but their consciences don't seem to bother them at all. They are not tormented by guilt or fear of divine retribution. They don't even try to be good. As anyone might, moral perfectionists bristle at the unfairness of it all. But by doing so, they are breaking their own rules and feel horribly ashamed of themselves. In fact whenever a negative and presumably unacceptable thought or feeling bubbles to the surface, they invariably redirect it at themselves, bombard themselves with self-criticism, and redouble their efforts to push down and rise above those feelings and impulses. Sometimes they cannot.

When moral perfectionists are tired, under more pressure than usual, in the midst of an exceptionally stressful situation, or just plain overdrawn at the bank of "goodness," they, like all human beings, will act on impulse: fly into a rage, slap a shrieking toddler, have a one-night stand, eat chocolate and watch soap operas instead of doing the laundry, or back out of a commitment and lie about the reason for doing so. With a sort of moral binge-and-purge mentality, some moral perfectionists will go on extended "ethical benders." As one moral perfectionist we interviewed put it, "When I was a kid, I'd sneak into the kitchen to get a snack before dinner, which I wasn't allowed to do. Then, after I'd eaten one cookie, I'd think, 'Since I'm going to get punished for eating that cookie anyway, I might as well have as many as I want,' and I'd grab a whole handful. I still think that way about things I shouldn't do. If I pick up a total stranger and have a one-night stand, I tell myself I might as well get it out of my system and pick up a different woman every night for a couple of weeks. Then I go to the opposite extreme and completely swear off women and sex." This moral perfectionist stuck to his vow of celibacy for as long as he could suppress his sexual urges, usually several months. Then he started the whole cycle over again.

Other moral perfectionists:

- Feel compelled to "confess" their sins immediately, talking about what they did and how horrible they felt to anyone who will listen.
- Must immediately do something to atone for their misdeeds or make amends to people they presumably harmed, often overcompensating for merely thinking about engaging in "sinful" behavior—as Beth did with her supposed prejudices. Another woman we interviewed paid for being sexually attracted to a colleague's husband by being exceptionally nice to her colleague, spending more time with her, buying her gifts, and assuming some of her workload—even though she really couldn't stand to be with that colleague.
- Feel so ashamed of their jealous feelings, hateful thoughts, or hurtful acts toward a friend, relative, or co-worker that they cannot face that person. They are cold and distant in the presence of the person they believe they have harmed or avoid that person altogether—even though they realize full well that they are causing more harm by doing so (and feel all the more ashamed of themselves as a result).

One thing moral perfectionists never do and indeed seem completely incapable of doing is simply letting go of their "misdeeds" and forgiving themselves. Instead they obsessively ruminate about them and cannot stop running through their opressive list of "shoulds, musts, and have-to's" until they rededicate themselves to being morally and ethically perfect and redouble their efforts to squelch any and all unacceptable thoughts, feelings, and actions.

Moral perfectionists' compelling urge to keep whole parts of themselves buried traps them in a time-consuming, self-defeating cycle of shame, self-punishment, and acts of contrition. In addition, their suppressed impulses and emotions may leak out in the form of veiled hostility (biting or sarcastic comments, daggerlike looks or icy silences that speak louder than words), passive-aggressive behaviors ("accidentally" forgetting or losing things, chronic lateness or double messages: "It's okay"—sigh— "I'll be fine here all by myself stuffing all of the envelopes for your mailing") or physical illnesses—all of which take their toll on moral perfectionists as well as everyone around them.

The Way Out for Moral Perfectionists

Like performance perfectionists, moral perfectionists need to find a healthier balance for their lives, maintaining the attitudes and behaviors that actually work for them, abandoning those that don't, and adding new experiences to their lives. In addition, like interpersonal perfectionists they can save themselves a great deal of misery by developing more tolerance for people whose value systems are different from their own. And because lightening up on themselves and others can stir up anxiety and bring other previously unexamined emotions to the surface, they, like appearance perfectionists, need to learn new skills for coping with those feelings. The following strategies, found in Chapters Nine and Ten, can be particularly helpful to them:

- Creating a well-balanced life-style (page 195)
- Adding fun (page 202) and humor (page 203) to their lives
- Developing tolerance (page 213) and empathy (page 214)
- Reducing obligations/increasing choices (page 221)
- Altering distorted thought patterns (page 224)
- Strategies to stop catastrophizing (page 230)

Chapter Eight

Fourteen Reasons to Stop Trying So Hard

At twenty-seven, Marty owns his own fitness consulting business, and thanks to that large corporate contract we mentioned in the introduction, he just bought a BMW and a new townhouse in a trendy neighborhood of the small midwestern city where he lives. Ever since he started writing a fitness column for the local newspaper (with his picture prominently displayed above it), he has been recognized everywhere he goes and admits that he is enjoying the "star treatment."

Of course he works seventy to eighty hours a week, and when he does socialize, it is usually with clients. But Marty says he doesn't mind that. After all, he's strived all his life to be where he is today, skipping grades in elementary school, winning an athletic scholarship to a prestigious college, excelling at baseball and ice hockey, and graduating magna cum laude as well.

So what's wrong with that picture? Nothing at all, if you overlook the stomach ulcer Marty's had off and on since the tenth grade or the fact that he hasn't had a steady relationship in years or so much as a date in the past six months. His mother isn't speaking to him (thanks to the proposal-typing fiasco that kept him from attending her birthday party) and at least once a week he wakes up in a cold sweat with his heart racing for no apparent reason. These are just a few of the unwelcome side effects of perfectionism that we will be describing in this chapter. Chances are that you suffer from one or more of them too.

If you are still thinking that, in the overall scheme of things, striving to be the best there is at everything you do and, in the process, pushing yourself and others "a little" too hard isn't such a big deal, we hope this chapter will change your mind. And if you are still telling yourself that what you have gotten by setting sky-high standards and relentlessly trying to live up to them has been worth the price you have paid thus far, we hope this chapter will make you aware of where you could be heading and convince you to take both preventive and curative measures: toning down your lofty expectations, breaking your self-defeating perfection-istic habits, and learning to be a healthy pursuer of excellence instead.

The problems you will read about in this chapter may seem extreme, but they are not farfetched. In fact in some of the research Miriam has conducted, not just some or many but *all* of the perfectionists studied reported problems in one or more of the following areas.

1. Stress and Stress-Related Illness

Like most perfectionists, Judy, the would-be superwoman we described in Chapter Four, does not know how to relax. "The minute I sit down, I get antsy," she said. "I feel like there's something I probably should be doing, and since I'm not doing it, I feel guilty." Yet Judy also knows that she needs to relax. "Sometimes, toward the end of an especially busy day, I'll notice my heart beating really fast or my ears ringing. And if I stand up quickly, I'll see spots in front of my eyes as if I'm about to pass out. That's when I know I'm overdoing things and have to slow down." Judy's symptoms (as well as her migraine headaches and occasional difficulty concentrating) are signs of excess stress. As a result of the pressure you place on yourself to be perfect and the constant vigilance required by your determination not to make mistakes, if you are a perfectionist, you probably suffer from it too.

Although stress—your body's response to any demand placed upon it—is a normal and necessary part of everyday life, excess stress is a killer that has been linked to high blood pressure, heart attacks, ulcers, diabetes, cancer, colitis, and various emotional disturbances. In hot pursuit of perfection, you not only cross your stress threshold on a regular basis but are apt to ignore most of the danger signs telling you that you are overloading your system: chronic headaches, back pain, cold hands and feet, fatigue, insomnia, irritability, rashes, eye strain, flulike symptoms, forgetfulness, gastrointestinal disturbances, frequent colds, and moodiness. If you allow those unrealistic expectations of yours and that insatiable desire to be, have, and do more, prevent you from acknowledging your limits, you will continue to push yourself beyond them until your body rebels (and you end up in the coronary care unit) or you burn out.

2. Burnout

Burnout is a syndrome, a cluster of physical, psychological, and behavioral symptoms, caused by prolonged excess stress. It is a condition that is quite common among dedicated, committed, achievement-oriented, and perfectionistic individuals who do and do and do without replenishing their energy supply through relaxation, recreation, or nourishing personal relationships. In addition to physical symptoms similar to those brought on by excess stress, people who suffer from burnout tend to be short-tempered, easily bored, perpetually worried, impatient, unproductive, and impulsive. Having done too much for too long, they "hit the wall" and make radical, often ill-advised moves, including

169

spur-of-the-moment decisions to tell off their bosses, quit their jobs, relocate, or deplete their savings accounts to pay for a six-month round-the-world cruise.

3. Anxiety and Panic Attacks

"I was in line at the grocery store when suddenly, for no apparent reason, I began to hyperventilate," Felicia, the moral perfectionist we described in the last chapter, recalled. "I just couldn't catch my breath and I was perspiring and shivering at the same time. My chest felt tight, and when my hands and legs started to get numb, I was sure I was having a heart attack." What Felicia was having was an anxiety or panic attack, and it had nothing to do with the condition of her heart but rather with her state of mind.

Anxiety attacks were what woke Marty in the middle of the night as well. Since he was asleep, he certainly wasn't aware of feeling anxious, and neither was Felicia. However, for reasons no one can adequately explain, all of their pent-up dread, worries about not doing enough well enough, and fear of failure simply chose that moment to rush to the surface, triggering the physical symptoms they along with an estimated twelve million other Americans experience.

It's generally acknowledged that the panic-prone are people who feel an overwhelming responsibility for getting things done and doing things right. They are people whose bodies have a low threshold for excess stress but who are so adept at mentally conjuring up worst-case scenarios and terrible visions of danger that they unwittingly push themselves past their threshold. More often than not they are also people with perfectionistic tendencies.

If you have ever had a panic attack, you know how terrifying they can be and can understand how someone who has them would be willing to do almost anything to prevent themselves from having another one. Associating their attacks with the physical setting in which they occurred, they may even avoid that

170

spot or locations similar to it at all costs, severely restricting their ability to lead normal lives, much less the exceptional ones they expect themselves to lead.

4. Obsessions and Compulsions

Nancy, a thirty-year-old medical researcher, weighs and measures every ounce of food she eats. At restaurants she interrogates her waiter to find out every ingredient that goes into the meal she is ordering, and when that meal arrives, pulls a small kitchen scale from her purse and weighs out the portions she will allow herself to consume. Nancy also works out for two hours a day: At precisely the same time each day, in all kinds of weather and in spite of injuries or illness, she jogs three miles to the gym, uses the Nautilus machines in a specific sequence, takes a thirty-minute aerobics class, and then jogs home. She will not work overtime or make plans with friends if doing so might disrupt her routine. And if, for some ungodly reason, Nancy can't get to the gym on time, the only way she can "feel okay" about it is by working out for an extra hour.

Ralph, the lawyer, we mentioned in Chapter Five, won't excuse himself from a meeting to use the rest room no matter how adamantly nature calls. It "bothers" him that other people would know where he was going and what he was doing. Ashtrays that are not emptied as soon as smokers put out their cigarettes also "bother" Ralph, and he cannot concentrate on what other people are saying or the business he hopes to conduct until he gets up, empties the ashtray, and wipes it clean.

Marilyn, the appearance perfectionist you first read about in Chapter One, cannot leave her house until certain tasks are completed. Even if she is running late, she must vacuum the carpets, dust the furniture, set the table for dinner, check to make sure all drawers and closet doors are shut, and, as she did during her own childhood, put her daughter's toys in their "proper" places. She must not only do those chores, she must do them in that

171

order. What would happen if she didn't? Marilyn doesn't know. "All I know is that when I don't, I get to the door and can't turn the doorknob. I tell myself. 'Just leave. No one's going to know you didn't vacuum. Who cares that you didn't check the closets? So what if the Ninja Turtles are in the kitchen instead of the playroom?' But it's like someone has a gun to my head. I *have to* go back and fix those things."

Nancy, Ralph, and Marilyn had become slaves to their perfectionism. Their preoccupation with making themselves and their worlds perfect have become an obsession: a recurring, persistent idea or impulse that shows up in their minds, stirring up anxiety and making it virtually impossible to concentrate on anything else. Their perfectionistic habits have become compulsions: repetitive, ritualistic behaviors that are clearly excessive, counterproductive, and usually not gratifying. Losing control of their thoughts and actions in this manner is a fairly common occurrence among perfectionists, and some may even develop a psychological condition known as obsessive-compulsive disorder (OCD).

Once considered a rare disorder, OCD is now thought to affect more than five million American adults, one-third of whom developed the problem during childhood. An unreasoning preoccupation with and irresistible internal demand to clean or wash or check things such as light switches or door locks, to avoid touching people or objects, or to repeat certain relatively meaningless actions in a specific sequence are some of the forms OCD takes. People with OCD may be plagued by intense feelings of self-doubt or dread, fearing that they have done something or will do something horrible even though there is no evidence to support their contention. They are usually well aware that their thoughts and actions do not make sense, but try as they might, they are unable to control or stop them. If this description fits you, we encourage you to seek professional help. OCD—which is obviously extremely frightening and debilitating—can be controlled and overcome with medication, therapy, or a combination of the two.

5. Alcohol, Drug, and Food Addictions

Whether to calm their nerves and manage their anxiety or for that extra energy boost they believe will increase their competitive edge, perfectionists have a tendency to self-medicate. They take downers for their tranquilizing properties and sometimes to make sure they don't "waste time" trying to fall asleep. They come to rely on amphetamines and cocaine for the burst of energy they produce, the false sense of confidence they create, their ability to suppress appetite, and their supposed power to increase concentration and motivation. Cocaine may also be used because it is fashionable in certain circles, giving onlookers the impression that the perfectionist user is sophisticated and also wealthy enough to afford the drug. Alcohol can loosen the uptight perfectionist's tongue, temporarily relieve stress, help the insecure perfectionist fit in with a crowd that also drinks, and numb feelings of disappointment or failure. Food, especially sweets, can serve that purpose, too, and it is frequently used by both performance and moral perfectionists as a reward or to fill them up after they have drained themselves dry while giving to others.

Because of perfectionists' tendencies to go to extremes, to think that more is better, and to be externally focused rather than inclined to look inside themselves and actually recognize or try to solve their problems, they are particularly prone not only to use drugs, alcohol, and food but to become addicted to them as well. In fact there are numerous similarities between the backgrounds and personalities of perfectionists and alcoholics, addicts, or compulsive overeaters. You need only spend a few hours in the rooms where members of Anonymous fellowships such as Alcoholics Anonymous, Overeaters Anonymous, or Narcotics Anonymous meet to hear dozens of people relate how the pressure to be perfect and the disappointment they felt each time they could not be led them to drink, take drugs, and go on eating binges.

Regrettably, because perfectionists so often believe they can handle everything on their own as well as fear rejection and harsh judgment by others, they will deny the existence or seriousness of a drinking, overeating, or drug problem long after it becomes obvious to everyone around them and starts seriously to damage their lives. The first of AA's Twelve Steps—admitting they were powerless and could not manage their lives—is exceedingly difficult for perfectionists to take, but it is a lifesaver, and if you even remotely suspect that alcohol, food, or drugs may be a problem for you, we wholeheartedly recommend that you find the willingness to take it.

6. Other "Addictions"

Approximately 5 percent of all men and women who exercise are exercise addicts. They are intensely preoccupied with slenderizing their bodies or adding bulk to them, devote excessive amounts of time and money to the pursuit of the perfectly toned or proportioned body, and actually experience such withdrawal symptoms as irritability, lethargy, difficulty concentrating, and nervousness if they are forced to stop working out. Their dependence on running, pumping iron, or swimming laps may be due in part to the pleasurable feelings created by the release of endorphins and other biochemicals. However, most exercise addicts are also perfectionists (usually in the area of keeping up perfect appearances).

Compulsive spending is yet another "addiction" that frequently plagues perfectionists. In their quest for the perfect outfit, accessory, or knickknack—the perfect "look" that will finally make them feel good enough—appearance perfectionists in particular tend to turn into shopaholics. They comb the malls alone instead of socializing with friends or developing intimate relationships. And believing that having the right image, living in the right home, driving the right car, and wearing the right clothes is of the utmost importance can be an expensive proposition indeed. Compulsively spending perfectionists often charge their credit cards to the limit and beyond, all too often finding themselves in serious financial trouble. In addition they are most likely to go on spending sprees when some aspect of their life other than keeping up perfect appearances is rife with problems that seem completely beyond their control.

7. Eating Disorders

Affecting primarily women between the ages of fifteen and forty, the eating disorders of anorexia nervosa and bulimia have reached epidemic proportions in this country. Anorexia involves self-starvation, whereas bulimia involves binge eating and "purging" by vomiting, taking laxatives, or excessive exercising. The two together afflict more than sixty million Americans.

The vast majority of people with eating disorders will deny that they have a problem. Their weight may drop to alarming lows. They may stop menstruating and suffer from malnutrition, early onset of osteoporosis, sleep disturbances, inability to fight off colds or other infections, and a decrease in overall fitness. Yet their distorted body image invariably convinces them that they could still stand to lose a few more pounds. Not until they experience a medical crisis or are forcibly admitted to an in-patient treatment facility will they acknowledge that they have gone overboard in their quest for the perfect body. Some will never admit it, literally starving or purging themselves to death. Between 5 and 18 percent of all eating disorder sufferers die as a direct or indirect result of the disorder.

Although being a perfectionist does not make someone develop an eating disorder, the vast majority of people with eating disorders are also perfectionists. In fact their scores on the Minnesota Multiphasic Personality Inventory, a psychological test, reveal high levels of the same self-doubt, guilt, worry, excessively high standards, and rigid beliefs that are the hallmarks of perfectionism.

8. Hooked on Work

Jay gets to his office at seven in the morning and stays until nine or ten at night. He works most weekends, and when he does take time off, he can't really relax. "I'm always thinking about work," Jay admits. "When I'm driving or watching TV, even in my sleep. I can't tell you how many times I've woken up in a panic in the middle of the night because I was dreaming about an important meeting where everything went wrong or a project that was going to be late because of all these bizarre things that were happening. I'll tell myself it's just a dream, but I can never get back to sleep afterward. Usually I get up and work for a while, sometimes for the rest of the night."

Over the years Jay's ambition, his high standards, and his relentless striving to reach new levels of success had taken on a life of their own. He no longer worked nights and weekends just to get ahead in his career or even to keep from falling behind. He overworked because working was the only meaningful activity in his life. It was the only thing he felt comfortable doing. It was the only thing that filled the empty spaces inside and distracted him from the loneliness, self-doubt, and self-loathing that seemed to pounce on him whenever he slowed down or stopped striving. When he was not working, he felt anxious, ill at ease, lost. So he kept working. He could not seem to stop.

Jay was a workaholic. Many perfectionists, especially performance perfectionists, are. Their never-ending struggle to succeed, the adrenaline rush it produces, and the rewards it delivers are habit-forming. Consequently workaholics spend more and more time working. But they do not necessarily get more work done. In fact most of their time is devoted to listing and worrying about the things they have to do, going over the things they've already done to make sure no errors were made, and justifying the time they are spending at work to themselves, their employers, their wives, or their kids.

On those rare occasions when someone can talk them into taking time off, workaholics' bodies may not be at the office but

176

their minds still are. "A couple of years ago I went to Bermuda with a bunch of guys I knew in grad school," Jay said. "It wasn't a great time to go because I was up for a promotion and couldn't really afford to be away for too long. But I brought work with me, only I never got around to doing it. I kept meaning to. I'd decide not to play tennis so that I could get some work done but would wind up staring at the scenery. Or I'd leave a nightclub early, take out my briefcase, and then fall asleep before I accomplished anything. I can't say I had any fun at all." In fact Jay was downright miserable, and instead of returning from his vacation rested and raring to go, he was exhausted, depressed, and disgusted with himself.

For workaholics who have them, their home lives are often rife with conflict, and that keeps their work addiction going. They go to the office to escape anything from marital strife to visiting in-laws and are oblivious of the fact that their habit of running away from their personal problems prevents those problems from being solved. The more they work, the worse problems on the home front get, and the worse those problems get, the more they work. The same basic cycle traps workaholics like Jay who have virtually no life outside of work. Because they have no social life or love life to speak of, their work life seems all the more appealing. Yet devoting all their time and energy to work leaves them with none left over to develop a social life or get involved in an intimate relationship.

In these and other ways the compulsion to work—which is such a natural outgrowth of a perfectionist's reliance on achievements as a source of self-worth—invariably backfires and can actually prevent performance perfectionists from achieving the success they so desperately desire. As one of Jay's superiors put it, "We can't afford perfectionists. It's as simple as that. While they're nitpicking and rewording memos, conducting efficiency studies, and getting two dozen opinions to help them make a decision, time's being wasted. We don't need perfect prose and perfect penmanship. We need people who produce, and Jay isn't one of them."

9. Unnecessary Sacrifices

"Social life? What social life?" Adele, the performance-perfectionist graphic designer from Chapter Three, laughed. "Except for award dinners, gallery openings, and other social functions that are more business than pleasure, I really don't get out much. I can't say I miss it. Who has time to stand around with a cocktail in one hand and a canapé in the other gossiping about people who aren't there to defend themselves? I can think of dozens of things I'd rather do." Of course Adele doesn't do those things either. Although she loves the seashore, she hasn't been to the beach in years. She can't remember the last time she took a "real" vacation, not just a business trip with a day or two tacked on for sightseeing. Browsing in department stores and specialty shops was another one of Adele's favorite pastimes that had fallen by the wayside. Nowadays she pays a professional to shop for her. Naturally an intimate relationship is out of the question.

"I tried that," Adele reminded us, and summed up her five-year marriage this way: "We hung in there duking it out for as long as we could, but when he began pressuring me about starting a family, I bailed out. I knew I wasn't ready to spread myself so thin, to try and be a successful businesswoman, a wife, *and* a mother." First things first Adele, who was then thirty, decided. There would be plenty of time to raise a family after she accomplished her lofty career goals, she thought. At forty-six, with no relationship in sight and still too much to do to begin looking for one, the chances that she would have children were virtually nonexistent. But Adele was philosophical about this lost opportunity and everything else she had sacrificed on her way to fame and fortune. "Most people can only dream of having the kind of success I've achieved," she said. "With everything I have to show for myself, how can I complain?"

Most performance perfectionists would agree with Adele. Driven to do things perfectly and achieve as much as possible, they willingly sacrifice anything that is not directly related to their goals. Fun, friends, family, recreation, relaxation, travel, other goals—these are all relegated to a category labeled "Things I'll Get Around to One of These Days." Since performance perfectionists always find one more mountain to climb, "One of These Days" gets pushed farther and farther into the future. In the meantime life passes them by, taking the possibility of fulfilling their dreams for the future with it. They lead one-dimensional lives devoid of pleasure and intimacy, neglecting, postponing, or completely cutting themselves off from every source of satisfaction other than their accomplishments or achievement-oriented activities and, as a result, become even more dependent on those activities to help them feel good about themselves.

Appearance perfectionists make similar sacrifices, for slightly different reasons. They postpone pleasure and social activities until that magical day when their bodies, wardrobes, homes, and ability to converse intelligently on any topic have been perfected. They turn down invitations because they have "nothing" to wear. They don't date because dating leads to sex and having sex means removing the clothes that conceal their flabby thighs or pot bellies. They won't invite guests into their homes because those guests might see that their wall unit doesn't match their dining room table or might set down a glass on their antique hutch. They put off vacations until they lose ten more pounds, tighten up those pecs, or pay off the plastic surgeon (whom they're still thinking of asking to fix the bags under their eyes). On the other hand, appearance perfectionists may fully intend to do any or all of the above but encounter so many "disasters" while preparing to do them that they wind up too upset or exhausted to actually follow through on their plans.

As you can see, if you are a perfectionist, while you are relentlessly pursuing perfection, life is passing you by. You are sacrificing present-day happiness for future flawlessness, a goal you will never attain and a decision you will invariably live to regret.

10. Loneliness and Isolation

Ironically perfectionists, who try so hard to impress people and want so desperately to be loved and accepted, are often perceived as distant and unapproachable or "uptight" and overly sensitive. Whether they are wearing their "I'm completely self-sufficient and need nothing from anybody" mask or overreacting to any hint of disapproval or criticism—even when none was implied—they are not much fun to be around for any length of time and almost impossible to develop a truly intimate relationship with. You see, an intimate relationship—one that is close, familiar, and usually affectionate or loving—asks two people to trust, depend upon, and share their real selves, innermost thoughts, and feelings with each other. That sort of self-disclosure is anathema to most perfectionists.

Afraid to reveal anything about themselves that might be seen as less than perfect, the best some perfectionists can do is alter their masks to reflect whatever they believe someone with whom they are interacting will appreciate and reward with approval or affection. As you may recall, that is what Amelia (the appearance perfectionist we described in Chapter Five) did. She agreed with whatever the man she happened to be dating said, did whatever he wanted to do, even feigned interest in the exact same topics and activities that interested him. She created an illusion of intimacy that no one interested in true intimacy was deceived by for long. The men she dated could sense that she was refusing to put herself on the line by revealing her own thoughts or feelings and interpreted that to mean she did not really want to be with them. "Can you imagine that?" Amelia bristled after one man conveyed that opinion to her. "There I was bending over backward to be the woman I thought he wanted and he thought I was giving him the brush-off!"

If you are a perfectionist, you, too, may have trouble getting both friendships and intimate relationships off the ground. You may keep people at arm's length the way Amelia did or simply because you seem too good to be true. Your effort to create an outward appearance of perfection may have worked too well, making other people feel uncomfortable in your presence and acutely aware of their own imperfections. Concluding that they are not and could never be good enough for you, they take themselves out of your life. So do people who feel like they are walking on eggshells when they are with you. Whether they neglect to mention how terrific you look, fail to chop vegetables to your exact specifications, or have the audacity to hold values that are different than your own, you get so upset so easily that they begin to feel as if they must keep their guard up at all times. Because they cannot relax and be themselves in your presence, they may start to avoid you. Your incessant demands, rituals, constant fishing for compliments, or tendency to sound like a walking résumé may get on people's nerves as well. But for whatever reason, thanks to your perfectionism, you get exactly what you did *not* want: disapproval, rejection, and more often than not, a lonely, isolated existence.

11. Impaired Personal Relationships

We do not mean to give you the impression that perfectionists don't have relationships. They do. Many are married, are active, interested family members, and have any number of friends. This does not, however, alter the fact that they are difficult to live with or love. As we alluded to in Chapter Six, interpersonal perfectionists are apt to have the most strife in their relationships, but no perfectionist is immune to the conflict that results from wanting themselves and everyone around them to be complete and flawless in all respects.

"I love Colin, I really do," his wife, Sarah, said. "But sometimes I could just wring his neck. He's so finicky about everything and he can't make a decision to save his soul because he's so scared that he'll make the wrong decision and ruin our lives. He's always ten miles ahead of himself like that and always imagining the worst. When he didn't have his new job down pat on the first day, he wasn't just mad at himself for that. He was already worrying about whether we would be able to make the mortgage payments on a house we hadn't even made an offer on yet and if our son would be irreparably damaged by being an only child since it looked like we'd never be able to afford to have another baby."

As she did with the infamous cover letter, Sarah often tired of waiting for Colin to make the perfect decision and took matters into her own hands. Colin would always get furious, "pitching a fit" and making many cruel comments he would later regret—especially when Sarah's decision proved to be a good one. Feeling guilty for his earlier tirade, he would fawn over his wife for days, bringing home surprise gifts and showing her a great deal of affection. "I can't say I mind that part," Sarah commented, "but I could definitely live without the rest. It's all so unnecessary and it makes our relationship seem like one long, gut-wrenching roller-coaster ride."

Barbara's husband, George, loved his spouse, too, but he hated the fact that she spent money on clothes she never wore. Her finickiness about their home left him feeling tense whenever he was in any part of it except his den—which Barbara was not allowed to enter. The more perfectionistic Barbara got, the more time George spent in the den. Sometimes he even slept in there, and they wouldn't speak to each other much less make love for weeks on end.

In these and other ways perfectionists throw a wrench into relationships that could work, that could enable them to feel safe, secure, and loved. *Every* perfectionist we have interviewed or counseled over the years has reported problems in this area of his or her life.

12. Sexual Dysfunction

A perfectionist's relationship difficulties and self-defeating habits all too often get carried into their bedrooms. Indeed, perfectionists tend to be prime candidates for sexual dysfunctions. As we mentioned earlier, appearance perfectionists are often too worried about the way their bodies look to relax enough to be sexually responsive, and moral perfectionists may have so thoroughly repressed their ability to experience pleasure or attached such negative connotations to sex that they can hardly be expected to enjoy it. But performance perfectionists tend to be hardest hit by sexual problems.

Their concentration on the adequacy of their own and their partner's performance diminishes pleasure, and regrettably performance as well. They engage in a behavior sex therapists refer to as "spectatoring": emotionally disconnecting themselves from and observing their sexual activity rather than fully participating in and experiencing it. This has repeatedly been shown to inhibit intimacy and sexual response as well as intensifying "performance anxiety"—the fear (and all too often the self-fulfilling prophecy) that they will suffer an "equipment failure" or otherwise be unable to feel sexually satisfied or to satisfy their partner. For someone who is compelled "always to do their best," someone who can't stop evaluating his performance or feeling inadequate if it rates less than a perfect ten, something as normal as the inability to get a full erection when he is physically exhausted or psychologically stressed out can be devastating. To make matters worse, perfectionists who fall short of their sexual standards once anticipate and obsessively worry about future failures, dramatically increasing anxiety *and* the potential for another less-than-perfect performance. This self-defeating cycle may in turn lead to inhibited sexual desire (ISD): a seriously diminished or total lack of interest in sex. ISD is the most prevalent sexual dysfunction brought to the attention of sex therapists today and is extremely common among overachieving time-pressured, results-oriented couples and individuals. Anxiety and inhibited desire may ultimately lead to avoiding sexual activity altogether and that, more often than not, creates additional *relationship* conflict between perfectionists and their spouses or lovers.

183

13. Passing It On

In a scene from the movie *Baby Boom*, Diane Keaton, playing an overachieving, work-obsessed marketing executive who inherits an eighteen-month-old baby girl, takes her child to the park, where she overhears several other equally success-oriented mothers discussing their young children's schedules (German lessons, piano, gymboree, etc.). Having never considered any of these things herself, Keaton, hoping to succeed as fabulously at motherhood as she has at marketing, immediately begins signing her child up for those "enrichment" activities as well. She tries, with a vengeance, to make sure her little girl is perfect and able, not to just keep up with, but to overtake other children in her "age group." Although Keaton soon learns the error of her ways and takes herself and the baby off the fast track, many, many parents today do not—especially if they are perfectionists.

Nowadays the pressure on a child to achieve often starts before birth, with expectant mothers playing classical music or Berlitz language records and talking to their unborn children in hopes of teaching them while they are still in the womb. Achievement-oriented parents put their infants through "stimulation exercises" soon after birth; educational toys and word-association cards are placed in babies' cribs practically before their eyes can focus. Naturally their names are placed on a waiting list at some prestigious kindergarten.

Competition begins early too. In some nursery schools and kindergartens if a child shows particular promise, he or she is tested, ranked, with other three- and four-year-olds, and pitted against them to see who's better at performing certain tasks. Youngsters' lives may be scheduled to the minute. There are music lessons, art classes, foreign-language instruction, gymnastics, swimming, reading. Kids are shuttled from one activity to the next, usually aware that their anxious parents are somewhere in the background expecting results. In *Atlanta* magazine, Tom Junod summed up this approach to childrearing as "the child as masterpiece," and perfectionist parents are most likely to view their children that way.

Fun is rarely the point of these activities; often, unhappily, it's to get ahead. And while some children, especially those with superior mental abilities, seem to thrive in this kind of environment, others merely go through the paces without much enthusiasm. Still others begin to develop stress-related illnesses. Pediatricians are now familiar with six-year-olds who suffer from digestive disorders as a result of this enormous pressure to perform.

Too much emphasis on achievement also tends to make children one-dimensional, so rigidly programmed to perform and "win" that they miss out on many of the joys of childhood. They can be so overscheduled that they are deprived of simple, unstructured playtime. Many therapists who work with perfectionistic children must actually *teach* them how to play.

Of course you may know all this already because you were pressured and prodded by *your* perfectionistic parents. In fact you may be a perfectionist today because you were pushed too hard, expected to do too much too soon, and made to feel that you had to earn your parents' love by being the very best—bar none—at everything you did. They passed on to you their perfectionistic thought patterns and habits as well as a legacy of neurosis and counterproductivity. Now you may unwittingly be passing it along to your children.

If you are a parent and a perfectionist, it is time to ask yourself some frank questions about the way you are raising your children:

- How do you reward your children? Only when they meet certain standards?
- How do you discipline your children? Are you stricter with them than most of your friends and relatives are with their kids? Do you also expect more from them?
- How do you talk to your children? Do you encourage them

to "think like a winner," and be smarter, faster, and more creative than everyone else? Do you compare them to their siblings or friends?

- How do you oversee your children? Are they allowed plenty of time to play and daydream, or is the entire day as rigidly scheduled as your own?
- Most important, how do you express your love to your children? Do you let them know that you love them no matter what, love them for who they are and not for what they do?

Although it was never your intention, your words and actions, all well-meaning, may be paving the way for future problems or contributing to ones that are already taking their toll on your child's physical health or emotional well-being. The list below, which was developed by Barbara Davis, Coordinator of Gifted Programs for the Eaton Intermediate School District in Charlotte, Michigan, outlines the signs and symptoms of childhood perfectionism. Have you noticed any of them in your child?

1. Unreasonably extreme response to poor grades or other evaluations
2. Inability to accept the "inferior" work of less-talented peers
3. Feelings of superiority accompanied by loneliness
4. Feelings of inferiority (not up to the task, not as good as the "perfect" ideal)
5. Relentless self-criticism
6. High levels of anxiety
7. Susceptibility to depression, especially following a productive period
8. Tendency to magnify and generalize his or her imperfections
9. Inability to share responsibility
10. Inability to cope with ambiguity and chance
11. Fear of the future

If your child is showing one or more of these symptoms of child-hood perfectionism, you may need to reexamine the way you're bringing him or her up as well as the way you are living your own life. Children learn by example, identifying with and acting out the attitudes and behaviors they observe. We can think of no better reason to break your own self-defeating habits than to make sure you don't pass them on to your offspring.

14. Giving Up

Bernie, the gifted and perfectionistic college student who became so anxious while taking tests that he "blacked out" in the middle of them, burned out before he turned twenty. "I was sick and tired of hearing about my potential," he said. "I was sick and tired of worrying about living up to it and trying to prove that I was as smart as everyone kept telling me I was. Maybe I was never that smart. Maybe some school secretary mixed up my IQ scores with someone else's and this whole living-up-to-my-potential thing was a setup. I'd kill myself trying to get straight A's, find the cure for cancer or whatever us smart guys were supposed to do, and then one day someone would show up and say, 'Sorry about that Bernie, but we made a mistake. Too bad you never had any fun or did anything you really wanted to do, but the truth is, you're just an average Joe.'" When he'd failed two tests because of his blackouts, Bernie decided not to stick around to find out that he wasn't so smart after all. Naturally it never occurred to him merely to lighten his course load or take a semester off. He was a perfectionist, and his all-or-nothing thinking left no room for compromise measures. He dropped out of school completely.

Although Bernie swears he never regretted his decision and insists that he's been quite satisfied ever since he quit school, the facts of his life do not support his contention. Five years after dropping out Bernie leads a rather lonely existence, spending most of his free time smoking marijuana or drinking beer while watching TV in his tiny, sparsely furnished apartment. He does not speak to his parents, who were understandably surprised and upset by his decision to quit school. He still has not forgiven his siblings for not backing him up. He drifts from job to job, never worrying about being good enough. "I'm usually the smartest guy they ever had in the position," Bernie explained. "And when I get bored, I move on." He also moves on when he distinguishes himself in any position and his supervisors start talking about promoting him or sending him back to college at the company's expense. "I don't need that aggravation," he said.

Wholeheartedly believing the old adage "If you can't do something right, don't do it at all," some perfectionists drop out of the race entirely. Having experienced more than their fair share of failure, frustration, and stress, they stop trying to succeed. Or they place themselves in situations that require so little of them that it is virtually impossible to fail. Like Bernie, they abandon ambition and opt for safety. They forgo challenges and stick with "sure things." Instead of winning or not losing, not competing becomes their goal. They escape the cycle of self-defeat by admitting defeat and overcome their fear of failure by giving in to it and, regrettably, giving up on themselves. This decision is often accompanied by depression, feelings of grief, lethargy, helplessness, and hopelessness that can in turn lead to the ultimate form of giving up—suicide.

Clearly, giving up is not the answer to the problems caused by perfectionism. Neither is trying harder to achieve your lofty goals. As we have been saying, there is another way out of the cycle of self-defeat and an alternative to resigning from life or traveling the same old path again and again and again. That alternative is the pursuit of excellence—learning to live a balanced, healthy, self-enhancing life. The remainder of this book offers you strategies and suggestions that will get you moving in a new direction and show you how to stop trying so hard so that you can start getting more out of life.

Part Three

A PRESCRIPTION

FOR THE

PERFECTIONIST'S

PREDICAMENT

F ew of us, whether we are perfectionists or not, enthusiastically embrace the prospect of changing ourselves
or our circumstances. In fact most of us perceive change
as being more painful than our present situation—no
matter how painful that situation may be. More often than not
we will resist change with a vengeance, as if we had sworn a
sacred oath to stay the same even if it kills us. Pulling out every
bit of ammunition in our psyche's extensive arsenal of defenses,
we tell ourselves (and others) that things are not so bad, that we
aren't really hurting anyone, or that we can change our ways
whenever we want to (but we just don't want to yet). A friend of
ours refers to this phenomenon as the "psychological law of
inertia": an irresistible force that turns us into immovable objects.
As you read through the remaining chapters in this book and
think about putting our advice into action, there is little doubt
in our minds that you will encounter that force.

For starters, our prescription for being less perfectionistic is based on three concepts that are alien to most perfectionists:

- *Balance:* Bringing the aspects of your life that you've ignored or neglected back into the fold; adding and subtracting behaviors, attitudes, and activities so that you can trade in your lopsided existence for a diverse, satisfying, and healthy lifestyle
- *Moderation:* Setting realistic goals and standards for yourself and others (instead of lofty, unattainable ones), making reasonable attempts to achieve those goals (instead of going to extremes), and being satisfied with your actual successes or progress toward your goals (instead of being chronically dissatisfied because nothing you or others do is ever complete and flawless in all respects)
- *Compromise:* Recognizing when you have reached a point of diminishing returns and finding a way to get *some* of what you want in a manner that enhances your sense of self-worth and does little harm to other people or your relationships (instead of taking the all-or-nothing approach that so often leaves you with nothing and damages both your self-esteem and your relationships)

Unfortunately perfectionists tend to equate balancing their lives with getting sidetracked from their goals, moderation with mediocrity, and compromise with caving in, giving up, or settling for something they don't want. They are reluctant to become less perfectionistic because they believe that relentlessly and single-mindedly striving to be complete and flawless in all respects is the *only* way to accomplish anything, overcome difficulties, or prevent disastrous consequences from occurring. If they were to stop trying so hard, they might even lose whatever ground they'd gained. If those thoughts have crossed *your* mind, let us assure you that we have no intention of asking you to abandon your ambitions, forget about your goals, settle for a life of mediocrity, or do less than your best in any given situation.

We won't suggest that you change any attitude or behavior that is actually working for you. In fact we hope you will use your analytical abilities, self-discipline, creativity, sensitivity, and other assets to help you break your unhealthy habits and develop new, positive thought and behavior patterns that will make it possible for you to get more of what you really want out of life.

If we have managed to convince you that your endless pursuit of perfection is defeating you, then a part of you wants to take the plunge and try a new approach. Still, another part of you may be shouting, "Wait! You're about to do a gainer off the high diving board and you don't even know if there's water in the pool!" That is the change-resisting part of you asking for an ironclad contract and a money-back guarantee. It wants to know that everything you try will work and that everything you do to be less perfectionistic will leave you better off than you were before. But there is no way of knowing that in advance. There are no guarantees. However, you can safely assume that if you don't change—making a few attitude adjustments and breaking a few self-defeating habits—then your circumstances and the results you've been getting by trying harder and harder to be the best there is at everything you do will not change either. At least not for the better.

Although we obviously believe that balance, moderation, compromise, and excellence-seeking is healthier and more sat-isfying than forever pushing yourself and others to be perfect, ultimately the decision to be less perfectionistic is a personal one. No one can make it for you. It is something you must choose for yourself. If you do make that choice, the following tips will come in handy as you travel in a new direction, face new chal-lenges, and periodically feel tempted to turn back:

1. *Concentrate on the here and now, not on your past history.* As you attempt the various prescriptive measures we will be sug-gesting, think of yourself as a blank slate, an unmolded piece of clay, an independent variable in an experiment. Your goal is to find out how a new behavior or attitude will work today—

not how it would have worked yesterday or how something similar to it failed to work for you in the past.

2. *Don't expect to undo a lifetime's worth of perfectionism overnight.* You won't change dozens of counterproductive attitudes and actions simultaneously and on a fixed schedule. Play for small percentage gains rather than huge, dramatic transformations. Pick a place to start, weave that new pattern into your life, then add something else.

3. *Don't let becoming less perfectionist create more ways for you to be hard on yourself.* There is no such thing as a perfect change effort or a perfect excellence seeker.

4. *Reward yourself for making progress.* Instead of focusing on how much farther you have to go, take a mental (or written) inventory of how far you've come and then savor your successes. Celebrate them with a friend or loved one. Give yourself a gift (a massage, permission to sleep in for an extra hour, a bouquet of fresh flowers, or anything else you could enjoy but so rarely allow yourself to). You may even want to make a list of possible rewards and then build them into your program for becoming less perfectionistic.

Change is never really easy. It will even scare the living daylights out of you from time to time. Every new behavior or thought pattern will feel unnatural and uncomfortable at first. You may experience the sensation of watching yourself participate in unfamiliar activities and wondering, "Am I doing this right?" Try to remember that change is not a competitive sport and that creating a more balanced, less perfectionist life-style is like wearing in a new pair of shoes. You have to walk in them awhile before they stop pinching, much less feel as comfortable as your old shoes did. Give your new approach a chance to work. However, if something makes you extremely uncomfortable or proves, over a period of time, to be of little use to you, *stop* doing it and try something else.

Chapter Nine

How to Stop
Trying So Hard
Part I:
Expand Your Horizons

Create a Vision of a Well-Balanced Life

What is a well-balanced life? One that provides many, diverse opportunities for satisfaction and fulfillment. A well-balanced life can supply you with enough positive input and ways to feel worthwhile to make perfectionism unnecessary. You do not have to keep trying to prove you are good enough because you will have enough self-esteem-enhancing habits and thought patterns to feel good enough the way you are. Like a well-balanced diet, a well-balanced life-style includes basic "nutrients" in the right proportions for your unique personality and leaves you feeling alert, alive, and prepared to handle whatever life throws at you.

Although that description may not fit you today, there were probably times in your life when it did. For Jay one such time was the summer after he graduated from high school, which he spent traveling around Europe as part of a student-exchange program. "I had already been accepted to college, so the pressure was off," he said. "The other kids I was traveling with were really terrific, and there was something new and different to do every day. I would actually wake up in the morning looking forward to whatever was going to happen, because I wasn't responsible for making it happen and could just enjoy it." Marilyn described the last six months of her first pregnancy in similar terms. "I wasn't obsessed with dieting," she said. "I just ate what the nutrition charts said was best for me and the baby. I took nice long walks, appreciating the scenery or joking around with another pregnant lady who sometimes walked with me. We called ourselves 'the Waddlers.' And since I knew I would be quitting my job when the baby was born, I didn't push myself so hard. I was competent. I got my work done. But I didn't feel like I had to be supersaleslady or anything like that."

If you were to take a quick mental trip back in your history, you would undoubtedly find days, weeks, maybe even months or years when you, too, felt *balanced:* not high on your latest achievement or hepped up over some goal you were closing in on, but simply content, at ease, and relatively self-confident and optimistic. In addition, if you were to picture those times in your mind clearly or to jot down a brief description of them, you would probably discover that most or all of the following ingredients for a balanced life were present in your life during those times:

- *Productivity:* Actually accomplishing various tasks you set out to do, being competent, although not necessarily a superstar
- *Recognition:* Having your efforts noticed by others and perhaps rewarded with praise, encouragement, appreciation, or affection; also patting yourself on the back for a job well done
- *Learning:* Expanding your horizons or mastering new skills that interested you—whether you were being "graded" or not
- *New Experiences:* Taking risks, trying things for the first time, exploring new territory
- *Unstructured Time and Activities:* Hours or days when there was nothing you *had* to do; pursuits that had no particular

plan or purpose to them other than the pure pleasure or relaxation they provided

- *Fun:* Solo and social activities that were lively, playful, humorous, and usually spontaneous; pursuits that made you laugh and that you did not feel pressured to excel at
- *Solid Relationships with Friends and/or Family Members*: A feeling of being accepted and liked by others as well as accepting and liking them
- *Intimacy:* A close, interdependent, affectionate (and possibly sexual) relationship with another person in which you felt free to share your real thoughts and feelings and were receptive to whatever the other person offered you
- *Physical Health:* A sensible diet; moderate excercise; adequate rest; relative freedom from aches, pains, illness, and over-indulgences
- *Giving of Yourself to Others:* Volunteer work, listening to other people's concerns, offering a helping hand, and so on
- *Receiving Emotional Support from Others:* A sense that there were people in your corner, willing and able to lend *you* a helping hand or be there to catch you should you fall
- *Being in Charge of Your Own Life, Decision-making Power, and Freedom of Choice:* Neither feeling like a powerless victim nor trying to control everything and everyone around you; having a say in the path you followed rather than acting out of a sense of fear or obligation
- *Order:* A certain rhythm to your life; a sense that things were as they should be; an absence of chaos or dread
- *Clarity:* A sense of where you were heading and faith that you would eventually reach your destination
- *Self-worth:* A belief in your inherent value, an acceptance of your strengths and your limitations, and a sense that you were okay the way you were

Now think about your life today. Would you consider it well balanced? Probably not. Thanks to your perfectionism, you may be putting almost all of your time and energy into getting or hanging on to some of the above ingredients while neglecting, ignoring, or completely eliminating others. As a result you are saddled with a lopsided existence devoid of the pleasures and energy replenishers that could actually help you feel safe, secure, and worthwhile. Worse yet, the more anxious, insecure, and doubtful about your own worth you feel, the harder you try *in the areas on which you are already placing more than enough emphasis*. It is time to correct that imbalance and start bringing new sources of satisfaction and self-esteem into your life instead of cutting them out to make room for more relentless and ultimately self-defeating striving in one or two areas.

Reread the list of ingredients for a balanced life. Choose three ingredients you would like to have *more* of in your life. Then choose three that you are currently trying too hard to have or hang on to and to which you would like to devote *less* time, energy, and attention. Please note that we did *not* ask you to choose things you think you *should* have more or less of. One of the reasons you spend sixteen hours a day trying to be productive, or obsessively worry about your health, or relentlessly attempt to control others and create order instead of adapting to the natural rhythms of your life is because you think that is what you are supposed to do. More "shoulds, musts, and have-tos" are the last things you need. Instead think in terms of what would bring you peace of mind, serenity, or a positive self-image.

For each of your choices make a wish, a statement that expresses your vision of that area as it will be when you have become less perfectionistic and created a more balanced life-style than the one you now have. Here are some examples:

> *I wish to have at least seven hours a week that is mine to do with as I please.*
> *I wish to feel more comfortable engaging in activities just for the heck of it, including things I used to enjoy but haven't gotten around to in a long, long time.*

*I wish to increase my decision-making power, worrying less about
   what will please others than I have in the past.*
I wish to be less obsessed with keeping things organized and in order.
*I wish to delegate more responsibility and waste less time and energy
   checking up on people or redoing their work.*

Whether you wish for more emotional support, to be less dependent on other people's approval, or to take more risks and
be more open to new experiences, your wishes are neither goals
you *must* achieve nor thinly disguised criticisms of your current
life-style. They are images to keep in mind as you read about
and try various strategies for becoming less perfectionistic. They
are visions of how you could be that can help you resist the
temptation to go back to the habits that have prevented you from
getting what you want out of life.

There are two basic avenues for creating a satisfying, well-
balanced life *as you personally define it*. The first—*adding* life- and
self-esteem-enhancing skills and experiences—will be discussed
in this chapter. The second—*modifying* or *eliminating* self-
defeating habits and thought patterns—is the subject of
Chapter Ten.

Take More Risks

Perhaps the greatest obstacle to developing a well-balanced life-
style is fear of failure. That is particularly true for perfectionists,
whose every failing deals a painful blow to their already shaky
self-image and whose broad definition of the term *failure* encom-
passes so much: making mistakes and actually falling short of a
goal as well as reaching it but not feeling calm, cool, and confident
in the process, looking foolish, finding themselves at a loss for
words, being unable to master a new task on the first try (no
matter how complex that task is) or anything else that is less than
complete and flawless in all respects.

199

Fear of failure stunts your growth, preventing you from taking risks or trying new things. You will not venture so much as an inch off the straight-and-narrow path you know like the back of your hand—not even when that path is getting you nowhere. Consequently you cannot do much to make your image of a well-balanced life a reality until you conquer your *fear*, for it is that fear rather than failure itself that is causing problems.

Failure is inevitable. Everyone experiences it repeatedly during the course of a lifetime. Although no one *likes* to fail, most of us realize that it is through our failures that we learn how to succeed. The route to any goal is like a labyrinth with many paths leading in many directions but only one that takes you out of the maze. The chances of finding the right path on the first try are slim. No matter how hard you try not to, you are going to take a few wrong turns along the way. However, by doing so, you actually improve your chances of finding the right path—because you now know several ways *not* to go.

By avoiding any and all situations that might lead to failure, you have done yourself a great disservice. You have robbed yourself of countless opportunities to venture into new territory, make mistakes, learn from them, and realize that the world did not come to an end and you did not fall apart at the seams. That realization is incredibly liberating. It enables you to do more, learn more, see more, and be more than will ever be possible by going for the safe bet and the sure thing.

Knowing that (and maybe even believing it) may lower your anxiety level a notch or two. Several techniques we will describe in the next chapter will further relieve the panicky feeling brought on by conjuring up worst-case scenarios prior to taking steps in a new direction. But when all is said and done, the only way to truly conquer your fear of failure is to feel it and take a risk or try something new anyway.

Prepare yourself for risk taking by making a long, long, long list of all the risks you have already taken: *everything* that was once new and unknown but is now so familiar that you have practically forgotten that it once posed a challenge for you. Go way back in your history and recall learning to walk and dress yourself and write your name. Move up through time and recall learning to ride a bicycle, drive a car, diaper a baby. You will find countless examples of risks you have taken both with and without experiencing a few or many failures in the process.

From your list pick several risks that you remember as being particularly difficult or frightening to take. Who or what helped you over the hurdle: having someone try the new experience along with you? reading or talking about it ahead of time? encouragement? visualizing yourself doing it? breaking it into smaller steps? Make mental or written notes on anything that helped you take risks in the past, and consider drawing upon those resources when you want to take risks in the future.

Then practice. Make a list of risks you could take or have avoided taking in recent years: going to the movies by yourself or calling a casual acquaintance and asking him to go to a movie with you; taking advantage of the free trial offer at a nearby gym even though you know you are not in the same physical shape as most of its members; saying no to a co-worker who wants to "bounce ideas off" you (if it means that she'll take your ideas and call them her own); answering or placing an ad in the singles column. The possibilities are limited only by your imagination (which we recommend you let run wild). The items on your list need not be major tests of courage and fortitude. Many can be relatively innocuous. Others can be things that are actually holding you back and preventing you from achieving your goals.

Once your list of possible risks is made, begin picking and choosing from it and actually taking those risks. Start small and work your way up to bigger, more challenging risks. Use the resources you listed earlier to help you bolster your resolve. And most of all savor your "victories" and celebrate *every* risk taken, even those that are not unqualified successes. There are few things as reassuring and generally gratifying as pushing past a fear and discovering what you *can* do when you are willing to take a chance.

Have More Fun

If you are a perfectionist, fear of failure is not the only force that holds you back. Your drive to be the best there is at everything you do is also a deterrent to a balanced life, keeping you too busy with achievement-oriented pursuits and making you too competitive to engage in countless pursuits that could help you feel good about yourself—or just plain feel good. You miss out on many of life's potentially pleasurable and replenishing experiences because you believe that anything you can't excel at isn't worth doing. You talk yourself out of trying many activities because you believe anything that doesn't advance you toward your goals is a frivolous waste of time.

To become less perfectionistic and lead a more balanced life, you need to recognize that there are some things that you can do better than others and some things that are more crucial than others *but that those other things are still worth doing*. Dare to be less than the best, to engage in activities just for fun and even though they won't help you get ahead. They *will* enable you to unwind, refuel, or lighten up on yourself, and over the long haul that will help you "win" more races than running all of the time will.

Think of ten things you used to enjoy but that you have allowed to fall by the wayside while you have been relentlessly striving to achieve your aspirations: walks on the beach, drives in the country, wandering through flea markets, horseback riding, watching and singing along with old movie musicals. Then come up with ten things you have thought about trying just to see what they were like or to find out if you would like them: going to the ballet or the opera, jogging, wind surfing, taking a cruise, playing a musical instrument. Finally think of ten things that you're fairly certain you would not do well but might enjoy doing anyway: baking bread, refinishing furniture, bowling, playing video games, square dancing, and so on.

Once you have a thirty-item list, go out and do some of the activities on that list. Don't justify what you do ("Since I've been working so hard, I deserve a night off to watch old movies") or arrange to "pay" for them ("I can leave work at six so I can get to my ceramics class on time if I work through my lunch hour tomorrow"). Just do them. Don't worry about how well you are doing them. Instead of evaluating your performance or the end result of the endeavor, concentrate on the *process* of engaging in that activity. If you are walking on the beach, focus on how the sand feels beneath your feet, the sound of the ocean, the sun glistening on the water, the squawking of the sea gulls, the "treasures" that have washed up on shore. At first you may have to silently talk yourself through activities in order to stay focused on their delights instead of their drawbacks.

Give yourself permission *not* to excel at the things you do for fun or relaxation. It's okay to botch up that batch of banana bread or bear absolutely no resemblance to Fred Astaire while you are out on a dance floor. You are not competing in the Betty Crocker bake-off or auditioning for *A Chorus Line*. The fate of the world does not rest on your skill at volleyball, and no one knows how many wrong notes you are hitting while singing along with the car radio. What's more, no one is actually going to think less of you for wiping out while wind surfing or being a barely competent furniture refinisher. In fact the people in your life may feel better about you if you goof up now and then. It's a relief to know that you are human.

Juggle More Scarves

Dr. Steve Allen, Jr., a physician and "humor consultant," often teaches his patients to juggle scarves. What on earth for, you may wonder. Because it is a thoroughly silly skill that keeps them from taking themselves too seriously. It is a way of exercising a muscle most perfectionists have allowed to atrophy from lack of use—their sense of humor. Although you do not have to actually juggle scarves (even though it *is* a lot of fun), the more you do to reactivate your sense of humor, the better off you'll be.

After years of perfectionism you may be so out of touch with your sense of humor that you'll need help and lots of practice to get it back into shape. Observe friends or colleagues who have a good sense of humor. What tickles their funny bone? When you think you are taking something too seriously, ask them to point out the humorous elements of your predicament. Go to comedy clubs, where other people's laughter can be contagious. Rent old Three Stooges, or Marx brothers, or *I Love Lucy* videos and watch them with friends or your kids. Listen to comedy albums (or watch the all-comedy cable TV channel). Comedians who make fun of their own flaws or get mileage out of their dysfunctional families will surely get a few knowing laughs out of you. Learn a few jokes, and the next time a group of people are involved in one of those "Did you hear the one about..." joke-telling round-robins, join in or really go out on a limb and recount something funny that happened to you. At first you will feel awkward and self-conscious—as if you are forcing yourself to laugh or be funny. That is exactly what you are doing, and that's okay. You'll loosen up as time goes by, and eventually you will even be able to laugh at yourself spontaneously, finding humor in foibles that have always made you cringe or set off a litany of self-criticism.

Manage Time

If you are a perfectionist, chances are that you cannot find enough hours in the day to do half of what you feel you must do, so how can you possibly find time to do the things we've been suggesting or anything else you want to do? Trade-offs are one answer. Effective time management is another.

Start thinking of time as a precious commodity and looking for things you would be willing to give up in order to get more of it. You might start by conducting a seven-day time study, actually jotting down everything you do and how much time you spend doing it. What unnecessary, pointless, or nonessential activities are literally eating up your time? Making breakfast for youngsters who are perfectly capable of doing that themselves?

Redoing your kids' or your spouse's household chores? Checking up on your staff or co-workers? Visiting your mother at the nursing home for an entire hour every single day even if she falls asleep fifteen minutes after you get there? Trying on a dozen outfits before you decide what you will wear and then hanging them all up again?

Many of your perfectionistic habits are literally stealing your time. Take back as much as you can. Make it a project. Try to find an extra hour a week, then two, then as many as you need to lead a more balanced life. Whittle fifteen minutes off your nursing-home visits or go every other day. Commit yourself to checking on your staff's progress half as many times as you do now. If a household chore is completed, let it be—even if it isn't done to your exact specifications. Believe it—the world will not end and you will have something you never allowed yourself before, time to do something you *want* to do and need to do for your own health and well-being.

Despite your penchant for organization and efficiency, there are a few basic time-management skills you probably never mastered. Learn them now. Prioritize. This is a real problem for perfectionists, who tend to see *everything* as crucial and requiring their immediate attention. Instead think of yourself as a doctor in an emergency room and your tasks as patients waiting for medical attention. Give priority to the patients who will survive if you attend to them and die if you do not—things that absolutely cannot be put off to another day. Make sure that no more than one third of the items on any "to do" list falls into that category. The second third should be things you'd prefer to get done today but that could wait, and the final third should be nonessentials. If you are a procrastinator, guard against your tendency to do your nonessentials first (and follow our advice on how to stop procrastinating, found in the next chapter). Once you have your priorities set, make a commitment to yourself: Allow nothing other than a top-priority obligation to take precedence over things you *want* to do for your health or well-being.

In addition *stop* trying to do everything yourself. Delegate responsibility when it is appropriate to do so (which is at least twice as often as you think). Ask for assistance, accept it, and if you think you'll need it again in the future, please don't criticize the help you get. There's really no truth to the old adage "If you want something done right, do it yourself." However, if you insist that something be done *your way* and refuse to "settle" for anything else, you *will* have to do it yourself and be overworked and overwhelmed for the rest of your days.

Learn to say no. If it is not your responsibility and you don't want to do it, don't. Take a course or read a book on assertiveness if you have to, but stop being suckered into "saving the day" or bamboozled into thinking that something won't get done unless you do it.

Here are two timesaving secrets:

1. *Do one thing at a time:* You will actually complete a task faster, make fewer mistakes, and derive more satisfaction from accomplishing it if you give it your full attention instead of trying to do two or three things at once. An exception to this rule of thumb would be combining compatible activities that you are attempting to add to your life-style (exercising with a friend, listening to soothing music while you are doing a crossword puzzle), especially if time constraints might prevent you from doing both separately.

2. *Keep your attention focused on the task at hand:* You could save many hours of precious time by simply concentrating on what you are doing at any given moment instead of allowing your mind to wander back over your past failings, forward to the tasks that lie ahead, or anywhere near a litany of self-criticism or listing of potential catastrophes. The instant you notice that happening, *stop. Think,* "Thank you very much for this information, but I have something else on my mind right now," and *picture* yourself setting those unbidden, unwelcome ruminations on a shelf where you can find them later (if you still want to).

Relaxation

As a perfectionist you live in a pressure cooker. You are constantly pushing yourself, doing something, going somewhere,
worrying about everything, and wondering if you are good
enough. You exceed your stress threshold on a regular basis and
have only the vaguest notion of what it means to relax, generally
equating it with doing nothing—which you rarely if ever allow
yourself to do. When you do permit yourself to slow down or
just sit around, you may find yourself awash in a sea of worry
and end up more agitated than you were beforehand. Although
we encourage relaxing activities—needlepoint, reading, golf, leisurely walks, listening to music, to name a few—we would also
like to offer you an alternative to those traditional forms of relaxation, one that numerous laboratory studies have shown to
relieve muscle tension, decrease heart rates, and increase alpha-
brain-wave activity associated with creativity and an overall sense
of well-being. It is not a particularly complex or difficult process
to master. Variations of it have appeared in many self-help books,
and relaxation audiotapes are also available at most bookstores.
Whether you use our instructions or some other approach to
active relaxation, rather than making you sluggish and lethargic
the way taking a nap so often does, the technique we are about
to describe leaves you refreshed and alert.

1. *Relax your body.* Set aside fifteen minutes of uninterrupted
   time and find a relatively quiet, comfortable place to sit or lie
   down. Close your eyes and focus your attention on your
   breathing. When you are tense and anxious, you tend to
   breathe shallowly, from your chest, and you may notice yourself doing that. Switch to deep breaths from your diaphragm.
   Picture yourself breathing out tension or worries and breathing in calm and relaxation. When your breathing has taken
   on a steady, soothing rhythm, switch your attention to your
   feet and, using all of your strength, tense the muscles of your
   feet as tightly as you can. Hold the tensed position for several

seconds and then release the tension, noticing the warmth and relaxation you feel. Moving up your body one group of muscles at a time, repeat the process until you are physically relaxed all over. If at any time during your relaxation sessions you notice tension in some part of your body, use the tighten-hold-release process on those muscles.

2. *Relax your mind.* While in your physically relaxed state, take yourself on a mental journey to the most relaxing place you can imagine. This secret resting place, as it is sometimes called, can be someplace you've actually been or a total fabrication. The important part is for it to be associated with peace and serenity and for you to visualize it in vivid detail. See it in living color. Hear the sounds you might hear if you were actually there. Feel wind against your skin or sand beneath your feet. Fully experience this place and the calming effect it has on you. (If you think you might find yourself straining to conjure up a "perfect" scenario on the spot, jot down some ideas or actually write a detailed description of your "secret resting place" ahead of time.)

Once you are in a physically and mentally relaxed state, you will begin to notice unbidden, sometimes negative or anxiety-provoking thoughts coming to mind. Do not struggle against them or try to force them out of your awareness. Simply accept that they are there and gently push them aside, returning your attention to your secret resting place.

3. *Send positive messages to your subconscious.* As the chattering thoughts become fewer and fewer and you become more and more relaxed, your unconscious mind becomes receptive to new ideas. Take a few moments to plant a few suggestions. Make them positive and simple: "I am happy and calm," "I am strong and well," or a variation on the serenity prayer— "I have the serenity to accept the things I cannot change, the courage to change the things I can, and the wisdom to know the difference." Repeat whatever message you choose to send several times and then, when you are ready, count slowly to

ten and open your eyes. You will emerge from your relaxed state feeling rejuvenated and often more self-confident as well.

Regular use of this relaxation technique will greatly reduce the impact of excess stress as well as enable you to re-create a relaxed, positively focused mental state on short notice. When you feel yourself becoming anxious during any interaction or feel nervous about an upcoming event, you can simply tense-hold-release a few selected muscle groups (your feet, hands, or shoulders, for instance) and conjure up an image of your secret resting place, centering yourself in preparation for whatever you may face (instead of working yourself up into a frenzy over it).

Visualizations and Affirmations

Steps two and three in the foregoing relaxation strategy incorporated two attitude-altering and anxiety-reducing techniques that you may have recognized from reading other self-help books or attending stress-management seminars: visualizations (sometimes called guided imagery) and affirmations. However, even if you have never heard those terms before, you have been using those techniques all your life to send messages and commands to your unconscious. All of us constantly think in vivid pictures. We silently chatter to ourselves all day long. Most of our "transmissions" are automatic: we barely notice ourselves sending them. And regrettably, for those of us with low opinions of ourselves and dim outlooks on life, many of those messages tend to be negative, self-critical, and pessimistic, perpetuating the sort of mind-set that keeps a self-defeating cycle of distorted thinking and counterproductive behavior in motion. An extremely effective way of breaking that cycle is to consciously send more realistic and positive messages to the unconscious. As renowned psychologist William James put it, "The greatest revolution of our generation is the discovery that human beings, by changing the inner attitudes of their minds, can change the outer aspects of their lives."

Visualizations are mental movies, and you are their writer, their director, and their star. Placing yourself in any situation you choose, you can use them to picture yourself accomplishing anything you want to do or be. Basketball players use visualizations to improve their foul shooting. Other athletes use them to play inner games of tennis or to picture themselves soaring over the bar when high-jumping or pole-vaulting. You can call upon them to imagine yourself calmly and effectively handling situations that typically provoke anxiety or self-doubt: job interviews, sales meetings, singles functions, Thanksgiving dinner with your hard-to-please in-laws. Visualizations associated with feelings of safety or self-esteem—baking cookies with Grandma when you were a child or reaching the top of a path you were climbing and drinking in the breathtaking scenery—can provide you with an overall sense of well-being. Or you might picture yourself achieving a goal or completing a task and basking in the glow of success. Be careful to use that particular visualization to savor the feeling of satisfaction and not to establish loftier standards for success.

Whether you visualize yourself serenely strolling through a meadow on your way to meet the person you love or picture yourself as a knight returning to your castle after successfully slaying a dragon, give your visualizations a plot, a theme, and a positive resolution. Rerun your mental movies repeatedly. Also call upon them whenever you face a situation that provoked anxiety in the past or you want to go into new situations with a self-confident attitude. With practice the new images you create will be as convincing as your old images were—but far less self-defeating.

Affirmations are mental statements that say, "At this moment I am the way I want to be." You can use them like visualizations to overcome specific problems, to counteract a spate of self-criticism, or to prepare yourself to take on new challenges. Because your unconscious is especially receptive to affirmations while in the alpha state, if you use them after relaxing your body and mentally going to your secret resting place, you can actually begin to reprogram yourself, incorporating new, positive, yet realistic ideas into your general belief system.

Always phrase affirmations in positive language. Rather than "I will not be afraid," think, "I am calm, steady, and strong." Instead of "I can feel okay about myself even if my thighs are flabby," try telling yourself, "At this moment I am the best me I can be." If you feel like you are lying to yourself, remember that you see what you believe. You cannot *be* calm, steady, and strong or *act* in your own best interest until you believe in those outcomes—and that is what an affirmation enables you to do. In addition, try not to use words like *should, must, have to,* or *supposed to.* Statements containing those words are internal demands, not affirmations.

Write out the affirmations you want to plant in your mind and repeat them to yourself as often as possible. Over time they, along with visualizations, bring about an overall attitude change that will ultimately carry over to your conscious thoughts and actions.

Be with People

Thus far, most of what we've suggested can be done alone, which may suit those of you who lean toward interpersonal perfectionism. However, loners, mask wearers, and nitpickers can never have truly balanced lives. They miss out on a whole range of positive input that other people could add to their lives if they let them.

If friendships, socializing, or merely getting along with people in general is a missing ingredient in your life, you can start to develop new or improved personal and professional relationships by simply having more contact with people:

- Think of friends or relatives whom you enjoy (or at least don't mind) hearing from when they call you. Call them for a change. Invite them to go somewhere or do something with you.
- Accept a few more lunch invitations from colleagues or co-workers. At least make an appearance at the "little parties" they give for mothers-to-be or retirees.
- Volunteer at a local hospital, youth center, shelter for the homeless, or other project in need of assistance (unless you are a moral perfectionist who is doing too much of that already).
- Take courses offered by community colleges, mental health centers, or the local YMCA, preferably ones that don't emphasize grades or competition among class members. For those of you who find shyness or fearing that you will say the wrong thing to be obstacles to getting along with others, courses teaching communication, assertiveness, or other social skills not only put you in contact with people but remedy an ongoing problem in your life.
- Work out at a gym instead of walking alone or exercising along with a videotape at home.
- Get involved in activities at your child's school, your church or synagogue, or a community group such as the Elks or Junior League, taking advantage of resources that are already part of your life. (Resist the urge to take over and run the show. Remember that you're there to be part of the group and not to take on more responsibilities or gather more accolades.)
- Join a self-help or support group. (See Chapter Eleven for further details.)
- If you are currently unattached, attend singles' functions. Although you may not meet the man or woman of your dreams, these semistructured group activities are less like junior high school dances than you'd think and singles-group veterans will almost always strike up some sort of conversation

212

with you, enabling you to practice and grow more comfortable with various communication skills you may be trying to learn.

Naturally if you are going to do any of the foregoing, you must leave your faultfinding glasses at home. We are not suggesting that the people you know or will meet won't have flaws or that you must always "turn the other cheek" and accept them no matter what they do. However, if you want more and better relationships, you must develop more tolerance and empathy than you have demonstrated in the past.

Develop Tolerance

Tolerance is the ability to see that circumstances or people are not exactly as you wish them to be, but nonetheless *let them be that way*. As you no doubt know, that is very difficult for perfectionists to do. Interpersonal perfectionists in particular are convinced that no imperfection should go uncorrected and generally expect other people not only to follow their unsolicited suggestions but to appreciate them as well. Since that rarely happens, perfectionists get aggravated with people and either push harder, creating unecessary conflict and driving people away, or give up and walk away themselves.

If you are interested in having a more balanced life, try setting aside your criticisms and advice. Mentally picture yourself slipping the negative or nitpicking comments you'd like to make into a folder and filing it away. Take out the file and mention the imperfection only if the behavior you have decided to tolerate actually poses a threat to someone or if the other person asks for your advice.

Try assigning a numerical rating to the supposedly glaring inadequacies you spot. Use a one-to-ten scale, with tens reserved for totally intolerable traits and ones assigned to entirely insignificant quirks or habits. Think of it as petty or a waste of time and energy to mention anything below a five, and make it a project to see how many "flaws" with higher ratings you can let slide over the course of a day or week.

Turning negatives into positives is another alternative for developing tolerance: temporarily relabel flaws, calling them differences or novelties, and then try to figure out if they have something to teach you about yourself, dealing with people, or approaching a particular problem.

Before You Criticize—Empathize

Tolerance-building measures are easier to take if you learn to empathize with people who are different from you or different from the way you expect them to be. Empathy is the ability to put yourself in other people's shoes, to see the world through their eyes and feel what they are feeling. It is not something that comes naturally to most perfectionists. They are generally too busy protecting their own fragile sense of self-worth or too focused on outperforming all "competitors" to consider other people's feelings or give credence to their points of view. With practice, however, you can begin to see the basic similarities between yourself and even the most mind-boggling or infuriating people in your life: a perspective that leaves you feeling less threatened by others and more receptive to them and their ideas.

Start with someone you do not know personally: a fictional character, a guest on a TV talk show, someone whose human-interest story you read in the newspaper or whom you observe in a shopping mall. As you learn about that person, try to imagine what he or she might be feeling. What needs or fears might be motivating his or her behavior? What ideas or beliefs may be behind his or her words and actions? Then look inside yourself for a match: a time, experience, or circumstance that provoked similar emotions for you, stirred up similar fears, or brought similar beliefs to mind. Once you locate the point (or points) where your own and another person's experience of the world intersect, you can *understand* their behavior—even though you would still behave differently yourself. That empathic understanding makes it easier to accept that other people can see and do things differently from you without being wrong or bad (or in desperate need of your advice or control).

If you use the same process to empathize with someone with whom you are frequently at odds, you will dramatically reduce your conflicts and power struggles with that person, paving the way to actually enjoying their company and the support, encouragement, or other pleasures they have to offer you.

Finally, taking a moment to empathize when you are in the midst of a conflict with another person can lead to a quicker, more satisfying solution to your mutual problem. Rather than accusing, blaming, or labeling the other person an idiot or a fool, try communicating your perception of that person's point of view. Always acknowledge that it is your perception: "It sounds like my suggestion offended you" (rather than "You're too sensitive," or "You shouldn't be offended. I was only trying to help."). Or "If I were in your shoes, I'd probably feel like I was being backed into a corner and left without much of a choice." Comments like these bring conversations to the common level of feelings, needs, and fears, almost always getting to the heart of the matter and resolving conflicts with a minimum of long-term negative consequences.

You now have ten positive, self-esteem-enhancing, energy-replenishing elements to add to your life, and the good news is that anything you do in any of the areas we've discussed *will* move you closer to the vision of a balanced life you created when you began reading this chapter. The not-so-good news is that your old habits and perfectionistic mind-set can prevent you from putting our advice into action—even when you sincerely want to take your life in a new, less perfectionistic direction. The next chapter will show you how to break some of those habits and refocus your distorted thought patterns so that you can finally break out of your cycle of self-defeat, stop trying too hard, and start getting more out of life.

How to Stop Trying

So Hard

Part II:

Kick Your Self-defeating Habits

Excellence seekers are self-accepting. They are aware of their strengths and their limitations, know that both contribute to their unique personalities, and set their goals accordingly. Excellence seekers do what is proper, correct, better-than-average, or the best they can do *in a given situation*. And when excellence seekers recognize that they have reached a point of diminishing returns, rather than trying harder and hoping that the same behavior will somehow produce different results they change their approach to the situation or modify their goals. Their *flexibility* enables them to learn from their mistakes, feel encouraged and motivated by their successes, and increase their competence, confidence, and sense of self-worth.

Trim Your Goals

Excellence seekers know something perfectionists do not: that there is no reason and no need to be the best, the brightest, or most meticulous and achievement-oriented at all times and under all circumstances. Sometimes it is enough to be competent. Sometimes it is better to have fun, to let someone else assume responsibility for getting things done, or to let go of a goal altogether in order to get more out of life overall. This attitude does not make them less ambitious or doom them to a life of mediocrity. It is not an excuse to do less than their best in situations that call for an all-out effort. What it does do is save excellence seekers from the chronic dissatisfaction, excess stress, and lopsided existences that plague perfectionists, whose lofty goals and sky-high standards rarely if ever take into account their actual limitations or the realities of a given situation.

If you are a perfectionist, you can stop setting yourself up for defeat and disappointment by toning down any of your expectations that are unrealistic, unreasonable, and therefore unattainable. You will actually get better results (and more out of life) by aiming for a little less and setting limits on the lengths to which you will go in order to achieve a goal.

GOAL-TRIMMING STEP 1: *Identifying Your Ideal.* Think about something you are currently trying to accomplish. It might be a specific goal: updating your résumé, finding the "perfect" outfit to wear to a friend's wedding, reorganizing your kitchen cabinets, or putting on a fund-raising event for a charitable organization. It can be an overall standard: being efficient or a good parent; demonstrating that you are intelligent, politically aware, or socially adept. Or it can be something you are trying to do to improve your body, your living environment, your reputation at work, or another person. In a notebook or on a sheet of paper write a description of the *ideal* outcome of your effort, an end result that you would consider complete and flawless in all respects and that would thoroughly satisfy you.

For instance Sharon, the hospital purchasing agent, wanted to end up with photocopying equipment that everyone in the hospital would give an A-rating on all counts. It had to be fast, durable, easy-to-use, and accompanied by an ironclad service contract. Moreover her boss would compliment her on the terrific job she had done as well as on the meticulous method she had used, and the hospital staff would thank her for saving them from the horrors of photocopying on less-than-perfect equipment. Nancy, the obsessive dieter and compulsive exerciser we described in Chapter Eight, wanted to weigh 102 pounds, wear a perfect size six, never again see anything "jiggle" anywhere on her body, and draw admiring looks wherever she went. She wanted to hear people say they were in awe of her discipline and determination and to "knock the socks off" any man whom she found attractive, "dazzling" him, drawing him to her like a magnet, and embarking upon a relationship that would fulfill all of her romantic fantasies.

GOAL-TRIMMING STEP 2: *Reality Checking.* Once you have described your ideal outcome, list the knowledge, skill, time, money, cooperation from other people, and any other resources that you need to bring about that exact outcome (and nothing less). Are those resources available to you now? Realistically speaking, how much of what you need would you be able to get if you worked at it? List any physical limitations, uncontrollable variables (e.g., other people's opinions, weather, or illness) or conflicting obligations that could prevent you from achieving your ideal outcome. Is it actually possible to overcome those obstacles? What sacrifices would you have to make in order to reach your ideal? What would your life be like while you were striving to bring about that perfect outcome? Is that what you really want?

To achieve her ideal outcome, Sharon needed unlimited time to "test" equipment, no budgetary constraints to prevent her from buying the perfect photocopying machines, all of her "report cards" completed and returned by anyone who used the machines, 100 percent agreement on which machines were best, and her boss to look at things the same way she did and believe her methodology was ingenius. She did not have these resources and, with the possible exception of haranguing people to turn in report cards, could not get them. Likewise, at a height of five feet six inches, 102 pounds was too low a goal weight for Nancy to achieve or maintain without remaining on a starvation diet indefinitely. Her bone structure, which included broad shoulders and broad hips, physically prevented her from being a perfect size six, and there was no way she could control other people's tastes in order to guarantee that heads would turn when she entered a room or that men she found attractive would be attracted to her. What's more, the fact that she rarely went anyplace where tempting but high-calorie food or alcoholic beverages would be served and spent three hours every day working out at a woman's health club severely limited her opportunities to meet a man with whom she could converse, much less fulfill her romantic fantasies.

Had Sharon and Nancy considered any of these factors in advance, they might have realized that actually making their ideal a reality was an unrealistic, unreasonable, and unattainable goal. But since they did not, they sincerely believed they could have exactly what they envisioned if they just tried hard enough. They devoted themselves to making a truly impossible dream come true, and chances are that your reality check showed you that you've been doing that too.

GOAL-TRIMMING STEP 3: *Finding Your Bottom Line.* Take out another sheet of paper and, based on the same potential accomplishment as well as the realities you have already listed, describe a *sure thing*: an outcome that you know you could achieve with the bare minimum of effort and few if any sacrifices. It should not be something you do not want at all, but rather something you could live with even though it it is considerably less than your ideal—for example, maintaining your current weight, dating and getting to know members of the opposite sex who don't necessarily fit your image of Ms. or Mr. Right, not being an abusive or hypercritical parent, or adding your most recent experiences to your résumé and leaving the rest as is. For Sharon the bottom line might have been reading about the photocopying equipment available in her price range and purchasing a reasonably priced machine that came with a "halfway decent" service contract. Nancy's bottom line might have been weighing 130 pounds, wearing a size ten or twelve, "pinching" less than an inch of flab anywhere on her body, and attracting "okay guys" (even though she still preferred "drop-dead gorgeous" ones).

For most perfectionists, accepting a bottom-line outcome is virtually impossible. Given the chance, they will always attempt to do more than the bare minimum, and that would be fine, indeed it would admirable and a valuable asset in most situations *IF their only alternative to merely getting by wasn't relentlessly striving for that unattainable, pie-in-the-sky ideal.*

GOAL-TRIMMING STEP 4: *Looking for In-betweens.* If you want to become less perfectionistic, locate and gear yourself toward goals and standards that fall somewhere between perfection and the bare minimum. Keep your ideals. Even though you cannot actually reach them, they do point you in the right direction, and you can use them as guides for decision making, asking yourself, "If I want to move toward my ideal (but not lose myself in trying to attain it), what course of action would be in my best interest right now?" Keep your bottom line as well. It can serve as your minimal measure of success. You will know you are getting off track if you fall below it. However, for your actual goal choose a standard of excellence, an outcome that is:

- Less than your ideal but one or several steps above the bare minimum
- Realistic because it takes into account your actual limitations and the parameters of your real-life circumstances
- Reasonable because it can be achieved without superhuman striving or enormous sacrifices
- An accomplishment because you will put some effort into it and do the best you can with the resources you have and the sacrifices you are willing to make in that specific situation

For Sharon excellence would have been investigating the photocopying equipment available in her price range, calling around for "references" from companies using various machines, signing a one-year lease agreement with an option to buy, and periodically checking with selected staff members to find out if they were satisfied with the machines. For Nancy, weighing 120 pounds, feeling comfortable in clothing regardless of its size, and following an exercise physiologist's program for a well-toned body could be a standard of excellence. Take a moment to identify yours, writing a reasonable, realistic, attainable goal for yourself.

As an alternative or in addition to this four-step method for toning down your expectations, you may also want to try adopting a *process* orientation rather than an outcome orientation: focusing on *what* you are doing rather than the results you are getting. Using that approach, Nancy might seek excellence by eating three moderate meals a day and exercising for forty minutes four times a week. Rather than trying to reach a certain weight, wearing a certain dress size, or eliciting a specific response from other people, her goal would be to follow her plan to the best of her ability and with enough flexibility to account for unforeseen circumstances. Or you might want to try breaking down your lofty goal into smaller steps, rewarding yourself for the progress you make toward your ideal and stopping after each step to ask yourself if you really *want* to move on.

Stop Taking on Obligations and Start Making Choices

If you are a perfectionist, your problems may not only stem from setting impossibly high standards for yourself but also from the standards set *for* you by other people whose acceptance or approval you crave or by those demanding inner voices with their seemingly endless list of "shoulds, musts, and have-tos." Consequently another way to stop setting yourself up for defeat is to become more familiar with and less of a slave to those demands.

Instead of trying to force yourself into doing the things you imagine you *must* do, try asking yourself about the things you are doing. Take a few moments to think of several obligations you are currently pushing yourself to fulfill. Then write out a half dozen demand statements associated with those obligations:

"I *must* pay my bills tonight," or "I *should* get to the gym every day," or "Married couples are *supposed to* make love at least twice a week," or "I *ought to* call my cousin on his birthday."

Then for each statement ask yourself a few pointed questions: Why should you? What makes you think you have to do those things? What do you think would happen if you didn't? If you didn't feel you had to do those things, would you choose to do them?

To put your answers (and your obligations) into perspective, you might try conducting a cost-benefit analysis. Take out a blank sheet of paper and divide it into four sections. Label the top left-hand section "Benefits of Doing What I Should," the top right-hand section "Drawbacks of Doing What I Should," the bottom left-hand section "Benefits of *Not* Doing What I Should," and the bottom right-hand section "Drawbacks of *Not* Doing What I Should." Then fill in each section with the applicable positive and negative consequences for each option. Guard against your natural inclination to magnify potential negative consequences. Although it is certainly in your best interest to pay bills on time, and your credit rating may be effected if you do not pay them until they are way overdue, thinking that your gas, phone, and electricity will be turned off if your payment arrives one or two days late is a magnification.

Here is a sample cost-benefit analysis:

BENEFITS OF CALLING COUSIN ON HIS BIRTHDAY

- I would feel like a good person
- It would keep my mother from criticizing me
- It might "guilt" him into not giving my kids such chintzy presents for Christmas

DRAWBACKS OF CALLING

- Cost of a long-distance call
- I would have to listen to him brag about his kids and his job and all the impressive things he's done lately

- My mother will want to hear everything he said and make a point of asking why my kids and my job and the things I do can't be that wonderful
- I'll resent the fact that I wasted my time this way and feel like a failure compared with him

BENEFITS OF NOT CALLING

- Save time and money
- Avoid resentment and feeling like a failure
- Could call a long-distance friend instead
- Wouldn't feel like a hypocrite for calling when he's one of the last people on earth I want to talk to

DRAWBACKS OF NOT CALLING

- Guilt
- Criticism from my mother
- Comparison with my sister (who will do the right thing and call)
- Need to come up with an explanation if he asks why I didn't call

Once you have your potential costs and benefits listed, go back and, using a one-to-ten scale (1 = makes no difference one way or another; 10 = will have a powerful impact on you, making you feel terrific or terrible), give each consequence you've listed a numerical rating based on how dramatically it will affect you. Then total your ratings in each section and compare them.

If the costs of doing what you should or the benefits of not doing it outweigh the benefits of fulfilling your obligation or the costs of not fulfilling it, then you know something that you did not know before: that what you think you *should* do is not necessarily the most beneficial (or the least detrimental) thing for you to do. And regardless of your numerical ratings, because you can see costs and benefits in black and white, you have something you did not have before: a choice. You can choose to fulfill the obligation (because it serves you or doesn't pay not to). You can choose not to fulfill it (because you don't want to and are willing to pay the consequences you have identified). You can even come up with a compromise: sending your cousin a birthday card, for instance, or paying the bills that are due immediately and scheduling the remainder of your bill paying for a more convenient time. No matter what you decide to do, you—and not the arbitrary demands of other people or your "inner taskmaster"—are in charge.

To reinforce your newfound decision-making power and freedom of choice, try removing as many "shoulds, musts, and have-tos" as possible from your vocabulary, replacing them with words that let you know you are in the driver's seat. Change "I ought to call my cousin on his birthday" to "I *can* call my cousin on his birthday"; "I must pay my bills tonight" to "I *may want to* pay my bills tonight"; "I should go to the gym everyday" to "I *have made a commitment to* go to the gym today"; "Married couples are supposed to make love at least twice a week" to "My spouse and I *may or may not choose to* make love twice a week." Even admitting that you *feel* obligated to do something reflects a more personally powerful point of view than a "should, must, or have-to," since it acknowledges that your feeling—rather than some irresistible external force—is the motivation for your actions. These word changes are much more than a matter of semantics. Even if you do not wholeheartedly believe it at first, by planting in your mind the idea that you are in charge and can choose which demands you will or will not comply with, you begin to counteract the "tyranny of oughts" and eventually the guilt feelings and perfectionistic behaviors that go along with it.

Alter Distorted Thought Patterns

Like the "shoulds, musts, and have-tos" that push you to your limit and beyond, distorted thought patterns—from all-or-nothingisms to making mountains out of molehills—are the driving force behind most (if not all) of your perfectionistic habits. They are the source of your low self-esteem and the idea that meeting impossibly high standards will cure it. They are what keep you relentlessly striving and prevent you from feeling satisfied with anything you accomplish no matter how remarkable your achievements may actually be.

Fortunately the beliefs and perceptions that generate self-defeating actions and emotions are only ideas—not absolute and unalterable truths. They can be revised to reflect reality more accurately or replaced altogether with more rational, realistic, and positive ideas. Moreover, altering distorted thought patterns invariably changes your feelings and behavior as well. In fact that process—known as cognitive restructuring—is one of the most useful tools available to anyone who wants to become less perfectionistic.

The mainstay of cognitive therapy (which has proven to be extremely effective in helping perfectionists lead more productive and less stressful lives), cognitive restructuring is based on the premise that once you can spot distorted thinking and see how far afield it is taking you, you will change the lens through which you are viewing reality, start thinking more clearly, and as a result engage in fewer counterproductive or neurotic behaviors. It involves learning to recognize your typical reaction to various situations, to identify the inaccurate underlying assumptions that contribute to that reaction, and to correct any misperceptions that may be defeating you.

Reframing

One useful cognitive-restructuring technique is *reframing:* changing your perspective on a troubling or anxiety-provoking circumstance by casting a new, more positive light on it or, to use a filmmaking metaphor, shooting it from a more flattering angle. You may recall how Tom Sawyer convinced his friends to white-wash a fence for him by acting as if it was a pleasure instead of a chore. That's reframing. So is viewing problems as opportunities (instead of obstacles) or mistakes as lessons on what not to do next time (instead of as irrefutable proof that you are a hopeless failure). Imagine how much time you'd save if you didn't look at a problem in terms of who you should blame for it but instead asked, "Is it fixable?" or "What can we do to fix it?" And just think how productive you could be if you stopped ruminating about *why* you did what you did wrong or *why* you didn't see something coming or *why* certain things always seem to happen to you and instead thought about *what* you did right or *what* you can do now or *what* you'll do differently in the future to keep history from repeating itself again.

Revising

Cognitive restructuring frequently involves *revising* self-defeating thoughts in some way, for instance changing crucializing thoughts and global indictments such as "I *never* do anything right," or "He *always* wants his own way," or "Now my *entire* day is ruined," to more moderate and accurate premises such as "Like any human being, I sometimes make mistakes," or "It looks like he won't be changing his mind this time," or "This is a setback and not what I wanted to have happen, but let's see if I can get back on track."

A good place to practice this skill is on the self-criticisms that are maintaining your negative self-image and fueling your relentless effort to perfect yourself. If you are a perfectionist, you routinely tell yourself that you are stupid, inadequate, incompetent, ugly, boring, you name it. When you make a mistake, you are a failure. When you find yourself at a loss for words, you are an idiot. When someone does not react exactly as you wish, you have made a fool of yourself. The ways you mentally punish yourself are limitless and entirely unnecessary. You wouldn't make such cruel and unrealistic comments to a friend, so stop making them to yourself. If you think you must criticize yourself to keep yourself in line, then at least focus your comments on your behavior—not your entire being. When you tell yourself that you *did* something stupid, the possibility of doing something differently remains. But when you tell yourself that you *are* stupid, the only avenue left open is to feel ashamed of or disgusted with yourself and neurotically worry about your flaws or counterproductively try to compensate for and conceal them. As you know by now, that gets you absolutely nowhere.

Replacing

As we pointed out in Chapter Three, most of your self-critical, self-punishing thoughts and negative, all-too-often self-fulfilling perceptions reiterate the messages you previously received from people who were important to you or reflect the ideas you psychologically inherited by modeling yourself after those people. They were inaccurate back then and are even more so now. You have more knowledge, skill, alternatives, freedom, and personal power as an adult than you did as a child or adolescent. You have accumulated more life experiences and have more resources available to you. Consequently many of your old "tapes" simply do not apply anymore. They do not accurately portray who you are today or your present-day capabilities.

Using the visualizations and affirmations we described in the last chapter, you can *replace* those tapes, substituting more up-to-date, realistic, and encouraging words and images for those old, obsolete, and self-defeating premises. Take out the list of risks you have taken that we suggested you compile while reading the last chapter. Or make a new list of your positive attributes, strengths, and talents. Ask people in your life to contribute items to that list. They may be more aware of your good points than you are. Read those lists daily and don't just skim over them. Concentrate on every word, maybe even read them out loud. Read them again whenever you are facing a challenge or feeling insecure. Add new items to those lists whenever you take a new risk or become aware of another positive attribute. This repetition is essential for developing new mental habits.

You may also want to gather facts, slogans, or inspirational messages that contradict or counteract old, self-defeating beliefs. For instance the fact that *it is statistically inevitable that a person's performance at any task will be below his average half of the time and above his average the other half* directly contradicts the assumption that doing anything less than the best is a failure. You are simply performing below your average at that moment—which everyone inevitably does from time to time. You can remind yourself that *perfection is an ideal, not an attainable goal*, or reduce the panic you feel before making a decision by telling yourself *the future is an open-ended set of possibilities* or that *a path is just a path, one of many: If you don't like the path you're on, try another one.* Even old chestnuts like *To err is human, to forgive divine* can be useful for combatting distorted thinking.

Writing It Down

To restructure distorted thought patterns, you must bring them out into the open, speaking your thoughts aloud, silently putting them into words, and carefully looking at them in your mind or, better yet, writing them down. Reframing, revising, and replacing self-defeating ideas is easier when you actually see those ideas on paper.

When you are feeling anxious or upset or are about to engage in compulsive perfectionistic behavior, get into the habit of doing spot checks. Ask yourself what you are thinking. Put your thoughts into words. Look for inaccuracies, premature conclusions, "fortune-telling," magnifications, broad generalizations, or phrases that sound an awful lot like the damning or demanding messages you previously received from influential people in your life. Then rewrite the distorted thought in a way that reduces its emotional charge, tones down an expectation, or moves you in a new, positive direction.

Writing is also calming when you are worried. Getting your fears out of your head (where they get bigger and bigger, like a snowball rolling down a hill) and onto a sheet of paper makes them more manageable. You can see the forest from the trees, picking out the realities and the distortions. Almost magically the real issue, the true source of your emotional distress, emerges and you can look for a way to deal with it instead of running around like a chicken with its head cut off trying to control or change things that have little or nothing to do with what's actually wrong.

As cognitive therapists often do, we highly recommend that you keep a journal and make a commitment to write something in it every day. Your entries need not be recaps of your day or problem oriented. You can use your journal to:

- Keep track of the positive feedback you've received
- Compile a sort of reverse "to do" list, recounting everything you *did* accomplish from the moment you got out of bed in the morning (including getting out of bed that morning)
- Jot down things you love to do or would love to try (and pick a few to weave back into your life)
- Recount a risk you took
- Practice empathizing: select an attitude or opinion that you feel strongly about and write from the opposite position with equal passion
- Write out affirmations or compose short stories about yourself doing or being what you want to do or be
- Carry on a dialogue between yourself and one of your "inner voices," yourself and one of your fears, or yourself and someone in your life with whom you ordinarily have difficulty conversing

Although we've tried to give you some strategies and suggestions to get you started on the road to clearer thinking, in a few short pages we could not possibly teach you everything you'll want to know about cognitive restructuring. We encourage you to learn more by consulting any of the excellent books—most notably

Feeling Good: The New Mood Therapy by Dr. David Burns—that have been devoted to the subject (and are available in most bookstores). You'll find other suggestions in the Bibliography.

Stop Catastrophizing

Because your goals and standards are so high and reaching them is the most important and sometimes the only measure of your self-worth, if you are a perfectionist, you spend a great deal of time worrying about what will happen if you don't live up to those lofty expectations. You are constantly on the lookout for things that could go wrong, things that might stop you from being the best there is, and thus deal yet another blow to your already shaky self-image. You live in fear of failing or being rejected, abandoned, criticized, ridiculed, ignored, or subjected to some other horrifying fate. And as we mentioned in the last chapter, that fear is one of the greatest obstacles to becoming less perfectionistic and leading a well-balanced life.

No matter what you are afraid of, your fears are so powerful—powerful enough to prevent you from fulfilling your needs—because you *catastrophize:* projecting your past failures or other painful experiences into the future in the form of worst-case scenarios. You turn the slightest hint of a potentially negative consequence into a nightmare vision of impending doom or disaster, and then you assume that what you envision will come to pass. This bit of distorted thinking raises your anxiety to intolerable and sometimes paralyzing levels, preventing you from taking the risks you need to take in order to succeed, convincing you to avoid any situation that includes even a remote possibility of experiencing what you fear or prompting you to engage in the compulsive and controlling behaviors you have gotten into the habit of using to relieve anxiety. By reacting in those ways, you not only reduce the odds that you'll achieve any goal but also keep yourself from figuring out that the catastrophes you fear are figments of your imagination. More important, you miss out on countless opportunities to learn that you

230

are quite capable of handling nearly any negative consequence that would actually occur. Plain and simply, to break out of your cycle of self-defeat, you must *stop* catastrophizing. Here's how:

1. *Catastrophize to your heart's content.* That's right, do what you were going to do anyway. In fact come up with the worst possible outcome you can imagine. Write out every gory detail of the most horrifying outcome you can picture for an anxiety-provoking upcoming event or challenge.
2. *Reality check.* By the time you finish putting your nightmare vision down on paper, you will have recognized how absurd it is. No matter how prone to catastrophizing you are, a part of you knows that failing to close one deal does not mean you are going to end up as a homeless bag lady sleeping on a steam vent. Canceling lunch with your mother will not prompt her to disown you. Your landlord is not going to pick the day you left your apartment without vacuuming to make a spot inspection and evict you. If the fund-raiser you are organizing is less than complete and flawless in all respects, your fellow PTA members are not going to drum you out of the group or run you out of town. And if you become tongue-tied during a dinner party or put your foot in your mouth, you are not going to fall apart at the seams and wind up in a padded cell somewhere. Look at the various absurdities in your worst-case scenario and have a good laugh. You'll start to feel better right away.

Although the possibility that your "nightmare" will actually come to pass is virtually nonexistent, there are probably a few grains of truth in it. The catastrophes you envision are almost always magnifications of consequences that actually might occur: If you cancel lunch with mom, she might lecture, remind you of all the sacrifices she's made on your behalf, or give you the silent treatment. If you make an offensive comment during a dinner party, you might feel mortified. If you work on commission, not closing a deal could affect your income. Using the catastrophe you imagined as a guide, list any consequences or problems that you really might encounter *which you feel you would have trouble handling*.

3. *Plan for contingencies*. Even though the possible repercussions you identified in step 2 are on a much smaller scale than the catastrophes you typically envision, the prospect of encountering them and being unable to handle them can still stir up plenty of anxiety. In fact for most perfectionists, even a remote possibility that a situation will not proceed exactly the way they want it to is enough to send their blood pressure soaring. However, there is usually more than one solution to any problem and more than one way to reach any goal. By learning to shift gears, change directions when you encounter an impasse or an unexpected opportunity, and come up with alternatives for handling negative consequences, you can dramatically reduce anxiety and feel more comfortable in almost any situation.

For each of the consequences you listed in step 2, come up with a contingency plan. Your plan might involve something (other than avoiding the situation altogether) that you can do in advance to decrease the chances of that consequence occurring: "sweetening" the deal in order to improve the odds of closing it, for instance, or putting more work into several smaller deals so that your income will remain about the same, or putting yourself on a budget today just in case the deal does fall through a month from now. Your contingency plan might include actions you can take on the spot should what you fear come to pass. For example, if you accidentally made an offensive comment, you could apologize then and there, or call upon a bit of self-deprecating humor ("Oops. I'd better shut my mouth before I put my *other* foot in it."), or pull the person you think you offended aside later and apologize. A contingency plan can also involve something you'll do after the fact to cope with a consequence you cannot prevent or do anything about. For instance, when you cancel that lunch date with your mother and she does lecture you or otherwise try to induce guilt, you might listen politely and then, when your conversation is over, scream at the top of your lungs, or call your sister to gripe about your mom, or write affirmations in your journal, or go for a brisk walk—repeating your affirmations to yourself along the way.

4. *Visualize your plans in action.* Sometimes just having a contingency plan will be enough to propel you past your fears. If it is not, you can prepare for a situation you are dreading by mentally walking yourself through it ahead of time. Doing so enables you to get the bugs out of your contingency plans as well as learn to lower your anxiety level at will. First, relax your body, mentally travel to your secret resting place, and repeat a few simple, soothing affirmations. Once you are calm and relaxed, visualize the situation you dread. Fantasize about it working out exactly the way you want it to. Then visualize it again, only this time imagine the negative consequence occurring. Picture yourself using your contingency plan to deal with those consequences or cope with their aftereffects. If, at any point in your visualization, your anxiety level rises above a five on a one-to-ten scale, take a few deep breaths, return to your secret resting place, and then repeat your visualization again from the beginning. It may take several sittings, but eventually you will be able to get all the way through the visualization with your anxiety level never rising above a five.

5. *Try it in the real world.* As we said in the last chapter, the only way truly to conquer a fear is to take a deep breath and do what needs to be done no matter how nervous you feel. Do what you can to prepare for anxiety-provoking situations. Remind yourself of your past successes. Flood your mind with affirmations. Then jump right in. Just do it. We can guarantee that nothing you encounter will be as bad as the disaster you imagined. And even if you do botch things up, the world won't end. In fact you'll learn something useful for dealing with similar situations in the future. Perhaps best of all, having survived a situation you once feared would destroy you, your courage to face new challenges will increase dramatically.

Will going through this five-step anticatastrophizing technique stop you from worrying? Probably not. We have yet to meet a perfectionist who was not convinced that worrying about everything that could go wrong was the only way to make things work out "right." And we have yet to change a perfectionist's mind about that. So what is the answer? We suggest restricting your worrying to a specific time each day. Permit yourself to worry for thirty minutes or an hour at the same time every day. If worries come to mind at other times, tell yourself you'll worry about that matter later. You are apt to discover that many of your concerns will have worked themselves out before your worry time arrives. You may even forget what you were supposed to worry about during your worry time. If it's important and you *need* to worry about it, you'll remember it eventually. Or maybe, just maybe, you'll find out that you don't *really* need to worry so much after all.

Gain Some Control over Your Obsessions and Compulsions

Obsessive-compulsive disorder (OCD) or addictive-type compulsive behaviors such as compulsive overeating, gambling, spending, and so on are rarely overcome without psychotherapy or participation in a structured recovery program (such as Overeaters or Gamblers Anonymous.) However, we can offer you a few stopgap measures for controlling unwelcome, anxiety-provoking thoughts or overwhelming urges to engage in certain activities.

Stop the thought. Thought stopping is exactly what it sounds like: putting a stop to an unwanted line of thinking that has invaded your consciousness at an inopportune moment. Simply imagine a voice shouting, "Stop!" or concentrate on the image of a giant stop sign. Then return your *full* attention to whatever you were doing. (It helps to be doing something that requires your full attention. If an unwelcome thought appears when you are daydreaming or engaged in an activity that leaves room for your mind to wander, you will have to think purposefully about

something else as well as stop the intrusive thought.) If the unwelcome thought reappears, simply repeat the process.

Write it out. Nagging thoughts often reflect unmet emotional
needs. Something that you are refusing to recognize is trying to
capture your attention through thoughts that are too disturbing
to ignore. If you take out a sheet of paper and write anything
that comes to mind, the true source of your distress may emerge.
If the problem involves a matter within your power to control,
deal with it. If you discover that you are stewing over a disagreement with your spouse that was not satisfactorily resolved,
bring the topic up for discussion again. If you learn that you are
still feeling hurt by a comment someone made that you did not
address at the time, talk to the person who made the comment.
If you feel guilty about an insensitive comment you made, apologize. Whatever you do, don't rebury your feelings (unless circumstances require you consciously to set them aside until you
get a chance to deal with the problem). They will just return in
symbolic form once again.

Turn it over. Many of the things perfectionists obsessively
think about are beyond their control: the weather on the day of
their outdoor fund-raising event, test results that won't be posted
for several days, if and when the man they met on Saturday will
call, whether the check their publisher insists is in the mail will
arrive in time to pay their estimated income tax, and so on. There
is nothing you can do about such thoughts except admit that you
are powerless to control the circumstances involved and let go
of the obsession, "turning it over" to God or some other concept
of a higher authority or force. You might visualize your concern
being carried away by a hot-air balloon and disappearing over
the horizon. Or you might get a large jar with a lid, call it your
"things I can't control" jar, write your concern on a slip of paper,
and put it inside. If you start obsessing again, remind yourself
that you have turned the matter over, that it is in someone else's
hands now. Then get busy with a more productive pursuit.

Set time limits. Most perfectionists can spend hours on end
cleaning their already spotless houses, organizing their offices,

trying on outfits, revising reports, calculating and recalculating their household budgets, or engaging in other habitual behaviors. Frequently the things they feel compelled to do keep them from doing things they actually need or want to do. If that is the case for you, try setting limits on the time you will devote to certain activities. Set a kitchen timer for ten minutes less than your allotted time. When the timer goes off, reset it for ten minutes and finish up whatever you were doing. When the timer buzzes again, stop what you are doing and immediately move on to something else. It helps to have a follow-up activity scheduled.

A kitchen timer is also useful for fighting the urge to engage in a behavior you are trying to discontinue—checking things, snacking, rearranging items on your shelves, and so on. When you feel compelled to do something you don't want to do, set your kitchen timer for fifteen minutes and tell yourself that you can engage in that behavior when the timer buzzes—if you still want to. Frequently you will not, and if you do, you can set the timer for another fifteen minutes. Again it is helpful to be involved in some other activity, preferably one that demands your full attention.

In general, obsessions and compulsions are convoluted ways of managing anxiety. Both not only distract you from the real problems in your life but also tend to increase when you are under pressure. Consequently regular use of the relaxation, visualization, and cognitive restructuring techniques we have already described can also help to diminish obsessive thinking and compulsive behavior.

Stop Procrastinating

Procrastination is one of the most self-defeating of all perfectionistic behaviors. By putting off anxiety-provoking tasks for as long as possible, procrastinating perfectionists naturally become more anxious and worried that they won't be able to complete the task flawlessly. Then, because they leave themselves so little time to get the job done, they end up rushing through it, making careless mistakes or doing less than their best work and reinforcing their feelings of failure and inadequacy—which leads to more procrastination the next time they have a task to complete.

Sometimes procrastination results from the faulty premise that there is no point in starting a project unless you have enough time to finish the whole thing. You focus solely on the completed task and not at all on the steps that lead to completion. Taking the exact opposite point of view could break your procrastination habit. Think of a task you have been putting off doing. Then write down all the steps you must take to complete the project. If any step has more than one element to it, break that step down into smaller steps. When you have the entire project divided into manageable pieces, take out a calendar or daily planner and schedule every step. Once you have all the steps scheduled, try not to give another thought to the whole project—just get each *part* of the project done on schedule.

Another way to combat all-or-nothing thinking about a project is to commit yourself to work on it for fifteen minutes. Tell yourself you do not have to complete the task. You do not need to worry about the results. All you have to do is put fifteen minutes' worth of work into it. Get out your kitchen timer, set it, and totally devote yourself to the task until the timer buzzes. Since you only committed to fifteen minutes, you can stop when your time is up. However, if you find that you are on a roll, feel free to continue and even complete the task.

Note: Fifteen minutes of staring at a blank sheet of paper, thinking about what you should be doing, or redoing a part of the task that has already been completed does *not* count. Your fifteen minutes starts when you start working. If you find that you can't start because you are afraid you won't do a good enough job, consider doing a bad job. Set out to write a rotten or mediocre cover letter, to add up a column of figures incorrectly, to come up with a lousy theme for your fund-raising campaign, and so on. You'll get past whatever's blocking you and probably discover that it's more difficult to mess up than you thought.

Although both of these techniques work well, to make a real dent in your procrastination habit, it helps to understand the driving force behind it. That information can often be found in the excuses you use to talk yourself out of starting or completing various projects. Take out a sheet of paper, draw a line down the middle, and then draw four narrow columns down the right side of the page. In the wide left-hand column list the excuses and rationalizations you use when you are procrastinating. If none come to mind right off the bat, try thinking about a task you have been putting off and ask yourself why you haven't gotten to it yet. Or think about a project you recently rushed to complete at the last minute. Why did you wait? The following excuses may ring a bell:

- I need more information.
- I don't have enough time today.
- I'm upset and can't concentrate.
- First I have to reorganize my files, lose ten more pounds, work out my relationship problems . . .
- I'm not very good at these things.
- I think I'll get a few more opinions from other people, just to make sure I'm on the right track.
- I don't know why I said I'd do this in the first place.
- How am I supposed to get this done when everyone is constantly interrupting me (or no one will cooperate with me)?
- No one else busts their buns to get things done around here, so why should I?

Once you've listed your excuses, you can identify the underlying issues: the fears or perceptions that are preventing you from getting started or sticking with a task.

In the first narrow column use the letter *D* to identify *distorted thought patterns* (all-or-nothingisms, magnifications, crucializations, catastrophizing, and so on). "How am I supposed to get this done when *everyone* is *constantly* interrupting me (or *no one* will cooperate with me)?" is an example of one such excuse.

In the second narrow column use the letter *I* to indicate excuses that reflect *insecurities*, low self-esteem, or fear of failure. "I'm not very good at these things" or "I think I'll get a few more opinions from other people, just to make sure I'm on the right track" are two examples.

In the third narrow column use the letter *O* to indicate excuses that reflect your resistance to completing tasks that you did not freely choose, but instead felt *obligated* to do. For instance, "I don't know why I said I'd do this in the first place." Excuses that convey resentment—"No one else busts their buns to get things done around here, so why should I?"—also fall into this category.

In the fourth narrow column use the letter *A* to indicate flat-out *avoidance:* problems or obstacles that you are focusing on so that you don't have to deal directly with your anxiety about the task at hand or worry about failing to perform it flawlessly. It is a safe bet that anything from "First I have to reorganize my files, lose ten more pounds, work out my relationship problems..." to "I don't have enough time today" is serving that purpose.

To eliminate the excuses that are prompting you to procrastinate, you must work on the issues they reflect, using cognitive restructuring on your distorted thought patterns; taking advantage of visualizations, affirmations, risk taking, and techniques to stop catastrophizing in order to combat insecurities and avoidance; or conducting the cost-benefit analysis we described on page 222 to decide whether or not the task at hand is one you truly want to accomplish.

Repair Your Relationships

In one way or another, perfectionism wreaks havoc on relationships. Although perfectionists may not mean to treat other people the way they do, their dissatisfaction with themselves, their nitpicking, pessimistic, always-going-somewhere-but-never-quite-getting-there natures and their seemingly insatiable desire for order, control, or approval make them harsh critics, demanding taskmasters, and hypersensitive worrywarts. Some hover, offering supposedly "helpful" hints or "constructive" criticism. Others dominate, rushing in to take over and control every imaginable situation. Still other perfectionists keep to themselves or incessantly talk about whatever they happen to be obsessively preoccupied with at any given moment. Interpersonal perfectionists in particular project their high expectations onto others, pushing everyone in their immediate vicinity to live up to their standards. But no matter how perfectionists go about it (and even if they are not consciously aware of what they are doing), the net results are relationships rife with conflict and power struggles or few if any nourishing relationships at all.

The saddest part of this situation is that, deep down inside, perfectionists long for peaceful, supportive, unconditionally loving relationships. They desperately want what they were deprived of at crucial points in their development: people to accept them for who they are and be there for them no matter what they do or how they look. If you are a perfectionist, as you begin to change your life and venture into unfamiliar territory, you will need that sort of emotional support and encouragement more than ever. Consequently it is imperative that you take steps to establish new relationships (using the techniques we described in Chapter Nine) and rebuild the relationships you have. At the very least you must make a concerted effort not to allow your perfectionism to do any more damage to the people around you or your relationships with them.

Bring your expectations of people and relationships down to a realistic and reasonable level. Use the goal-trimming strategy that opened this chapter to help you accept that your ideal is unattainable in the real world. There is simply no way you can force a person or a relationship to fulfill your perfect fantasy. Relationships wither and die when you try to control them. People have minds, wills, and needs of their own—and the right to be who they are no matter how much better you think they could be if they just tried a little harder. You also have a right not to take something you *don't* want from people or relationships. The goal-trimming strategy can help you draw your bottom line. In between those two extremes you will find reasonable, realistic expectations for people and relationships. However, you must also come to realize and eventually to accept that you cannot go about fulfilling those expectations in the same way you achieve other goals.

Be less critical. Think about your own life. How much truly constructive criticism have you received? Did having someone pick at and harp on you or deliver scathing reviews of your conduct actually build character or endear you to your critic? Absolutely not. It damaged your self-esteem, undermined your confidence, and set you on the perfectionistic path you are pursuing today. What's more, your relationship with that pushy, hypercritical individual was not based on trust, sharing, interdependence, or even mutual respect. You merely did what you had to do to avoid more criticism and, if you were lucky, obtain a few crumbs of affection or approval. Is that how you want your spouse or lover, children, friends, and colleagues to relate to you?

If you put into practice our suggestions for developing tolerance, your urge to nitpick and correct every imaginable imperfection will naturally decrease. However, making critical comments and pointing out flaws is a habit, an automatic behavior that you stopped paying conscious attention to long ago. You must start paying attention to it again, stopping to think before you speak and editing out "constructive" criticism that isn't really constructive at all. When you feel an urge to find fault or offer unsolicited suggestions for improvement, ask yourself the following questions:

> *Will telling this person what I think he or she did wrong or could have done better actually accomplish anything of value?*
> *Will it strengthen our relationship and help us live or work together more comfortably?*

Is it something that the other person needs to hear so she will not *seriously harm herself or others and* not *something I need to say in order to control this situation or feel superior?*
Is this new information and not *something I have mentioned at least once (and probably many times) before?*
Have I already tried other ways of expressing my dissatisfaction and requesting a behavior change?

If you answer no to *any* of these questions, do *not* deliver your criticism. Either tolerate the imperfection or try the following "I've got a problem" approach. It acknowledges that being bothered by the behavior is *your* problem (which it usually is) and involves the other person in the problem-solving process (which usually increases their commitment to changing the behavior in question).

At an appropriate moment, and not in the heat of battle or when you are too aggravated to think straight, calmly convey that you have a problem. Define that problem in terms of how you feel when the other person engages in the behavior that bothers you. For example, "I get nervous when you leave your desk (or the house) without telling me where you're going," or "I get anxious and worried when you are late," or "It's difficult for me not to lose my temper when I see that you haven't gotten to something I asked you to do right away." Then convey your interest in solving the problem and ask the other person to help you come up with a solution that will work for both of you. Be willing—and this is the hard part—to accept a solution other than the one you had in mind. Remember, there is always more than one path to any goal, and your goal is to solve the problem— which you have repeatedly failed to do by trying to force the other person to live up to your standards.

In addition, *validate* the people in your life as often as possible. By validation we do not mean praising them for doing things to your satisfaction, but rather letting them know that you value them for who they are. "I appreciate your kindness and am delighted that someone so sensitive and thoughtful is part of my life," "I admire your courage and creativity. I'm always amazed by your grace under pressure," and a simple "You're terrific. I love you," are just a few examples of the kind of unconditionally accepting messages you could start conveying to the people in your life.

Give up some control. Perfectionists in general, and interpersonal perfectionists in particular, consistently run themselves ragged and alienate everyone around them by trying to control everything under the sun. If they are to be the best there is at all they do, they cannot afford to let things happen. They must *make* things happen. Unfortunately what usually happens not only fails to meet their expectations but also creates bitter conflicts, resentments, and blatant or subtle power struggles in their personal or professional relationships. People simply do not take kindly to being controlled. In fact they will do everything in their power not to be controlled or to make perfectionists pay for trying to control them. If you are a perfectionist, chances are that you will never be able to stop controlling completely. However, you *can* cut down on this truly infuriating, ultimately self-defeating behavior.

Identify several things you try to control that are really not that important: how your spouse chops vegetables, the neatness of your ten-year-old daughter's dresser drawers, your secretary's method of taking dictation (which works for her), the way the supermarket cashier bags your groceries, and so on. One at a time stop trying to control those things. If something disastrous happens, you can always start controlling them again.

Identify several areas where you could eliminate your need to control by lowering your standards or coming up with compromises. For instance, instead of endlessly nagging your teenage son to clean his bedroom, could you let him keep it any way he wants provided there are no health hazards and he doesn't expect you to, on a moment's notice, wash or iron clothing he has left crumpled on the floor for days? Could you stop looking over your staff's shoulders if they have agreed to give you progress reports at the beginning or end of the work day? Be creative.

Experiment. You'll be amazed at the time you save and the co-operation you receive from people who used to fight you every step of the way.

Or try sharing control. You and your spouse, lover, or col-league could be in charge of cooking, cleaning, running meet-ings, or any other source of conflict on alternating days. On your day things get done your way, and the other person is not to criticize or complain. On the other person's day things are done his way—imperfect as that may be—and you must not criticize or complain.

Like cognitive restructuring, there is far more to building or rebuilding relationships than we could possibly cover here. We have merely suggested a few simple ways to stop trying so hard to perfect your relationships and start getting more of what you truly need from them.

We encourage you to continue strengthening your relation-ships, your interpersonal skills, and indeed all the areas of your life that have been damaged by your perfectionism. Creating a more balanced, less perfectionistic life is an ongoing process, and your efforts in that regard will not end when you reach the final page of this book. In addition, at various times, for various rea-sons, you may discover that you need help staying on your new path or breaking an old habit. The next chapter tells you where you can turn for that help.

Chapter Eleven

Guides on the Path
to Excellence:
Where to Find Help
for Overcoming Perfectionism

We hope the last two chapters have shown you that there *are* ways to control your perfectionistic tendencies and add positive, balancing experiences to your life-style *without* completely abandoning your goals, standards, and ambitions or being doomed to mediocrity. We hope you have begun to think a bit differently from the way you have in the past and to see that if on occasion you do fall short of your goals, it isn't the end of the world. There are worse things than failing or making mistakes—shortchanging yourself and other people while relentlessly pursuing unattainable ideals, for instance.

That's not to say that you shouldn't have ideals or that there are not times when you should make an effort to perform at a near-flawless level. However, wanting and trying to do the best you can in situations that require an all-out effort makes it even more important to recognize the many other times when you *can* relax a little and give yourself and those around you some slack. That flexibility, that willingness not only to go after your goals but also to enjoy the fruits of your labor and share your life with other people is the foundation for excellence seeking and a well-balanced life.

As a perfectionist you have always had the desire and energy to pursue your goals. You've just overshot a little, tried too hard, concentrated on one area of your life to the exclusion of all others. Once you rein in all that ambition, the things you have previously taken to extremes can be used constructively. As a perfectionist you are quick to recognize your own deficiencies and eager to remedy them. This also gives you a certain advantage when it comes to breaking old habits and developing new ones—even with your tendency to procrastinate, pine over past mistakes, and resist change. Indeed, as you move along a path to excellence, many of the instincts and abilities that were part and parcel of your perfectionism will come in handy. Your intelligence, creativity, eye for detail, ability to spot potential problems, and so on will be great assets in your struggle to overcome the unhealthy habits associated with relentlessly pursuing unrealistic goals. So will the resources we are about to describe. No one—no matter how smart, determined, or self-sufficient he or she may be—can truly break out of and *stay out of* the self-defeating cycles of perfectionism all alone.

Bibliotherapy

Once you have defined a problem, reading can be a good place to begin the process of solving it. We have found this to be true in our own lives and have seen it work wonders for our clients as well. In fact many, many therapists routinely recommend that their patients read everything from self-help books like this one to biographies of individuals who have overcome various adversities.

To be effective, bibliotherapy requires *active* reading: putting yourself into the "story" being told in a book and trying to figure out how the information fits into your life. Ask yourself the following questions:

- Do the symptoms, the mind-sets and thinking patterns, the destructive actions described apply to me?
- Are the people in the case studies—their attitudes, their frustrations, their behavior—familiar?
- Is that the way I think?
- Do I do those kinds of things?
- Have my friends, relatives, or co-workers previously mentioned some of these things to me?

You may also want to keep a log of advice and suggestions given by the author or thoughts and feelings conveyed by people described in a book that make a particular impact on you. If the books include exercises like those you found in this one, give them a try. They will not change your life instantaneously, but they may get you moving in a direction you never before considered going. The Bibliography offers a broad selection of books that have proved helpful both for our clients and for ourselves.

Psychotherapy

When you picked up this book, you embarked upon a journey away from the self-defeating pursuit of unreachable perfection and toward the self-enhancing world of excellence. Reading other books and putting what you read into practice can take you farther down that road to a well-balanced life. But reading alone may not be enough to get you where you want to go. Somewhere along the line you may encounter a roadblock that the advice you find in books and the support you receive from friends or relatives cannot dismantle. You may discover, for example, that no matter how hard you try to stop your obsessive thoughts and reduce your anxiety through relaxation and visualizations, you still can't seem to leave your home without performing certain chores in a specific sequence or checking to make sure that every drawer and closet door is shut. You might absorb every bit of written information on intimacy but continue to find fault with every potential lover or destroy budding relationships by incessantly nitpicking and endlessly trying to control people. Lifelong patterns and deeply ingrained habits may persist in spite of your best efforts to alter your distorted thought patterns. Eating disorders, panic attacks, workaholism, addictions, compulsive rituals, and other problems that were an outgrowth of your perfectionism but have now taken on a life of their own may simply be too much for you to unravel and overcome by yourself. You need help. Professional help.

If you are a perfectionist, you may resist the idea. In fact, if you are like many of the perfectionists we have known or treated, you will put off getting professional help for as long as you can. You may be afraid that by probing your psyche you will uncover a deep, dark secret, a lifetime's worth of anger and resentment or a truly fatal character defect that will utterly destroy you. The pain might be unbearable. You might have a nervous breakdown. Or you might be forced to give up *all* of your familiar routines, leaving you defenseless and without a clue as to how to function in a world where those old routines at least brought you some measure of success, if not happiness. Therapists will try to assure you that these worst-case scenarios will not come to pass. But you may not believe them. Or you may want them to guarantee that therapy will solve all your problems forever. Their inability to make that promise is your "out." After all, if your life won't be perfect when you are finished with therapy, why should you bother with it at all?

You may stubbornly cling to your belief that you should be able to solve all your problems yourself, that you can handle anything if you just try hard enough. Emotional well-being is like any other goal, you think—if you set your mind to it, you can achieve it, without using therapy as a "crutch" or depending on people who probably don't know what they're talking about anyway. Whether you feel that asking for help is admitting defeat, are skeptical about the value of therapy in general, or doubt that you could find a truly competent therapist, you talk yourself out of seeking any kind of professional help and, as a result, miss out on an opportunity to actually be helped.

Or you may believe that being a perfectionist isn't a big enough problem to present to a therapist. A therapist with a waiting room full of people with *real* problems would probably laugh you right out of his office. Fearing ridicule or rejection, you decide not to bring your "little idiosyncrasy" to a professional's attention. But as you now know, perfectionism is a *real* problem that can bring on more and more serious problems. You can wait until the enormous pressure you place on yourself and others leads to a physical or emotional crisis that forces you to wake up and realize outside help is needed, and needed badly. Or you can choose to seek psychotherapy at any time (including the present) simply because you feel you could benefit from it. Many, many perfectionists have.

If you do decide to take advantage of this useful and sometimes even lifesaving resource, it helps to know a bit about the various therapeutic options available to you. We'd like to offer you a few basic facts now and encourage you to talk to friends, your family doctor, or therapists themselves in order to learn more.

Individual Therapy

Individual therapy involves a one-on-one exchange between you and your therapist. It is frequently the most intensive form of therapy since the therapeutic hour is devoted entirely to you and your concerns. It tends to be the best option for obtaining insight into unconscious thought processes as well as ferreting out and clarifying the ways your past experiences affect your present-day attitudes and actions. Even if you end up in another form of therapy, you can expect to have at least one and usually several individual sessions with your therapist so that he or she can find out about your background and the nature of your difficulties.

Group Therapy

Group therapy brings people with similar problems together to form a mutual support system in which group members can encourage and help one another as well as be helped by the psychotherapist guiding the group process. Many perfectionists find that the give-and-take among people who have personal experience with and intimate understanding of the difficulties they confront both helps them feel less isolated and provides them with "recovery role models" to emulate. Group therapy is especially beneficial for interpersonal perfectionists, helping them to develop social skills and learn to accept flaws in others as they also learn to cope with their own.

Couples and Family Therapy

Couples and family therapy enables you to resolve many of the difficulties your perfectionism has contributed to on the home front. If you are married or involved in an ongoing intimate relationship, joint counseling gives both you and your partner a forum for frank expression and a place to learn new ways of communicating and resolving conflicts. It may provide your partner with his or her first opportunity to truthfully tell you about feelings that have been bottled up inside and to convey resentments openly that have been coming out in passive, sullen ways that only raised your anxiety level (and led to more perfectionistic behavior). You may not like what you hear, but once the cards are layed on the table, you will finally be able to deal with your interpersonal problems effectively and compassionately. Perhaps for the first time in your relationship your conflicts and power struggles can actually get resolved.

Over the past few decades psychologists have come to realize that any serious psychological or emotional difficulty causes trouble for more than just the individual. That person's problem inevitably affects everyone close to him and frequently disrupts entire family units, creating a system in which spouses and other relatives unknowingly and certainly unintentionally tend to sustain or "enable" one family member's problem behavior to continue. Consequently more and more psychotherapists are treating the "system": including family members in therapy sessions, directing attention away from individual problems, and focusing on the context in which those problems occur. By examining family roles, assumptions, expectations, or unacknowledged "agreements" to maintain the status quo—no matter how destructive it may be—and prescribing corrective measures for all family members, family therapists eliminate the dysfunctional patterns that support perfectionistic behavior, reducing the likelihood that the perfectionist will continue it in the family setting.

Therapy procedure, in individual, group, and family counseling alike, often involves versions of the you-talk-the-therapist-listens-and-occasionally-comments-and-asks-questions technique with which you are probably familiar. But within that basic framework there are many variations. Two that perfectionists seem to respond to in a particularly positive manner are described below.

Cognitive Therapy

Cognitive therapy is designed to bring to light the beliefs and distorted thinking that rule your life from the subconscious part of your mind. By making these negative thoughts explicit, their power can be checked or subdued. And by learning to become conscious of what you are doing and why you are doing it, you can start to pay attention to what you are thinking under various circumstances, to identify problematic distortions and incorrect underlying assumptions, and to replace self-defeating, negative misperceptions with more accurate, rational, positive ideas.

Originally developed by Aaron T. Beck, M.D., to treat depressed patients at the Mood Disorders Clinic at the University of Pennsylvania School of Medicine, cognitive therapy generally requires three or four months of weekly sessions, each with a set agenda, followed by monthly meetings for another six to twelve months. At the outset and throughout your involvement in therapy, cognitive therapists explain exactly what they are doing, what they are asking of you, and why. They will teach you to use cognitive restructuring techniques similar to those we described in the last two chapters as well as have you try "cognitive rehearsal" and role-playing, both to clarify your typical reaction to new challenges or negative experiences and to test out new ways of handling those situations. You will also receive homework assignments: keeping a record of your activities and feelings, for example, or trying out new behavior and positive thought patterns in specific real-life situations. This practical, straightforward approach along with cognitive therapy's short-term structure, noticeable results within a few weeks, and emphasis on logic and reason, make it one of the most attractive and effective forms of counseling available to perfectionists.

Reality Therapy

Developed by psychologist William Glasser, reality therapy is a counseling technique that can teach you how to plan and prepare for the future effectively, amend and alter behavior that prevents you from getting what you want out of life, and take calculated risks that will enable you to achieve specific goals. It is an action-oriented approach that involves the following:

- Therapists who interact with you, rather than analyzing you in a detached manner. Most will reveal details about their own lives and by doing so encourage you to discuss your problems and concerns openly.
- A here-and-now focus rather than a lengthy reexamination of your past history.
- Practical assistance in formulating plans of action for the future and making commitments.
- Concentration on behaviors rather than feelings so that you can deal with specific hurdles and logistics instead of conjuring up worst-case scenarios or dwelling on your fears and

insecurities. Instead of asking why—"Why did you do that? Why do you think that way?"—reality therapists ask what, as in "What are you going to do about it?"

- Learning to evaluate and correct your actions without condemning or beating up on yourself. Not all commitments will be kept, nor will all plans be successful. Accepting that enables you to make modifications or a new plan instead of making excuses, assigning blame, or seeking absolution.

Reality therapy is about figuring out what works for you and what doesn't, doing what works and, instead of trying harder when a plan of action fails to produce the desired outcome, trying something different. As we have emphasized throughout this book, that is precisely what perfectionists need to do and why reality therapy may prove enormously helpful to you.

As you no doubt know, there are dozens of other therapeutic approaches available to you: from traditional psychoanalysis to problem-specific treatments for sexual dysfunction, phobias, or obsessive-compulsive disorder. Choosing the approach that will work best for you will take some effort on your part and some trial and error. Naturally it helps to know what you want from therapy *and* from your therapist. Indeed your relationship with the professional you turn to for guidance is at least as important as the type of therapy that professional provides.

Choosing a Therapist

Keeping in mind that there are no perfect therapists and accounting for your perfectionistic tendency to look for flaws in others, shop around for a good therapist. Ask for recommendations from your friends or your doctor. Contact a local mental health clinic, an information and referral service, or your state licensing board. They can give you names of qualified therapists in your geographic area.

Although it doesn't always occur to new therapy patients to

do so, you would be wise to interview any therapist thoroughly prior to entering treatment with that person. Ask questions during your initial telephone conversation and make sure any concerns you may have are addressed during your first session. Reputable therapists will answer your questions willingly and will also do some emotional probing of their own. They want to determine if they can help *you*, and if they feel they cannot, they will often be able to refer you to someone who can.

Generally speaking, you will want to:

- Tell the therapist about the specific areas in your life where you are having difficulty.
- Tell the therapist what you hope to accomplish in therapy and ask if he or she thinks those goals are attainable.
- Ask what kinds of treatment approaches the therapist uses, and how you can benefit from those methods.
- Ask if the therapist has worked with other people who had problems like yours, and try to get some ideas about the therapist's attitudes about perfectionism and how to overcome it.
- Have practical concerns—such as how often you'll be seen and over how long a period—addressed.

At the same time you should be asking yourself several questions: Does the therapist seem empathetic? Does she understand your problem and recognize its legitimacy? Are you comfortable with the therapist's comments about perfectionism? Does the therapist talk as though he doesn't think perfectionism can/should be controlled?

Does the therapist listen to you? Does he let you speak, even ramble, without interrupting you or acting bored? Does the therapist answer your questions (even if the occasional answer is "I don't know")? Is she frank (without being curt)? Or does the therapist seem merely to be saying what she thinks you want to hear? Does he sound like a used-car salesperson, singing the virtues of his method and how it's just right for you? Or does the therapist offer an honest, reasoned analysis of how he will—and will not—be able to help you? Finally, given the general discomfort you will feel being in any therapist's office for the first time, do you feel comfortable talking to this person? Can you picture yourself sharing your thoughts and feelings with him or her and somewhere down the line trusting his or her advice?

Don't reject therapists who cannot give you a precise cut-and-dried formula for recovery. In fact you should probably be skeptical of anyone who can. Skilled and experienced therapists know that until therapy actually begins, they cannot predict exactly how—or how well—you'll respond. In addition, despite your careful screening and even an encouraging start, you may find that you and your therapist don't "fit" as well as you had hoped. He may not be able to grasp the ideas you are trying to convey. His methods may not work for you. If you feel that you are not being helped, share those feelings with your therapist. He may be willing and able to change his approach. If he is not or if, after half a dozen sessions, you still have not "clicked," exercise your prerogative to terminate counseling with that therapist and find another. Believe us, you will not be the first or the last person to do that.

Peer Support and Self-help Groups

Having watched far too many perfectionists struggle unsuccessfully to break their self-defeating habits on their own and having tried that ourselves at various times in our lives, we can assure you that, as frightening or distasteful as seeking outside assistance may seem right now, it is a far better option than going it alone. That assistance can be found in books or therapists' offices but also in the church basements and community centers where peer support, self-help, and Twelve-Step recovery groups meet.

Self-help and peer support groups are excellent resources for your continuing journey toward excellence and a well-balanced life. They engage you in a process of helping yourself while helping and being helped by others who have similar problems—relieving your sense of isolation; offering new perspectives on your problems; helping you develop trust, tolerance, and empathy; and giving you an opportunity to improve your communication and social skills. There are peer support groups for victims of abuse, victimizers, widows and widowers, divorcées, adult children of alcoholics, families of the mentally ill, and almost any other population imaginable.

As we pointed out in Chapter Eight, addictive or compulsive behavior often goes hand in hand with perfectionism. If you take a cold, hard look at yourself and recognize that you have (or might have) a drinking or drug problem; an eating disorder; or a compulsion to gamble, spend, exercise, or engage in sexual activity you feel ashamed of after the fact, we strongly recommend that you get involved with perhaps the most effective of all peer support and self-help groups: a Twelve-Step recovery program based on the principles and practices of Alcoholics Anonymous. We make the same recommendation to those of you who are now or at some time in your life have been involved with an addicted, compulsive, or otherwise dysfunctional person. The coping strategies you developed to survive in a household that was turned upside down by that person's problem may be the driving force behind your perfectionism, especially your compulsion to control everyone and everything in your immediate vicinity and your seemingly insatiable need for other people's approval.

Alcoholics Anonymous, Narcotics Anonymous, Overeaters Anonymous, Gamblers Anonymous, Sex Addicts or Sexaholics Anonymous, and groups for codependents and family members affected by another person's addiction or compulsive behavior (Al-anon, Alateen, Nar-anon, etc.) promote physical health, emotional well-being, and spiritual growth. They charge no dues or fees and have no membership requirements other than the desire to discontinue your addictive, compulsive, or codependent behavior. In addition to helping you overcome a specific problem, involvement in a Twelve-Step recovery group will teach you honesty, self-respect, and compassion for others. You will learn to accept the things you cannot change, to have faith in a higher power, to trust yourself and others, and to derive satisfaction from making progress rather than seeking perfection.

On any day of the week, in communities throughout the United States, Twelve-Step recovery and other self-help groups meet. To locate groups in your area, check the telephone book, call your local mental health clinic, or contact:

The National Self-help Clearinghouse
33 West 42nd Street
New York, New York 10036
(212) 840-1259

Chapter Twelve

When Someone Else's

Perfectionism

Is Your Predicament:

Survival Strategies for Living or

Working with a Perfectionist

There's no doubt about it. Perfectionists can be very difficult people. They are difficult to work with—"impossible," Bob, an exceptionally talented, normally even-tempered, graphic artist, would say. After six months as an assistant to Adele, the performance perfectionist we introduced in Chapter Four, he is ready to scream. Or quit. Or strangle Adele, whom he once admired and viewed as a potential mentor. "She's a brilliant graphic designer," Bob said. "One of the best when it comes to sheer creativity. So naturally I jumped at the chance to assist her. I knew I'd learn amazing things from her." What Bob did not know was how demanding—and unappreciative—Adele would be.

"She expects you to work nights, weekends," he continued, "thinks nothing of calling at two A.M. to tell you something that could have waited until you got to work the next morning. You'll completely exhaust yourself trying to live up to her expectations and she'll never, ever say 'Thank you' or 'Nice job,' or anything else that remotely resembles a compliment." Put-downs, on the other hand, come as naturally to Adele as breathing. "She criticizes everything," Bob claimed. "Not just your work but your grammar, your posture, even the clothes you wear. Once she made me go out and buy a new tie right before an important meeting. She said the one I had on reflected badly on her and the firm."

But what frustrated Bob the most were Adele's work habits. "She won't let me in on a project until the last minute," he said. "I have no idea what she's working on until she shows up in my office with a completed design and precise instructions for executing it. She won't listen to suggestions and she'll usually give me about half the time I need to do the artwork. Then, after I kill myself to get the job done on time and do it exactly the way she told me to, she'll take one look at it and decide it isn't quite right or that she's changed her mind about this color or that line or sometimes the entire concept. But does she discuss any of that with me? Or have me do sketches to test out different ideas? Not Adele. She changes her design herself, comes back to me with new instructions, and then ends up hating the finished product *again*. We'll go through this half a dozen times, and when we miss our deadlines, she blames it all on me."

Understandably Bob is finding it more and more difficult to perform his job. "It's pretty tough to feel enthusiastic about my work when I know that no matter how good a job I do, I'll have to do it over," he grumbled. "And I'm not too thrilled about all the firm's clients thinking that *I'm* the one who's holding things up and wasting their time." If well-paying jobs in his field weren't so hard to find and if his wife hadn't just left her job to give birth to and stay home with their first child, he might have resigned months ago, Bob told us. "As it is, I can't afford to quit," he said with a sigh. "But I may have to, because I really don't know how much more of Adele I can take."

Perfectionist Employers, Employees, Colleagues, and Co-workers

If you regularly come in contact with perfectionists in the workplace, you probably know exactly how Bob feels. With their tendency to overschedule and procrastinate, pay painstaking attention to every last detail, and demand the same superhuman effort from others as they expect from themselves, perfectionists in the workplace are indeed hard to take. Alternately pushing you to do more (and do it better and faster) than humanly possible or showing a complete lack of confidence in your ability to do the job for which you were hired, perfectionists in the workplace are impossible to please. They may check up on you repeatedly or simply do your job themselves because they are too impatient to explain what they want or too controlling to delegate responsibility. They haggle over proper protocol, need constant praise and reassurance, are indecisive and afraid to take risks, or fly off the handle whenever anything unexpected occurs. Thorns in your side, the banes of your existence, they may make every workday more stressful and every project more difficult to complete. Is it any wonder that you so often feel like wringing their necks, spiking their coffee with arsenic, checking the want ads, or running for cover as soon as you see them heading in your direction?

As one of Colin's co-workers put it, "Colin's like a ticking time bomb. If one little thing doesn't go according to plan, if one misspelled word gets past a copy editor, or, God forbid, someone puts a pen in his pencil drawer, he explodes. I don't think he realizes how cruel he can be when he's chewing someone out over something that really wasn't that big a deal or how crazy he sounds when he's worrying out loud about the horrible things that could happen a month or a year from now, when those things probably aren't going to ever happen at all. It's tough not to laugh at him when he gets like that or to grab him by the shoulders and shout, 'Get a grip on yourself, Colin. This is *not* the end of the world!'" Colin's "temper tantrums" disrupted many an otherwise peaceful workday and hurt many people's feelings, making almost everyone reluctant to deal with him in any way, shape, or form.

Perfectionist Friends, Relatives, Spouses, and Lovers

Perfectionists can hardly be considered team players in their personal relationships either. "My marriage was more like a contest than a relationship," Adele admitted. "We were both ambitious and trying to make it in our professions. And we played an endless game of one-upmanship with each other. Even though we were in entirely different fields, he wanted to think he was more successful than I was and I wanted to think I was more successful than he was." When Adele's husband "won," she felt like a loser and when she "won," she thought he was a loser and wasn't sure she wanted to be with someone who couldn't "keep up" with her: A no-win situation if ever there was one.

This sort of competition in a friendship, family, or intimate relationship as well as a perfectionist's nagging, nitpicking, mood swings, obsessions, and seemingly insatiable need for control, leave a trail of recurring conflicts, brutal power struggles, hurt feelings, anger, and frustration in their wake. Take Elise and Barbara's friendship, for example. When Elise moved in next door to Barbara and was befriended by her, she had no idea what she was in for. She had no way of knowing that Barbara's exquisitely coordinated outfits, meticulously organized household, impeccable manners, and sophisticated repartee were the trappings of her appearance perfectionism or that Barbara's lofty standards for saying and doing the right thing would soon be applied to her. Perceiving Barbara as far more worldly and "together" than she was herself, Ellen initially took Barbara's mostly disapproving comments and frequently condescending lectures on etiquette and attire to heart. But soon enough she grew tired of hearing about her imperfections. "Sometimes I get so annoyed with Barbara that I want to scream, 'Lighten up already. People have better things to worry about than whether I ironed the jeans I wear to the grocery store! I don't care if my condiments aren't arranged alphabetically! And I'm sick and tired of you telling me what I should do!'"

If you live with, love, or are in any way personally involved with a perfectionist, you may want to scream too. Or tear your hair out from sheer frustration. Or retaliate in some way. As John, one of "born again" moral perfectionist Paul's former roommates put it, "I wanted to throw that darn Bible of his out the window. Paul was always quoting from it or running off to read it whenever I did something or said something that wasn't exactly saintlike. He was just so uptight. So self-righteous and judgmental. Sometimes he got on my nerves so badly that I'd say things just to shock him, just to shake him up and get back at him for acting like he had a one-way ticket to heaven or something." As Adele, John, and Elise did, you and the perfectionist in your life may duke it out for the duration of your relationship, losing more than you gain from those battles and ultimately calling a halt to the hostilities by ending the relationship altogether. Or you may fall into the trap of trying to please the perfectionist in your life, failing and trying harder, failing again and trying harder still. Laura, the most recent ex-girlfriend of Peter, the interpersonal perfectionist we introduced in Chapter Six, did.

"Peter was so particular. And so critical," she explained. "Not in a loud way. He wasn't a yeller. In fact I don't think I ever heard him raise his voice. He would look at me and shake his head or roll his eyes as if to say he couldn't believe how stupid and inept I was. Or he'd lecture me in this very soft, extra-patient, condescending tone of voice. Sometimes he'd give me the silent treatment until I figured out what I did wrong and apologized. And most of the time he just took over—turning off the TV while I was watching it, taking a knife or spoon out of my hand while I was trying to get dinner ready, or making announcements like 'We won't be going to the movies again until you learn not to laugh so loudly.'"

At first Laura protested. "But after a while I just gave in and went along with whatever he wanted," she said. "I could never win an argument. He either walked away and refused to talk to me or kept at me until he wore me down." Besides, under the constant onslaught of Peter's criticism and controlling behaviors, Laura had begun to doubt herself. Maybe she should watch less television, she thought. Maybe she did laugh too loudly. Perhaps she could be a better housekeeper or cook or conversationalist— if she tried. And try she did. "I bent over backward to make him happy with me," Laura claimed. "I was always trying to figure out what he wanted me to do and how he wanted me to do things. But as far as Peter was concerned, I could never do anything right. No matter how hard I tried, I couldn't please him." And the harder Laura tried, the more her self-esteem suffered. "I hated the things I did to get Peter to let up on me. I totally lost myself in trying to be who he thought I should be and I ended up thinking that I was a hopeless case, that I was always wrong, and that I was the one with all the problems."

In addition to blaming and berating yourself for the problems in your relationship with a perfectionist, you may walk on eggshells in an explosive perfectionist's presence, censor yourself when dealing with a perfectionist who is extremely sensitive to criticism, or resent the unsolicited advice and helpful hints you are constantly given, periodically throwing a tantrum of your own and feeling guilty about it afterward. And if you are involved with a perfectionist who is working, starving, exercising, or drinking himself to death or showing signs of the serious physical or emotional problems that can stem from perfectionism, you may spend most of your waking hours worried sick or feeling utterly powerless to stop your loved one's downhill slide.

"Marilyn's always been insecure," her husband, Carl, told us. "But lately it's gotten so bad that I have to watch everything I do or say. She constantly wants me to prove that I love her, that I think she's beautiful, that I appreciate how hard she works to take care of our home and our kids. If I don't say those things over and over again or, worse yet, if I don't notice something she wants me to notice, she'll sulk for hours."

According to Carl, Marilyn will take an innocous comment

like "I thought we were having chicken for dinner tonight" as criticism and do something rash, such as throwing out what she had cooked and cooking chicken—or refusing to cook anything. An offer to help her with the laundry or the grocery shopping is apt to be be misconstrued as a negative comment on her ability to handle her household responsibilities (and she might stay up half the night scrubbing and polishing to prove Carl wrong). The slightest hint that he is growing impatient while waiting for Marilyn to decide what to wear can cause a fight. And even when Carl watches his step and keeps all of his comments and feelings to himself, he can never be sure that he won't get home from work to find Marilyn in tears and talking about "checking out of this miserable life" because something upsetting had happened to her during the day. "I'm at the end of my rope," he said sadly, helplessly. "I don't know what else I can do"

Coping with Other People's Perfectionism

Whether or not your circumstances resemble Carl's or Bob's or Laura's, if there are perfectionists in your life, you may be at the end of your rope too. Indeed, you may have picked up this book because living or working with a perfectionist was driving you crazy. The survival strategies you will find in this chapter can help restore your sanity and prevent other people's perfectionism from adversely affecting your health and happiness in the future.

As a result of reading this book, you now have a better understanding of why perfectionists do what they do and how difficult it can be for them to behave in any other way. You know that they have been the way they are for a long, long time. You realize that they may not choose to change and that even if they do, their transformation into more realistic, reasonable excellence seekers will not take place overnight. Unless you intend immediately and completely to cut yourself off from the perfectionists in your life (which is always an option), you are going to have to cope with their nitpicking and obsessive worrying, their compulsive and controlling behavior, their intrusive advising, nagging, and reminding for at least a while longer. The best way to do that is to reduce the emotional impact other people's perfectionism has on you by changing *your* perception of it and assumptions about it.

Develop a New Attitude

A good place to start your journey toward a more peaceful co-existence with perfectionists is to use what you now know about perfectionism to *stop taking their behavior as personally as you have in the past.* Yes, the perfectionists in your life are directing their criticism at you. Yes, their pushiness, procrastination, and paranoia are putting pressure on you, making you look incompetent or feel like an idiot. Yes, they are expecting you to live up to their standards and are, in one way or another, "punishing" you for falling short of their expectations. But hurting you is rarely, if ever, their intention, and it does not help you to look at their actions in that way. Remind yourself that perfectionists act out of habit. They are not out to get you. They are not willfully and maliciously trying to make you miserable. They are merely doing what they typically, automatically do to manage their emotions, boost their sense of self-worth, compensate for their insecurities, and feel safe, comfortable, and in control of their own lives. Reframe your perception of them so that they seem less like villains or slave drivers or thorns in your side and more like relatively harmless robots with their wires crossed. Instead of getting knocked off your feet by the emotional undertow of an angry tirade, think of those shouting, foot-stomping, name-calling perfectionists as if they were children throwing tantrums to vent the frustration they do not know how to deal with in any other way.

You will also save yourself a great deal of aggravation by *shelving the idea that perfectionists are bad or wrong for acting the way they do.* Try a more neutral message, such as "They certainly deal with things differently from the way I do." Then use what you have learned about the distorted thought patterns behind perfectionism to help you look at your situation from the perfectionist's point of view and to accept that neither your viewpoint nor theirs is necessarily the "right" perspective (or the only way to think about your circumstances).

Finally try to stop buying into their portrayal of you and blaming or beating up on yourself for being less or different from how they expect you to be. No matter how inept, unmotivated, unsophisticated, or inadequate the perfectionists in your life imply or come right out and say you are, do not automatically assume that they know what they are talking about or that they wouldn't say the things they say if there wasn't at least a grain of truth to them. Even if you have messed up or *could* use some improvement in the area they have brought to your attention, *you are not the problem*. They are criticizing and trying to change you out of their need for control or their desire to confirm their own superiority, and feeling disgusted with yourself or changing yourself to please them will not get them to let up on you. If you want to change, by all means do so. But if you do not want to or are not ready to correct the "flaws" perfectionists point out to you, thank them for their unsolicited advice but disregard their suggestions.

Naturally, taking on this new detached and depersonalizing point of view is not easy to do. But since the alternative is living in a near-constant state of anger, frustration, resentment, and anxiety, it is certainly worth trying, and with a bit of cognitive restructuring you can actually pull it off.

Revise Your Thinking

Like perfectionists themselves, you increase your anxiety and reduce your ability to handle difficult situations effectively, by catastrophizing, jumping to conclusions, magnifying your problems, and minimizing your coping skills, projecting past experiences into the future and falling prey to many other inaccurate assumptions and distorted thought patterns. Consequently the same cognitive restructuring techniques we recommended to perfectionists can help you contend with other people's perfectionism.

If, based on your past experiences with the perfectionists in your life, you anticipate future problems in dealing with them and dread your encounters with them, the uncatastrophizing strategy found on page 230 can work wonders for you, helping you realistically to assess the risks you are facing, create contingency plans, and use visualizations to reduce your anxiety. You may want to familiarize yourself with your typical reactions to a perfectionist's words and actions, jot down your thoughts, identify distortions, and rewrite them in a way that will increase your confidence and reduce self-criticism. Writing and repeating affirmations can help you replace ideas that make it easier for perfectionists to get to you ("He probably knows more about this than I do, so I should do what he says," "If I were smarter, prettier, more careful, etc., she wouldn't be so hard on me," or "Anger scares the dickens out of me, and I'll do whatever it takes to calm him down") with ones that build up your immunity to their habits: "I have the inherent wisdom to know what is best for me," "I am lovable and capable," or "I am safe and sure of myself and able to handle whatever gets thrown at me."

Relaxation and visualization can also be beneficial, especially if contending with a perfectionist creates excess stress and tension for you or if you find yourself feeling intimidated by people who present themselves as superior to you. While in a relaxed and receptive state of mind, you can remind yourself that no matter how powerful and sure of themselves those intimidating perfectionists appear to be, they are subject to the same laws of the universe you are. They cannot walk on water. Then you can reinforce that idea by picturing the people who intimidate you in different settings or doing different things. Think of your perfectionist boss diapering a baby or your perfectly put-together neighbor changing the oil in her car or your pompous in-law delivering a lecture and having the audience walk out on him or fall asleep. The images you conjure up may make you laugh or help you empathize with someone with whom you've been butting heads. And they will certainly make you less anxious the next time you actually have to deal with that person.

Find an Emotional Outlet

Although the perfectionist in your life may "blow a gasket," throw a tantrum, burst into tears, or make cruel, hurtful comments at the drop of a hat, it is not particularly useful for you to do the same. In the workplace, giving vent to your anger or frustration can cost you your job, further strain your relationship with the perfectionist, or earn you a reputation as a hothead. Fighting fire with fire on the home front escalates conflicts instead of resolving them. Besides, perfectionists, who are hypersensitive to criticism and threatened by obvious displays of emotion, are liable to shut down or become defensive whenever you try to express undiluted anger, fear, pain, or dissatisfaction directly. They won't hear what you are saying or they'll misunderstand you, perhaps even using your "emotional outburst" against you ("You're overreacting as usual," they'll say, or "I don't see any point in discussing this if you can't be rational about it"). When dealing with perfectionists, simply letting your feelings fly generally backfires in these or other ways. But so does trying to bury your feelings or pretend that they don't exist. Not only do suppressed emotions leak out in passive-aggressive ways (through sarcasm, forgetfulness, lateness, and other "accidents") but stifling your feelings and censoring yourself over an extended period of time can cause ulcers, depression, panic attacks, and other physical or emotional ailments.

To deal with other people's perfectionism effectively and cope with your feelings without doing yourself and others more harm than good, you can get distressing thoughts and unsettling emotions out of your system by talking to someone other than the person who stirred them up—a therapist or a supportive friend. Or discharge them by beating on a pillow, walking briskly, throwing darts at a dart board, or watching a tearjerker movie. Laughter can be a release as well. You can also get into your car, roll up the windows, and scream at the top of your lungs or write down everything you *wish* you could say and then rip up your poison-pen letter or burn it.

Learn When and How to Walk Away

By adopting a new attitude, revising your thinking, and releasing your pent-up emotions in relatively harmless ways, you reduce the emotional charge on your interactions with perfectionists. They simply do not get to you the way they once did, and as a result you are better equipped to deal with them. Or *not* to deal with them. The fact of the matter is that under certain circumstances there is nothing you *can* do about the pushy, picky, obsessive, compulsive, or excessively controlling people in your life.

For instance the "mirror-polishing" interpersonal perfectionists we described in Chapter Six treat you like objects because that is the way they see you. You are not someone with whom they have a relationship. You are *something* that can either gratify them or get in their way, a mirror that can reflect positively on them or an albatross hanging around their necks and slowing them down. They want what they want when they want it and are not particularly concerned with the effect their actions have on you. Your best bet is to stay out of their way and have as little to do with them as possible.

Then there are perfectionists who, for one reason or another, have absolutely no interest in doing things any differently from the way they have always done them. No matter how much you wish they would (or how hard you try to get them to), they do not *want* to change. They are entitled to their position. You know they feel that way. So why waste your time and energy struggling with them?

Other perfectionists in your life periodically go so far overboard and get so worked up that they cannot be dealt with *at that time*. Likewise certain situations make confronting a perfectionist too risky. In other instances you will feel too anxious or angry to think clearly and do what is best for you. Under any of these circumstances you can *choose* not to deal with the problem—either for the time being or at all.

In addition to encountering situations where there is nothing you can do, there are times when doing nothing is the best thing to do. In fact not dealing with perfectionists directly is an excellent alternative more often than you might think. Life is simply too short to mess around with perfectionists if you don't have to, and as you've probably realized by now, a great deal of perfectionistic behavior is so ridiculous and unimportant in the overall scheme of things that there's really no reason to take it seriously. You can teach yourself to accept and tolerate it (see page 213). You can literally walk away—physically leaving the scene, ending a telephone conversation, excusing yourself to go to the rest room, or, on a larger scale, getting a new job or getting out of a bad marriage. We also recommend spending less time with perfectionists who get to you: Don't call your chronically dissatisfied mother *every* day. Don't accept all of your nitpicking neighbor's invitations to come over and chat. Stop carpooling with a colleague who spends the entire drive telling you how to do your job. Learn to overlook things that may be irritating but don't really hurt you, to allow perfectionists to sulk or pout without repeatedly asking them what's wrong or trying to make them feel better, to ignore sarcastic comments, and to stop asking for perfectionists' opinions (after all, you know you aren't going to like what you hear).

Work from the Plus Side

Just as we recommended that perfectionists add pleasurable, energy-replenishing experiences to their lives in order to become less perfectionistic, we recommend that you use the time you save by no longer butting heads with them to increase your peaceful or pleasurable interactions with them. Reinforce their positive attributes and nonperfectionistic behaviors with words of praise and gratitude. Perfectionists thrive on approval and acceptance. By validating the things they say or do that are pleasing or helpful, you are fulfilling their needs and virtually guaranteeing that the behavior you praised will be repeated, thus fulfilling your needs as well.

Reread our discussion of ways of having more fun and bringing more laughter into your life. Engage in those sorts of activities with your perfectionist friend, relative, spouse, or lover. Take care to choose endeavors that are as noncompetitive as possible: dancing, fishing, hiking, visiting art museums, attending concerts, and so on. If necessary, allow the perfectionist to play "expert," and if he becomes critical or competitive, make light of it, perhaps exaggerating your klutziness or jokingly doing the opposite of what you've been told. (When he accuses you of not taking things seriously, remind him that you are not supposed to be serious about that particular activity.)

Know Your Bottom Line

Naturally there will be times when you cannot or do not want to let perfectionistic behaviors slide. An important project might be jeopardized if you can't get your perfectionist co-worker to make a decision or stop procrastinating. Or a valued employee might leave you in a lurch if her immediate supervisor doesn't curb his criticism or let her do her job without interference. Your children may be showing serious symptoms of excess stress because of the unreasonable demands your spouse is making of them. Or your social life may be nonexistent because your lover finds fault with all of your friends and refuses to have anything to do with them. In addition each and every one of us finds certain behaviors intolerable and we are entitled to voice our opinions about them as well as do what we can not to be subjected to them. However, many of us fall into one of two traps in this area. We confuse irritating habits with intolerable ones and kick up a fuss more often than necessary. Or we bury our true feelings about things we truly cannot tolerate, pretending that they do not bother us until we can't stand it anymore and explode. Both traps can be avoided by identifying your bottom line: the nonnegotiable limits that separate circumstances you can tolerate from those you cannot.

Use the goal-trimming strategy on page 216 to identify the *best* you can hope for and the *least* you could accept from a person or situation without losing your self-respect. The former probably involves needs or wishes that you cannot expect the perfectionist in your life to fulfill, but that you will want to reward and reinforce whenever that person tries to or actually does come through for you. The latter is your bottom line and probably describes a situation that is the same as or slightly better than the one you have now.

With a specific perfectionist in mind, make a list of a dozen or so of that person's perfectionistic quirks or habits and decide if they fall on, above, or below your bottom line. Try to be as honest as possible about what you can and cannot tolerate. Clarity in this area gives you a solid foundation on which to stand while negotiating, compromising, setting limits, or otherwise attempting to resolve conflicts with perfectionists who violate your boundaries and treat you in ways that you cannot tolerate.

Rules of Thumb for Confronting and Requesting Changes from Perfectionists

Although you have a right to protect your bottom line and put your foot down when the perfectionists in your life cross it, you also have a responsibility to confront problems and request behavior changes in the least destructive, most constructive way possible. To avoid making matters worse instead of better, we suggest that you adhere to the following general guidelines:

- Don't let wounds fester or allow resentments to simmer below the surface until they boil over and come rushing out in a furious tirade. At the first available (and appropriate) opportunity after you've been treated intolerably, bring the topic up for discussion.

- Address the problem in terms the perfectionist in your life can best understand and appreciate. State the dilemma as clearly as you can. Be frank, coming to the point as quickly as possible. If you beat around the bush, hesitate, or speak in vague, wishy-washy generalities, perfectionists will grow impatient and exasperated with you. Be practical, whenever possible appealing to the perfectionist's interest in achieving a goal, being helpful, doing what is politically or morally correct, making a good impression, or not making a mistake that will be difficult to remedy at a later date. Rather than rehashing every detail of the perfectionist's failings, concentrate on solutions.
- Be prepared. Rehearse what you're going to say. Make sure you have specific suggestions for solving the problems you are experiencing. Acknowledge your feelings, but be able to back them up with facts and examples. Do not, however, haul out a whole grocery list of grievances that you've been saving up for the occasion. Deal with one issue at a time.
- Use effective communication skills. For instance, "I" messages ("I need to know about upcoming projects so that I can schedule my time," or "I'd prefer not to be called a lame-brained idiot") are usually more effective than accusatory or demanding "You" statements ("You've got to give me some advance notice about upcoming projects," or "You bastard, you have no right to call me a lame-brained idiot"). Avoid crucializations: "This *always* happens," "You *never* think about my feelings," or "I'm sick of being criticized for *everything* I do." If you feel you might not be as skilled as you need to be in this area, consult the many available resources on effective communication or consider taking a course or attending a seminar on the subject.
- Do not assign blame. Pointing the finger at the perfectionists in your life and trying to make them feel guilty for treating you in a certain way is counterproductive. They will freeze up or become defensive, neither of which is going to help

matters. You want to have an action-oriented discussion that will supply both of you with ideas for improving your relationship. That is not what you will get if you resort to name-calling or playing "district attorney": building an airtight case against the perfectionist in order to prove beyond a shadow of a doubt that you are right and he is wrong.

- Finally, be flexible and willing to accept approximations of your goal or steps (even teeny, tiny ones) toward the outcome you desire. Don't expect to make more than a dent in the perfectionist's attitude or actions the first time out. You may have to discuss the matter many times over before you actually notice a significant change. That is the nature of the beast. You know that. So just do the best you can during a given interaction. You may have better luck the next time around. Or you may have to try a different approach.

Helping the Panicky Perfectionist

Although nagging, criticizing, correcting, advising, and making unreasonable demands tend to be the first aggravating perfectionistic behaviors that come to mind, they are not the only ways perfectionists can get to you. Some, like Marilyn, are so insecure and overly sensitive that they constantly come apart at the seams—leaving you to pick up the pieces or drag them out of the pits of depression. Others, like Colin and Marty, ruminate and catastrophize, working themselves up into a near-paranoid frenzy that is painful to witness. At times their panic becomes contagious, and you find yourself conjuring up your own anxiety-provoking visions of doom and disaster. Or like Sharon and her photocopier study, perfectionistic behaviors are sometimes so obviously counterproductive that you cannot stand idly by and watch people set themselves up for defeat, or sabotage a project that is important to you.

Under such circumstances the perfectionists in your life need your objectivity, sympathy, and assistance in regaining their equilibrium. Your clearheaded guidance can help them see options, steps, and a light at the end of the tunnel that they—in the midst of a crisis—cannot find for themselves. By engaging panic-stricken perfectionists in a nonthreatening, nonjudgmental, open-ended dialogue, you let them know that "everyone" won't reject or think less of them when they remove their perfect-person mask or fall short of their lofty expectations. Your re-assuring, reasonable, and realistic perspective may actually take root and help perfectionists avoid similar crises in the future.

You can help the panicky perfectionists in your life—and in the process help yourself—by neither getting caught up in their breathless catastrophizing nor dismissing their concerns as ri-diculous, irrational overreactions. What looks like "nothing" or "no big deal" to you may seem monstrous in a perfectionist's mind. Remember that they are probably light-years ahead of themselves, reeling from the impact of both their immediate circumstances and the repercussions they are convinced they will suffer in the future. They feel as if the financial ruin, personal humiliation, public embarrassment, or anything else they are imagining is actually happening to them, and at that particular moment they have virtually no control over their reactions. So, rather than telling them to calm down and get a grip on them-selves or immediately offering them your sage advice for solving their problems—which they are too distraught to grasp or pro-cess—take time to listen to them.

Encourage panicky perfectionists to express their feelings. Since self-disclosure is not their strong suit, you may have to pave the way for it: "If I were in your shoes, I'd feel pretty scared right now. Is that how you're feeling?" you might say, or "You sound really hurt. Did something bad happen?"

Listen actively. Nod. Maintain eye contact. Pay attention and periodically reflect back to the speaker the messages you are receiving. Try not to plan your reply while the other person is talking. And whether or not you agree with the perfectionist's *ideas* (or even think they're completely insane), acknowledge the validity of their *feelings*. Summarize their position in a way that reinforces the fact that their perceptions rather than any concrete reality are at the heart of the matter: "You were fifteen minutes late for your interview and *felt like* the interviewer would hold that against you," or "You *thought* you were the only one at the party who didn't have a full-time job and that everyone knew it and looked down on you."

Use questions—"Specifically, what convinced you that the interview was a flop?"—and comments—"I'm not sure I understand what you are most afraid will happen"—to clarify the problem. Slip in a few encouraging words: "If *you* got a B, that test must've been impossible," or "When I got passed up for that promotion last year, I thought my career was over. But it wasn't. Six months later I was offered a much better position. Which just goes to show, that you never know exactly what tomorrow will bring."

Help them gain some perspective, slowly shifting their focus from disaster predicting and self-punishment to solution finding. Steer them away from obsessing, in hindsight, about the "why's" that are useless now—"Why did she leave me?" "Why didn't I realize the boss was disappointed in my work?"—toward considering the practical "whats," namely "What should I do now?" and "What can I do to keep this same thing from happening again?" Offer suggestions and, together, brainstorm alternatives that could constructively solve the problem.

Since perfectionists tend to be goal and achievement oriented, they often respond well and quickly to the idea of making a new game plan for the future. If they don't—if they seem intent on wallowing in self-pity or continuing to go over their flaws and failings with a fine-tooth comb—allow them to do that, although you need not stick around for the recap. Keep the lines of communication open, letting the perfectionists in your life know that you are available to help them when they are ready to look at some options. Then check back with them in a few hours or a few days.

Resolving Conflicts Constructively

Judy, the would-be superwoman we've talked about throughout this book, and her husband, Ron, a lighthearted, "laid back" college professor, have a mixed marriage of sorts. She's a perfectionist. He's a free spirit. She's into order, rules, control, precision. He's into emotional expression. She folds grocery bags and puts rubber bands around them before storing them neatly under the sink. He pays almost no attention to his surroundings, and things could be strewn from one end of the house to the other for weeks before he'd notice, much less pick them up. She has a jam-packed schedule and, even though she cannot always stick to it, knows exactly where she should be and what she should be doing during every waking hour of every day. He is aware of where he absolutely must be—in class, at a faculty meeting, on the racquetball court—but otherwise "plays it by ear," allowing circumstances or his feelings to dictate what he does and when he does it.

Conflict between these two very different individuals was inevitable. Judy's needs for order, cleanliness, predictability, and perfection and Ron's need for flexibility, creativity, spontaneity, and little or no pressure were incompatible. If Judy allowed Ron to be true to his basic nature, she would have to lower her standards, which, being a perfectionist, she found impossible to do. Yet to completely meet her needs, Ron would have to completely sacrifice his. The only other alternative appeared to be for Judy to assume full responsibility for keeping their household in order and organizing both of their lives. For years that is what Judy has tried to do, running herself ragged making sure that she *and* Ron live up to her expectations: that they look good, are on time, are seen in the right places, socialize with the right people, you name it. She exhausts herself compensating for their differences and resents it. Although Judy always denies that anything is wrong, her resentment nonetheless gets conveyed to Ron in icy silences, mixed messages, weary sighs, and excuses not to make love. Every few months she reaches the end of her rope, lashes out at Ron, hits him with a lenghty list of complaints, and demands that he "pull his weight around here." He tries. He does the best he can. But that is never good enough for Judy, and she takes over again.

After fifteen years of marriage the time it takes to go through this cycle has decreased dramatically. Nowadays Ron and Judy bicker and battle almost all the time. But is their situation hopeless? Not necessarrily—and if you are currently struggling with a perfectionist who seems intent on having his way at your expense—your situation is not hopeless either. No matter how a perfectionist's needs or wishes appear to be different from or incompatible with your own, there is almost always a way for both of you to get some of what you want without giving up more than either of you is willing to sacrifice—*if you learn to negotiate and compromise*.

The Art of Compromise

Perfectionists unquestionably prefer to do things their way. They want what they want when they want it and precisely as they have unilaterally decided it should be. But marriage or coupling obviously involves *two* people and won't survive, let alone thrive, under such conditions. Relationships require give-and-take, mutual understanding, respect. Sometimes you get to indulge. Sometimes you have to share. Sometimes you put your needs on hold so that your partner's needs can be fulfilled. Nobody in a healthy, balanced relationship gets the whole pie at all times. Compromise comes with the territory.

Every compromise has its own features. For instance, Judy is determined to be on time. She schedules herself right down to the minute. And she expects this same kind of time consideration from others, especially her husband. While Ron is usually good about calling Judy if he's going to be late, he sometimes forgets, and his idea of being on schedule is to arrive within thirty minutes of the appointed time. Naturally this makes Judy a nervous wreck while she is waiting for Ron and furious at him when he finally arrives.

With the help of a counselor they came up with a compromise that required each of them to give a little. Ron allowed himself his regular leisurely agenda with others, but made a commitment to be no more than five or ten minutes late meeting Judy. Judy in turn factored Ron's five or ten minutes into her schedule, and in fact planned for him to be fifteen minutes late.

Another approach to compromising is what we call the one-third solution. Choose a category of contention; one that is not too emotionally charged but has the battle lines specifically drawn. It should involve decisions you regularly have to make: choosing a movie to see, deciding where to go for weekend get-aways, who cooks, how laundry gets taken care of, and so on. Establish a time frame, a period long enough to be facing this decision many times. One third of the time you do it his way. One third of the time he does it yours. One third of the time you creatively compromise. One couple we interviewed used this strategy to resolve their struggle for control of the kitchen. The perfectionist husband cooked one day, his wife the next, and on the third day they either ate out or prepared a meal together. They added an extra ground rule: The perfectionist was barred from the kitchen when it was the nonperfectionist's turn at the stove!

This was a new experience for them, as it will undoubtedly be for you—and an enlightening one. With the stakes—and risks—kept small, divvying up responsibility into thirds—with one third involving shared control—teaches both you and the perfectionist in your life that you *can* work out methods for effective give-and-take, even when one partner's inclination is to take, take, take and the other's is to give, give, give.

In some areas you may find it easier simply to take turns. Many couples use that method of compromise on that eternal source of disagreement: household cleanliness. Judy and Ron did. One week Ron would clean and Judy agreed to live with his more laid-back style, without carping or complaining or taking charge. The following week Judy was in control of the house-keeping duties, and during that week Ron would live up to her standards, putting things away and trying to be more orderly.

To coexist peacefully and develop a healthy relationship as well, you and the perfectionist in your life will have to adjust to each other continually. That process is made easier when you put your differences to work for you rather than letting them split you apart. Decide which duties each of you is most comfortable with and assign them accordingly. For example, a detail-minded performance perfectionist who is adept in financial matters and devoted to orderliness could do budgeting, taxes, and cleaning while her nonperfectionistic mate with his creative bent and flair for bargain hunting could be responsible for shopping, cooking, and child care. If you make sure the roles aren't automatically assigned but are rather the result of a mutual decision, you will relieve a lot of tension as well as take advantage of your own and your partner's strongest skills and talents.

The Skill of Negotiation

Compromise may be an art form, but it cannot take shape without skilled negotiation. This is particularly true when one of the people being asked to compromise is a perfectionist. Believing that settling for anything but the whole pie counts as a failure, perfectionists generally *hate* the mere thought of compromising. In addition they are decidedly reluctant to give up so much as an ounce of the control they need to feel safe and secure. Consequently you cannot wait for the perfectionists in your life to suggest a compromise. You are going to have to make the first move, open negotiations, and in all probability assume full responsibility for keeping the bargaining process going—at least in the beginning. Perfectionists, who are fast learners and generally motivated to please the people who matter to them, usually get the hang of negotiating fairly quickly.

Begin the negotiation process by acknowledging that a difference of opinion—not necesarrily a problem, certainly not a catastrophe, but simply differing and at least somewhat incompatible viewpoints—exists. Agree to discuss the matter. You can do so right then and there, or you make an appointment with each other. At the bargaining table you will clarify your own and the perfectionist's needs or goals and hammer out a deal that allows both of you to get at least some of what you want. That will involve the following:

1. Specifying that your goal is to come up with an *imperfect* solution. Both of you will get some, but not all, of what you want, and each of you will probably have to give up something as well. Agree to do your best to come up with a solution that leaves neither of you beaten and both of you content.
2. Establishing ground rules such as no yelling, name-calling, or bringing up problems that are not related to the specific matter being discussed.
3. Defining the issue—use the rules of thumb we mentioned earlier to be as clear and specific as possible.
4. Proposing possible solutions. Brainstorm options without judging them yet. The more options the better, even if some of them seem ridiculous at first glance.
5. Talking about the pluses and minuses of various solutions and agreeing on one that both of you are willing to try.
6. Making a *time-limited* commitment to that option. We emphasize the words *time-limited* because no compromise solution needs to be etched in stone. Think of it as an experiment and set a date to evaluate the results.
7. Following through. Do what you've decided to do, evaluate the outcome on the agreed-upon date, and decide whether you will renew your agreement or renegotiate it.

Setting Limits on Intolerable Behavior

If all else fails, you are going to have to take a no-nonsense, nonnegotiable stand, setting clear, firm, reasonable limits on behavior that you simply cannot tolerate a moment longer. Begin by identifying the intolerable behavior. Be very specific and direct. Then explain the effect that behavior has on you:

> "When you shout at me, especially in front of the rest of the staff, I feel too furious and humiliated to listen to what you are saying."

Immediately follow with a request:

> "I would prefer that you meet with me privately to discuss your concerns calmly."

Then explain what the perfectionist will get by fulfilling your request:

> "If you do that, I will be able to give you my full attention and do my best to correct the mistakes I made."

You can also identify the costs to the perfectionist if he chooses not to fulfill your request. Sometimes you won't have to. Because perfectionists are often unaware of the effect their actions have on you, simply pointing that out may be enough to set them straight. Or you may not have to *state* the consequences, since perfectionists are apt to assume that they will suffer certain consequences anyway (usually imagining things far worse than you would propose). However, some perfectionists just won't get your message or take it seriously unless you let them know what you will do if their intolerable behavior persists *and actually do it*.

If you define consequences but for one reason or another cannot carry them out, this strategy will not work. Whenever possible, choose logical consequences that are natural outgrowths of the behavior you want discontinued or the effect you have already stated it has on you:

> "Although I can't stop you from shouting at me in front of other people, I can't guarantee I'll hear enough of what you're saying to avoid making the same mistake again."

Make sure the consequence is believable. Don't make idle threats—to quit a job you won't quit, for instance. In addition make every effort to sound as nonthreatening as possible. Because you might say things you'll later regret, it is also best *not* to use this technique in the heat of battle when you are feeling frustrated or angry. Wait until both of you are calm and thinking rationally, possibly using the "I've got a problem" technique we described on page 242 to open up the discussion.

Getting More Help

Like the perfectionists to whom the bulk of this book was addressed, you may need or want more information, advice, or assistance than this book alone can provide. If your marriage to or an ongoing intimate relationship with a perfectionist is rife with conflicts that do not respond to the strategies found in this chapter, couples counseling may be in order. If you cannot get your partner to go into therapy with you, consider going by yourself, especially if your self-esteem has sustained significant damage as a result of relentlessly trying and repeatedly failing to please the perfectionists in your life. Communications and assertiveness-training courses may be helpful to you as well. And if you are coping with a perfectionist who is also an addicted or compulsive person, we highly recommend that you get involved with a Twelve-Step recovery program for codependents such as Al-anon or Nar-anon.

Finally, the Bibliography, which follows, lists some books that may be of special interest and value to you.

Whether you are or someone in your life is a perfectionist, it is our hope that this book has shown you that life in an "imperfect" world is intrinsically worth living and that instead of relentlessly striving for a mythical pot of gold at an illusory rainbow's end, you can start right where you are and build a real fortune— physical health, emotional well-being and close, lasting relationships.

Bibliography

The Psychology of Perfectionism
•
BOOKS ON HUMAN BEHAVIOR AND OTHER FACTORS THAT CAN
LEAD TO PERFECTIONISM

Adderholdt-Elliott, M. R. *Perfectionism: What's Bad About Being Too Good*. Minneapolis, MN: Free Spirit Publishing Co., 1987 (on perfectionism in children/teens).

Adler, Alfred. *Understanding Human Behavior*. London: George Allen and Unwin, Ltd., 1928.

Glasser, William. *Reality Therapy: A New Approach to Psychiatry*. New York: Harper & Row, 1975.

Horney, Karen. *Our Inner Conflicts*. New York: W. W. Norton, 1966.

Kiersey, David, and M. Bates. *Please Understand Me: Character and Temperament Types*. Buffalo: Prometheus Press, 1988.

Kirkland, Gelsey. *Dancing on My Grave*. Garden City, NY: Doubleday, 1986.

Leman, Kevin, M.D. *The Birth Order Book: Why You Are the Way You Are*. New York: Dell, 1985.

Miller, Joy, and M. Ripper. *Following the Yellow Brick Road: The Adult Child's Personal Journey Through Oz*. Pompano Beach, FL: Health Communications, 1987.

Peck, M. Scott. *The Road Less Traveled*. New York: Simon & Schuster/Touchstone Books, 1978.

Potash, Marlin. *Hidden Agendas*. New York: Delacorte, 1990.

Tschirhart, Sandford; Linda and M. E. Donovan. *Women and Self-esteem*. New York: Penguin, 1984.

Woititz, Janet G. *Adult Children of Alcoholics*. Pompano Beach, FL: Health Communications, 1985 (applicable to anyone from any kind of dysfunctional family).

Related Issues

•

BOOKS ON PROBLEMS ASSOCIATED WITH PERFECTIONISM

Braiker, Harriet B. *The Type E Woman: How to Overcome the Stress of Being Everything to Everybody*. New York: Dodd, Mead and Co., 1987 (on overachievement).

Burka, Judith, and L. Yuen. *Procrastination: Why You Do It, What to Do About It*. Reading, MA: Addison-Wesley, 1990.

Clance, Pauline Rose, M.D. *The Imposter Syndrome: When Success Makes You Feel Like a Fake*. New York: Bantam, 1985.

Ellis, Albert, and William J. Knaus. *Overcoming Procrastination*. New York: New American Library, 1979.

Freudenberger, Herbert. *Burnout: The High Cost of High Achievement*. Garden City, NY: Anchor Press, 1980.

———, and G. North. *Women's Burnout: How to Spot It, How to Reverse It and How to Prevent It*. New York: Penguin Books, 1986.

Handly, Robert, and Pauline Neff. *Anxiety and Panic Disorders: Their Causes and Cures*. New York: Fawcett Crest, 1987.

Knaus, William J. *Do It Now: How to Stop Procrastinating*. Englewood Cliffs, NJ: Prentice Hall, 1979.

Levenkron, Steven. *The Best Little Girl in the World*. New York: Warner Books, 1978 (on eating disorders).

———. *Treating and Overcoming Anorexia Nervosa*. New York: Warner Books, 1978.

Milam, James Robert, and K. Ketcham. *Under the Influence: A Guide to the Myths and Realities of Alcoholism*. Seattle: Madronna, 1981.

O'Neill, Cherry Boone. *Starving for Attention*. New York: Dell, 1983 (on eating disorders).

Orsborn, C. *Enough is Enough: Exploding the Myth of Having It All*. New York: G. P. Putnam and Sons, 1986 (on overachievement).

Rappaport, Judith. *The Boy Who Couldn't Stop Washing: The Experience and Treatment of Obsessive-Compulsive Disorder*. New York: Dutton, 1989.

Woolfolk, Robert L., and F. C. Richardson. *Stress, Sanity and Survival*. New York: New American Library, 1978.

Advice and Self-help

Beck, Aaron T. *Love Is Never Enough: How Couples Can Overcome Misunderstanding, Resolve Conflicts and Solve Relationship Problems Through Cognitive Therapy*. New York: Harper & Row, 1988 (on intimacy, interpersonal perfectionism).

Burns, David D., M.D. *Feeling Good: The New Mood Therapy*. New York: William Morrow, 1980 (on cognitive therapy strategies).

———. *Nobody Is Perfect* and *Feeling Good About Yourself*. Audio tapes numbers 20268 and 20269 of the Psychology Today Series.

Charlesworth, Edward A., and R. C. Nathan. *Stress Management: A Comprehensive Guide to Wellness*. New York: Atheneum, 1984.

Earle, Ralph, and S. Meltsner. *Come Here, Go Away: How to Stop Running from the Love You Want.* New York: Pocket Books, 1991 (on intimacy).

Ellis, Albert, and R. Harper. *A New Guide to Rational Living.* Hollywood, CA: Wilshire Book Co., 1975.

Galway, Timothy W. *The Inner Game of Tennis.* New York: Random House, 1974 (on visualization/affirmations).

Gawain, Shakti. *Creative Visualization.* New York: Bantam Books, 1983.

Gravitz, Herbert, and J. D. Bowden. *Recovery: A Guide for Adult Children of Alcoholics.* New York: Simon & Schuster, 1987.

Halverson, Ronald S., and V. H. Deilgat. *Twelve-Steps—A Way Out: A Working Guide for Adult Children from Addictive and Other Dysfunctional Families.* San Diego: Recovery Publications, 1982.

Hyatt, Carole, and Linda Gottlieb. *When Smart People Fail: Rebuilding Yourself for Success.* New York: Penguin Books, 1988.

Lakein, Alan L. *How to Get Control of Your Time and Your Life.* New York: New American Library, 1989.

Lazarus, Arnold, Ph.D. *In the Mind's Eye.* New York: Guilford, 1984 (on relaxation, visualization, anxiety control).

Simon, Sidney B. *Getting Unstuck: Breaking Through Your Barriers to Change.* New York: Warner Books, 1988.

Smith, Manuel J. *When I Say No I Feel Guilty.* New York: Dial Press, 1975 (on assertiveness).

Viscott, David, M.D. *Risking.* New York: Pocket Books, 1983.

Walker, Charles Eugene. *Learn to Relax: 13 Ways to Reduce Tension.* Englewood Cliffs, NJ: Prentice Hall, 1975.

Coping with Other People's Perfectionism

Bach, Dr. George R., and Peter Wyden. *The Intimate Enemy: How to Fight Fair in Love and Marriage.* New York: Avon Books, 1968.

Beattie, Melody. *Codependent No More.* Center City, MN: Hazeldon, 1987 (one of the most popular books on the subject, but there are many others. Check the addiction and recovery section of your bookstore).

Bramson, Robert M. *Coping with Difficult People*. New York: Dell, 1981.

Elgin, Suzette Haden. *The Gentle Art of Verbal Self-Defense*. Englewood Cliffs, NJ: Prentice Hall, 1980.

Leman, Dr. Kevin. *The Pleasers: Women Who Can't Say No—and the Men Who Control Them*. New York: Dell, 1987.

Piaget, Gerald. *Control Freaks*. New York: Doubleday, 1991.

Index